# Self-Esteem and Foreign Language Learning

# Self-Esteem and Foreign Language Learning

Edited by

Fernando Rubio

CAMBRIDGE SCHOLARS PUBLISHING

Self-Esteem and Foreign Language Learning, edited by Fernando Rubio

This book first published 2007 by

Cambridge Scholars Publishing

15 Angerton Gardens, Newcastle, NE5 2JA, UK

British Library Cataloguing in Publication Data
A catalogue record for this book is available from the British Library


ISBN 1-84718-215-1; ISBN 13: 9781847182159

This book is dedicated to Jane Arnold.
For her support, wit, enthusiasm, patience and love.

# Table of Contents

# FOREWORD

ELAINE K. HORWITZ
(THE UNIVERSITY OF TEXAS AT AUSTIN)

Self-Esteem. Self-Concept. Self-Image. Self-Confidence. Anxiety. Willingness to Communicate. Language-Ego. Integrative Motivation. Acculturation. Language Learning Stories. Identity. Self. Selves. These are all terms that have been used in this volume and elsewhere to describe the relationship of learners to the endeavor of language learning and to the new language. We have truly come a long way from the early years of language aptitude research when the likelihood for success in language learning was conceived of primarily in cognitive terms. At this moment in language teaching history, the role of affective variables and the necessity of focusing on the emotional states of learners are readily acknowledged by the language teaching community. As this volume clearly attests, this understanding of the emotional vulnerability of language learners is shared by many language teachers and researchers around the world.

Questions remain, however, as to why language learning is so much more ego-involving than other fields of study, and moreover, what can be done to assist the learner's emotional journey. The authors in this volume have done an impressive job addressing these two issues; they offer a wealth of interesting and useful theoretical frameworks from which to understand the place of self-esteem in language learning as well as an abundance of truly creative and humanistic approaches to supporting and encouraging positive self-esteem in language classrooms. Many teachers intuitively understand the importance of supporting their students' self-esteem, but without the specific guidance offered in this volume, they are at a loss as to how to provide this support while at the same time accomplishing more conventional language teaching goals.

I like to think of language learning as a journey. All learners do not take the same route or travel at the same speed. When considering the learner's self-esteem, it is necessary to recognize that how learners feel about themselves and about language learning is likely to be different at different points in the language learning process (Horwitz 2008). It is not necessarily the case that more advanced learners will have higher levels of self-esteem. It is entirely possible that as learners become more competent, they will also become more aware of limitations in their language ability. I have argued elsewhere (Horwitz 2000) that many learners experience anxiety when they feel that they are unable to "be themselves" when speaking a new language, and more advanced learners may actually be more sensitive to differences between their true identity and the version of themselves they can communicate in the new language (Horwitz, Horwitz and Cope 1986). In terms of ultimate impact on language teaching, it is also important to recognize that lack of self-esteem in learners can in short order become a lack of confidence in language teachers. When advanced language learners become language teachers, low self-esteem can limit the experiences they offer to their students (Horwitz 1996).

The authors in this volume have made numerous suggestions as to how language teachers can help guide their students' language learning journey by incorporating reflection, group work, and discussion into language classrooms. To their voices, I would propose the addition of counseling components to language programs. Students could meet with a "counselor" when they begin language studies, throughout their studies, and again at the termination of their language studies. Language counseling would help students develop specific personal goals for language learning and a plan to reach their goals. Most importantly from the perspective of this volume, language counseling would help "legitimize" learner's feelings and offer a regular forum to consider these feelings. While language counseling is seen as fundamental to self-directed language programs, it is seldom available to students in traditional school-based programs. In addition, since it is generally recognized that the amount of language proficiency that can be achieved in a classroom is limited, language teachers must encourage their students to take more responsibility for their own learning, that is, to become more autonomous. The development of autonomy in and of itself may be a source of self-esteem for many learners.

Learner feelings of self-esteem may also benefit from more realistic goals for language learners. I have often thought that language programs err by making native-like competence the goal for their students. My colleague Carl Blyth (2003) has written that language professionals should look to functioning bilinguals within various language communities as models for language learners rather than to native-speakers. By re-envisioning language teaching in this way, I believe that students will see more value in their language studies—they will come to understand that less than perfect competence can be very useful—and see themselves as more competent language learners. When learners compare themselves and are compared to native speakers, they will inevitably come up short. Such comparisons, in turn, likely contribute to poor self-esteem. When learners subscribe to common overly perfectionistic beliefs about language learning, they may erroneously interpret their progress as abnormally slow and conclude that they lack aptitude for language learning (Gregersen and Horwitz 2002; Horwitz 1988).

The many roles, classroom levels, and cultural contexts of the contributors are a true strength of this volume. Many of the authors view themselves primarily as language teachers while others tend to see themselves more as researchers or teacher trainers. All are deeply rooted in and committed to language classrooms. Thus, the suggestions offered here are both practical and doable. I sincerely hope that language teachers will take these papers as a guide and find culturally appropriate ways to encourage positive self-esteem in their students.

## Works Cited

Blyth, C. 1995. Redefining the boundaries of language use: The foreign language classroom as a multilingual speech community. In. C. Kramsch, ed. *Redefining the boundaries of language study*, 145-183. Boston: Heinle.

Gregersen, T., and E. K. Horwitz. 2002. Language learning and perfectionism: Anxious and non-anxious language learners' reactions to their own oral performance. *The Modern Language Journal* 86: 562-570.

Horwitz, E. K. 1988. The beliefs about language learning of beginning university foreign language students. *The Modern Language Journal* 72: 182-193.

—. 1996. Even teachers get the blues: Recognizing and alleviating non-native teachers' feelings of foreign language anxiety. *Foreign Language Annals* 29: 365-372.

—. 2000. It ain't over til it's over: On foreign language anxiety, first language deficits, and the confounding of variables. *The Modern Language Journal* 84: 256-259.

—. 2008. *Becoming a language teacher: A practical guide to second language learning and teaching.* Newton: Allyn & Bacon.

Horwitz, E.K., Horwitz, M.B., and J. A. Cope. 1986. Foreign language classroom anxiety. *The Modern Language Journal* 70: 125-132.

# ACKNOWLEDGEMENTS

The editor and contributors are grateful to the authors and publishers who have given permission for the use of copyright material in the text. Every effort has been made to trace sources of all the materials used. Apologies are expressed for any omission.

Fig. 4-2. The Components of Motivational Teaching Practice in the L2 Classroom (Dörnyei 2001, 29). Fig. 4-3. (Littlejohn 2001, 4). Fig. 4-4. Kohonen (1994, 61).

The editor thanks Cambridge Scholars Publishing for their professional work, especially Andy Nercessian, Carol Koulikourdi and Amanda Millar.

The editor also wishes to thank Bob Reasoner, Douglas Brown and Elaine Horwitz for their contribution and helpful suggestions.

To all the contributors of this book, thank you for the encouragement and cooperation.

To all the members in my family, thank you for your patience and understanding for the stolen time.

# Part I:

# An Overview

# CHAPTER ONE

# SELF-ESTEEM AND FOREIGN LANGUAGE LEARNING: AN INTRODUCTION

FERNANDO RUBIO[1]
(UNIVERSITY OF HUELVA, SPAIN)

*This chapter introduces **Self-Esteem and Foreign Language Learning**. First, it briefly reviews the antecedents and the conceptual entity of self-esteem and then discusses the controversial effects some self-esteem programs have raised. The chapter then examines the influence of self-esteem in schools and specifically in the language classroom. A short review of each chapter of the book has also been included.*

## 1. Introduction

It was spring 2004 and I was attending a weekend course on self-esteem in the language classroom at El Molino, a lovely place hidden in the mountains of Huelva, in southern Spain. Veronica de Andrés, the presenter, stimulated my interest on the topic and showed some interesting classroom applications. She also stressed the importance of not considering self-esteem as a fashionable bandwagon to jump upon for a while, but rather an enduring concern for educators. Reflecting on the ideas we had been discussing, I felt that the topic certainly deserved serious research. However, I searched and found that there are no publications covering self-esteem in the foreign language classroom in a comprehensive manner, that is including theory, research and classroom applications. If the truth be told, there are very few articles dealing with self-esteem and the foreign language classroom.

---

[1] Fernando D. Rubio Alcalá teaches in the English Department at the University of Huelva. His research interests lie in affective factors in language learning, new technologies and teacher development in foreign language teaching and learning. E-mail: fernando.rubio@dfing.uhu.es

This book aims to bridge this gap between the areas of self-esteem and foreign language learning. In order to do so, it provides a theoretical background, a review of the existing literature and applications for classroom instruction.

## 2. Antecedents

Self-esteem is considered an indispensable concept in the literature of the social sciences (Wells and Marwell 1976). From William James' pioneer work in 1890 up to now, there exist thousands of studies that report the influence of self-esteem on human behaviour. Feelings of inadequacy, a sense of unworthiness, increased anxiety, depression, suicide, child abuse, mental disorders and other negative phenomena have been closely related to lack of self-esteem (Coopersmith 1967; Skager and Kerst 1989).

A considerable amount of research has also been carried out within the field of educational psychology, especially that which has been devoted to studying the relationship between self-esteem and academic achievement. Two main issues have been discussed:

1. Whether self-esteem is a cause or an outcome of academic achievement.
2. Whether correlations between both are positive, negative or insignificant.

Findings for both issues are diverse. Harter (1983), Beane and Lipka (1984), Chapman (1988), Marsh, Byrne and Shavelson (1988) maintain that self-esteem influences achievement; and a positive correlation is found in many studies (Solley and Stagner 1956; Covington 1989; Klein and Keller 1990; Rennie 1991; Auer 1992; Benham 1993; Lawrence 1996; Lerner 1996). Conversely, other studies sustain that self-esteem is mainly an outcome of achievement (Calysn 1971; Hoge, Smit and Crist 1995), or report a negative or absent correlation (Mecca, Smelser and Vasconcellos 1989; Roy et al. 2003).

This disparity of conclusions implies the difficulty involved in understanding the implications of the concept of self-esteem. As a matter of fact, numerous authorities have described it as an "impure phenomenon" (Mruk 1999, 34) connected to many other self-related phenomena and processes (Coopersmith 1967; Wiley 1974; Wells and Marwell 1976; Jackson 1984; Mecca et al. 1989; Ross 1992). Let us take a look at different conceptualizations.

## 3. What is self-esteem?

James (1890), White (1959), Coopersmith (1959) and (1967), Rosenberg (1965) and (1979), Branden (1969) and (1994), and Mruk (1999) and (2006) have been the main contributors to the development of the theoretical concept of self-esteem. Basically, their definitions point to six major components or dimensions of self-esteem:

- Competence and worthiness.
- Cognition and affect.
- Stability and openness.

Research indicates that all components are included to a certain degree and may affect a person depending on individual traits and context circumstances. *Competence* has been studied extensively under different labels (efficacy, success, etc.) and can be a major influence in school settings regarding academic achievement (Bandura 1987). Developmental psychology places the emergence of competence in middle childhood. On the other hand, *worthiness* develops in early childhood and comes originally from parental value, for instance, when parents show acceptance and approval after a child does something successfully. Worthiness is making judgment about oneself. Both phenomena exert influence on each other.

Also, part of the literature regarding the conceptualization of self-esteem has dedicated attention to whether to label it as being related to cognition or affect. Since evaluation is necessarily involved in our sense of worthiness and competence, cognition is then a central factor. However, neuro-scientific studies have shown that cognition and affect are distinct but inseparable (Schumann 1994) and have stressed the connections between the neocortex, involved in thinking and the limbic system which is related to emotions (cf. LeDoux 1996).

Finally, perhaps the most difficult issue researchers have faced on the conceptualization of self-esteem has been its dynamicity in terms of stability or openness. Is self-esteem open to change? Does change happen rapidly or slowly over time? In White's psychodynamic view, most openness occurs during childhood and then self-esteem becomes relatively stable, but still subject to change to a lesser degree. In that sense, self-esteem can fluctuate more than other stable characteristics like personality and intelligence (Sigelman and Shaffer 1995).

## 4. A definition of self-esteem

It is not my intention to add another definition of self-esteem here to the existing ones, but to briefly summarize the main components of the term. "The disposition to experience oneself as being competent to cope with the basic challenges of life and of being worthy of happiness" (Branden 1994) is one of the most accepted definitions. However, because self-esteem is a complex construct, a short definition cannot possibly grasp the whole concept and phenomenological process.

Basically, self-esteem is a psychological and social phenomenon in which an individual evaluates his/her competence and own self according to some values, which may result in different emotional states, and which becomes developmentally stable but is still open to variation depending on personal circumstances.

A definition is very "useful in making the distinction between authentic or healthy self-esteem and pseudo or unhealthy self-esteem" (Reasoner 2004), an issue to be dealt with in the next section.

## 5. Self-esteem and controversy

Many studies on self-esteem come from the USA. This has been in part due to the actions that have been carried out in schools as part of government programmes. Then, it is not surprising that political opponents and the media have taken any opportunity to criticize aspects of the programme which have had less than optimal results. This criticism, however, has led to discussion and development.

Most of the controversy could have been avoided if all involved had started from a sound definition. Most criticism comes from journalists, not always well informed, who misunderstand self-esteem as a phenomenon only related to worthiness[2]. Possibly, the main misconception has been associating high-self esteem with certain negative behaviours, such as narcissism or aggression. Mruk's matrix (1999, 164) is useful to comprehend the relationship between competence and worthiness and the resulting behaviours. Individuals can have a sense of high and low worthiness and competence combined in different ways:

a. High worthiness and high competence leads to high or authentic self-esteem.

b. High worthiness and low competence leads to Type I Defensive self-esteem, resulting in a self-centred behaviour.

---

[2] See instances in most articles at http://www.illinoisloop.org/selfesteem.html

c. Low worthiness and high competence leads to Type II Defensive self-esteem, resulting in overachieving behaviour.

d. Low worthiness and low competence leads to low self-esteem, resulting in negativistic behaviour.

In more extreme forms Types I and II can lead to narcissistic and antisocial behaviours respectively, and low self-esteem to depression. Thus it is not the case that individuals with high self-esteem show narcissistic behaviours.

Some of the criticisms of the anti-self-esteem movement may be legitimate since some school programs, probably implemented by uninformed educators, have tried to boost self-esteem artificially. For instance, praising students no matter what their effort or resulting work, instead of providing students with objective feedback and accurate evaluation of their competence. As Reasoner points out

> Programs and efforts limited to making students feel good are apt to have little lasting effects, because they fail to strengthen the internal sources of self-esteem related to: integrity, responsibility and achievement. Only addressing these areas can one effectively build self-esteem (Reasoner 1992, 24).

It is one thing to discuss the ways self-esteem work has been implemented in the schools and another to deny that self-esteem is of vital importance to an individual. We may still need to find better ways to deal with self-esteem in the classroom, but there is no doubt from all research available that self-esteem is crucial for personal and academic growth.

## 6. Self-esteem development and school

Although personal development and behaviour is influenced by a large number of factors, parental involvement can be decisive (Coopersmith 1967). For instance, Rosenberg (1965), Coopersmith (1967), and Clark (1994) found a positive correlation between children with lower levels of self-esteem and parents who were indifferent toward their children or absent for short or long periods of time. Parental warmth, expectations, respect, consistency and birth order are other factors affecting the development of self-esteem (Mruk 1999).

In addition to the family context, social settings can have an important influence on self-esteem, especially during adolescence. However, the early school years are associated with the most influential stage for the development of self-esteem. Fostering adequate early patterns which lead to healthy self-esteem is very important. Research in psychology and the neurosciences shows that the years from childhood to adolescence comprehend the critical period for personal formation. While nurturing within the family is the most important factor in early childhood, school progressively gains importance as a determining influence on the individual's self-esteem. In school, students are constantly evaluating their competence in classroom tasks and performances. Accordingly, self-efficacy, which is the perception people have about their competence, is fostered mainly in schools (Bandura 1987).

Inside the school context there are many factors that may affect the students' self-esteem. The type of subject to be learnt can be a significant issue, and specifically, learning a language. In the next section we will explore some of the reasons for this.

## 7. Self-esteem and the language classroom

Arnold (1999) and many other researchers refer to the importance of affect in the language classroom. Language learning is an anxiety-provoking experience for many students (Muchnick and Wolfe 1982; Horwitz et al. 1986; MacIntyre and Gardner 1991; Rubio 2004). As Horwitz et al (1991, 31) note,

> The importance of the disparity between the "true" self as known to the language learner and the more limited self as can be presented at any given moment in the foreign language would seem to distinguish foreign language anxiety from other academic anxieties such as those associated with mathematics or science. Probably no other field of study implicates self-concept and self-expression to the degree that language study does.

Generally speaking, self-esteem is one of the central drives in human beings. When the level of self-esteem is low, the psychological homeostasis is unbalanced, creating insecurity, fear, social distance and other negative situations. Self-esteem can exercise a determining influence on a person's life, for good or bad; when there is very low self-esteem, this may even bring about a need for clinical treatment. However, though in the context of language learning low self-esteem is a non-clinical phenomenon, it can have serious consequences. Students may avoid taking the necessary risks to acquire communicative competence in the target language; they may feel deeply insecure and even drop out of the class.

Taking these effects into consideration, in the language classroom it is important to be concerned about learners' self-esteem. However, this implies more than doing occasional activities to make students reflect about their worthiness and competence. As a first step, teachers themselves need to be aware of their own self-esteem, to understand what self-esteem is, what are the sources and components, and how applications can be implemented in the language classroom. This implementation should be based on a valid framework. In this book, many authors have adopted Reasoner's model (1982), which comprises security, identity, belonging, purpose and competence as the main components of self-esteem. Applications of a self-esteem model should be pre-planned in the teaching units and integrated within the foreign language curriculum.

## 8. Content of the book

Given that until now little has been written on self-esteem and the language learning context, this volume aims to bring together work on the topic that integrates both a theoretical and practical point of view, with the hope of attracting the interest of academic theoreticians and classroom teachers. While empirical research is not stressed in the book, hopefully researchers will also find inspiration for carrying out studies which can further illuminate the field.

This book is organized into three main parts. Part I serves as an introduction to self-esteem. Part II is dedicated to report the existing literature on the theory and research dealing with self-esteem in the language classroom. Finally, Part III includes general procedures for implementation and a wide range of activities for classroom applications.

Jane Arnold explores in Chapter 2 the territory giving an account of the connection between self-esteem and the affective domain in the language classroom. She stresses the importance of focussing on what is happening inside the learner rather than on other external elements in order to achieve goals for language learning, pointing out the importance of beliefs for the learning process. After analysing what realistic implementation should be, Arnold introduces Reasoner's model of self-esteem components and gives examples of how to deal with each in the language classroom.

In Chapter 3, Veronica de Andrés, one of the first researchers in the field of self-esteem and language learning, reports her experience with self-esteem implementation programs. Apart from explaining some of the theory regarding self-esteem, she includes a description of an action-research project, which includes details of the procedures used and examples of activities to promote self-esteem.

In Chapter 4 Javier Ávila delves further into the theoretical aspects of self-esteem. He reviews the existing literature, offering evidence that levels of self-esteem in the language classroom have impact on other process phenomena, such as motivation, anxiety, information processing, and learner autonomy.

From Avila's individual perspective on self-esteem Chapter 5 moves on to a more social or collective one. Sonia Casal describes the social dimension of self-esteem in the language classroom and claims that group work in itself does not necessarily foment socializing and learning. Cooperative work, where there is interdependence, is a step in the right direction. She specifies that classroom activities which incorporate goal interdependence, resource interdependence and role interdependence can help to foster healthy self-esteem on a personal and a social dimension.

In Chapter 6, Ana Ortega examines the relationship between self-esteem and anxiety. Both phenomena exert influence on each other and affect students in a subtle way so that they avoid participating in class.

Chapter 7 studies the role of self-esteem in adolescents. Carmen Fonseca and Carmen Toscano explain that the difficulties involved in teaching teenagers may well relate to the special characteristics of learners in this age group who are involved in a critical period for the construction of their identity. After presenting an analysis of different factors affecting adolescents, they offer Smith's model as a guide to improving teenagers' attitudes towards learning a foreign language.

Andrew Wright offers in Chapter 8 an analysis of the connection between self-esteem and storytelling. Following an introspective method and relying on his extensive experience in the world of language teaching, Wright explains that storytelling helps in the creation of positive values that would eventually form part of a person's identity. He also gives an account of how to create, adapt and apply stories in the language classroom with the aim of enhancing self-esteem.

In Chapter 9 Marina Arcos provides a wide range of activities to develop children's self-esteem. She suggests that through these activities young learners both improve their self-concept and acquire English in a way that is personally meaningful and thus more effective for learning. Chapter 10 presents some ideas and activities for enhancing teenagers' self-esteem in the language classroom. Eva Díaz and Concha Julián also include some tips for classroom procedures, taking into account the difficult age students are going through and their resulting problematic behaviour in the classroom.

Finally, Chapter 11 turns our attention to teachers. Inmaculada León deals with the topic of teachers confirmation, which is described as the process by means of which teachers make students feel valued, recognized and acknowledged. She also examines some of the problems that affect teachers today and offers a scale of teacher behaviours that lead to confirmation.

## Works Cited

Arnold, J. 1999. *Affect in language learning*. Cambridge: Cambridge University Press.

Auer, C.J. 1992. A comparison of the locus of control of first and second grade students in whole language, basal reader, and eclectic instructional approach classrooms, *Dissertation Abstracts International* 53, (11): 3856 PhD diss., Northern Illinois University.

Bandura, A. 1987. *Pensamiento y acción. Fundamentos sociales*. Barcelona: Martínez Roca.

Beane, J.A., and R.P. Lipka. 1984. *Self-Concept, self-esteem, and the curriculum*. Newton: Allyn and Bacon.

Benham, M.J. 1993. *Fostering self-motivated behaviour, personal responsibility, and internal locus of control,* Eugene, Oregon. Office of Educational Research and Improvement (ERIC Document Reproduction No. ED 386 621).

Branden, N. 1969. *The psychology of self-esteem*. New York: Bantam.

—. 1994. *The six pillars of self-esteem*. New York: Bantam.

Calsyn, R.J. and D.A. Kenny. 1983. Self-concept of ability and perceived evaluation of others: Cause or effect of academic achievement? *Journal of Educational Psychology* 68: 136-145.

Chapman, J.W. 1988. Learning disabled children's self-concept. *Review of Educational Research* 58: 347-371.

Clark, J. 1994. Adolescents in post divorce and always married families: Self-esteem and perceptions of father's interest. *Journal of Marriage and the Family* 56.

Coopersmith, S. 1959. A method for determining types of self-esteem. *Journal of Abnormal Social Psychology* 59: 87-94.

—. 1967. *The antecedents of self-esteem*. San Francisco: Freeman.

Dornëy, Z. 2005. *The psychology of the language learner*. Mahwah: Laurence Erlbaum Associates, Inc.

Harter, S. 1983. Developmental perspectives on the self-system. In *Handbook of Child Psychology*, ed. E. M. Hetherington, 275-385. New York: Wiley.

Hoge, D.R., E.K. Smit, and T.J. Crist. 1995. Reciprocal effects of self-concept and academic achievement in sixth and seventh grade. *Journal of Youth and Adolescence* 24, (3): 295-314.

Horwitz, E.K., M.B. Horwitz, and J.A. Cope. 1986. Foreign language classroom anxiety. *Modern Language Journal* 70: 125-132.

Horwitz, E.K., and D.J. Young. 1991. *Language anxiety. From theory and research to classroom implications*. Englewood Cliffs: Prentice-Hall.

Jackson, M. 1984. *Self-esteem and meaning: A life historical investigation*. Albany: State University of New York.

James, W. 1983. (Ed. 1890). *The principles of psychology*. Cambridge: Harvard University Press.

Klein, J. D., and J.M. Keller. 1990. Influence of student ability, locus of control, and type of instructional control on performance and confidence. *Journal of Educational Research* 83, (3): 140-46.

Lawrence, D. 1996. Enhancing self-esteem in the classroom. London: PCP Ltd.

LeDoux, J. 1996. *The emotional brain*. New York: Simon and Schuster.

Lerner, B. 1996. Self-esteem and excellence: The choice and the paradox. *American Educator* 20, (2): 9-13.

MacIntyre, P.D. and R.C. Gardner. 1991. Methods and results in the study of anxiety and language learning: A review of the literature. *Language Learning* 41: 85-117.

Marsh, H.W., B. Byrne, and R.J. Shavelson. 1988. A multifaceted academic self-concept. Its' hierarchial structure and its' relation to academic achievement. *Journal of Educational Psychology* 80: 366-380.

Mecca, A.M, N.S. Smelser, and J. Vasconcellos. 1989. *The social importance of self-esteem.* Berkeley: University of California Press.

Mruk, C. 1999 (2nd ed.). *Self-esteem: Research, theory and practice.* New York: Single Publishing Company.

—. 2006 (3rd ed.). *Self-esteem: Research, theory and practice.* New York: Single Publishing Company.

Muchnick, A.G., and D.E. Wolfe. 1982. Attitudes and motivations of American students of Spanish. *The Canadian Modern Language Review* 38: 262-281.

Rennie, L.J. 1991. The relationship between affect and achievement in science. *Journal of Research in Science Teaching* 28, (2): 193-09.

Reasoner, R. 1982. *Building self-Esteem: A comprehensive program.* Palo Alto: Consulting Psychologists Press.

—. 2004. The true meaning of self-esteem. http://www.self-esteem-nase.org/whatisselfesteem.html

Ross, A. 1992. *The sense of self.* New York: Springer.

Roy F., J.D. Baumeister, J.I. Campbell, I. Krueger, and D.V. Kathleen. 2003. Does high self-esteem cause better performance, interpersonal success, happiness, or healthier lifestyles? *Psychological Science in the Public Interest* 4, (1): 1–44.

Rosenberg, M. 1965. *Society and the adolescent self-image.* Princeton: Princeton University Press.

—. 1979. *Conceiving the self.* New York: Basic Books.

Rubio, F.D. 2004. *La ansiedad en el aprendizaje de idiomas*. Huelva: Universidad de Huelva.

Schumann, J. 1994. Where is cognition? Emotion and cognition in second language acquisition. *Studies in Second Language Acquisition* 16: 231-242.

Sigelman, C.S., and D.R. Shaffer. 1995 (2nd ed.). *Life-span human development.* Belmont: Brooks/Cole.

Skager, R. and J. Kerst. 1989. Alcohol and drug use and self-esteem: A psychological perspective. In *The social importance of self-esteem*, ed. A.M. Mecca, N.J. Smelser, and J. Vasconcellos, 248-293. Berkeley: University of California Press.

Solley, C.M., and R. Stagner. 1956. Effect of magnitude of temporal barriers, types of perception of self. *Journal of Experimental Psychology* 51: 62-70.

Wells, E.L., and G. Marwell. 1976. *Self-esteem: Its conceptualization and measurement*. Beverly Hills: Sage.

White, R. 1959. Motivation reconsidered: The concept of competence. *Psychological Review* 66: 297-333.

Wylie, R. 1974. *The self-concept* (Vol. 1). Lincoln: University of Nebraska Press.

# CHAPTER TWO

# SELF-CONCEPT AND THE AFFECTIVE DOMAIN IN LANGUAGE LEARNING

JANE ARNOLD[1] (UNIVERSITY OF SEVILLE, SPAIN)

*Recent years have seen the growth of interest in affective factors, which influence the process of language learning in many ways. These may be of a facilitating or inhibiting nature and can often determine the outcome of this process. In the classroom affect may be apparent in the relationships established there but it may also relate to learner-internal aspects, and one of the most prominent of these is self-esteem. Learners' self-concept–their perception of themselves, what they see when they look "inside"-and their self-esteem–their evaluation of this self-concept and their affective experience of it-are closely related to their learning. In this chapter we will explore how they influence language learning and see some implications for the classroom.*

## 1. Affect and learning. The role of self-concept

There can be no doubt today about the importance of affect for learning. As Rodríguez, Plax and Kearney (1996, 297) explain, "Affect is by definition, an intrinsic motivator. Positive affect sustains involvement and deepens interest in the subject matter". It can lead to more effective learning and, in fact, may be essential for learning to occur.

If we were looking for a golden rule for language learning, one possible candidate would be Stevick's (1980, 4) statement about how success in this process depends "less on materials, techniques and linguistic analysis and more on what goes on inside and between the people in the classroom". This often quoted phrase has been used to organize the area of affect in language learning

---

[1] Jane Arnold is Professor of English Language Teaching Methodology at the University of Seville. She has published *Affect in Language Learning* with Cambridge University Press, and is actively involved in programs of foreign language teacher training. E-mail: arnold@us.es

and teaching, where we can consider that there are two basic aspects, the "inside", or internal characteristics which are a part of the learner's personality, and the "between", or the relational factors which focus on learners and teachers as participants in an interactional situation (Arnold and Brown 1999). Among the learner internal factors, of central importance is the image we form of ourselves, our self-concept. As human beings, at all times and in all places we inevitably form an image of self. How we evaluate that self–negatively or positively–will determine our self-esteem. Researchers in communication studies, an area very relevant for language teaching, affirm that "the overwhelming conclusion from both research and theory is that the perceptions one has of self significantly affect attitudes, behaviours, evaluations, and cognitive processes. In classroom research the concept an individual has of self has also played an important role" (McCroskey et al. 1977, 269).

In an early approach to the topic Coopersmith (1967, 4-5) described self-esteem in this way:

> By self-esteem we refer to the evaluation which the individual makes and customarily maintains with regard to himself; it expresses an attitude of approval or disapproval, and indicates the extent to which the individual believes himself to be capable, significant, successful, and worthy. In short, self-esteem is a personal judgment of worthiness that is expressed in the attitudes the individual holds towards himself; it is a subjective experience which the individual conveys to others by verbal reports and other overt expressive behavior.

Based on work by researchers such as Coopersmith, Reasoner (1982) and others, the incorporation of a concern with self-esteem has proved to be an important direction in education. Yet in the process it may have come to be considered a band-wagon to jump on or even a panacea which is alleged to be able to solve complex problems that have very diverse and unrelated roots. Thus, there have been misunderstandings of the essence of work on self-esteem in education. Critics have affirmed that dealing with self-esteem can lead to egocentric behaviour and to unrealistic expectations. However, for productive work on self-esteem it goes without saying that what is being considered is what we could term "healthy" self-esteem, where students have both a positive, **accurate** belief about themselves and their abilities and also the **commitment** and **responsibility** that comes when they see themselves as able to complete worthwhile goals. It is never a case of giving students false beliefs or of telling them that "anything goes". Quite the contrary, work with self-esteem and other affective issues is connected to providing a supportive atmosphere in which we can better encourage learners to work hard to reach their learning potential unhindered by the negative affect Krashen (1982) referred to with his metaphor of the affective filter.

Rosenberg, the originator of one of the most commonly used self-esteem measurement scales, adds an important point in his formulation of the concept: "High self-esteem... expresses the feeling that one is *good enough*. The individual simply feels that he is a person of worth; he respects himself for what he is, but *does not stand in awe of himself nor does he expect others to stand in awe of him*" (Rosenberg 1965, 30-1, emphasis added). So it is not, as some have affirmed, a case of an unhealthy ego. What we are referring to is a balanced view of self worth from which it is easier to carry out learning tasks in whatever subject matter of the curriculum we are dealing with.

## 2. Self-esteem and beliefs

Self-esteem can, as Rosenberg (1965, 15) states, be thought of as one's *attitude* towards oneself. Secord and Backman (1964) use three categories to define our attitude about something: *affective* (our feelings about it), *behavioural* (how we behave regarding it), and *cognitive* (our beliefs about it). To reframe this somewhat in the context of language learning, we could say that our attitude about the self as a language learner includes what we believe ("I am capable of learning the language" or "I can never learn") which leads to our feelings about the learning process ("pleasure" or "pain") and this in turn will determine our behaviour (approaching or avoiding opportunities to further our learning).

Puchta (1999b, 66) has stressed the importance of beliefs for any learning experience. "Beliefs are strong perceptual filters. They serve as explanations for what has happened and they give us a basis for future behaviour". They are so influential in the learning process because they operate on the level of our identity. Thus, if we, for example, correct students' errors in an insensitive manner, what they may perceive is not that we have given them an opportunity to see how to bring their interlanguage closer to the target norm, but instead that we have reinforced their belief that they are not capable of learning the target language or even that they are not valuable human beings. Their identity and their self-esteem are compromised, they may become unwilling to try again, and future learning experiences will be less productive.

Low self-concept makes it hard to be fully on task, as energy is split between the task and an excessive concern with a belief about one's lack of ability or worth. It creates a doubly disadvantaged learning situation: there is less energy for the task at hand and the negative feelings generated make the learning experience unpleasant, less motivating and thus less effective. Ehrman and Dörnyei (1998, 257) point out that according to motivation theory, "the highest human priority is the need for self-acceptance". Thus, we cannot ignore this factor in any activity that is as motivation-dependent as language learning.

A student who has formed a belief that he can't learn languages is right-he can't... unless he changes this belief. As long as he maintains it, he may even have a vested interest in doing poorly. It may be that in the language classroom all he has left to protect his self-concept is the small satisfaction that comes from being right about something: his failure proves he made a correct appreciation of his language ability. Deutsch and Solomon (1959) have shown that an individual with low self esteem may view a negative evaluation by others of himself as more favourable than a high evaluation. Puchta (1999a, 257) maintains that "negative beliefs influence our student's expectations. Low expectations lead to a low level of motivation and every failure is seen as confirmation of the initial beliefs". The inner speech or self-talk of this type of individual may go something like this: "I'm right again. I am a terrible language learner. I knew it right from the start". This feeling that is generated does not depend on objective, observable facts but on our beliefs, often very subjective, but, for this very reason, fortunately amenable to change.

There are different ways to change, to reframe these limiting beliefs. One possibility is through mental imagery. Brown (1991, 86) presents students who are trying to learn to speak a foreign language with what he calls the visualization game: "Visualize yourself speaking the language fluently and interacting with people. Then when you are actually in such a situation, you will, in a sense have been there before". As there exists a very close relationship between our feelings and our mental images, including self-images, if students experience a strong mental image of themselves performing language learning tasks successfully, this can reduce negative beliefs and provide a good starting point for effective bottom up work on the language.

In psychology the concept of "ideal selves" is very relevant here. As Markus and Ruvolo (1989, 213) claim, "imagining one's own actions through the construction of elaborated possible selves achieving the desired goal may thus directly facilitate the translation of goals into intentions and instrumental actions". Dörnyei (2005, 102) cites further work by Ruvolo and Markus (1992) where they "provide empirical evidence that imagery manipulations (in their case, asking participants to imagine themselves as successful or unsuccessful before a task) increased the accessibility of possible selves and this was reflected in the subjects' performance". He applies this idea to language learning where the concept he proposes of the *Ideal L2 Self* can broaden our understanding of motivational factors at work in a wider variety of learning situations than other models which are closely tied to a context in which the learner has significant contact with the L2 outside the classroom. Describing his model of the L2 motivational self system, Dörnyei (2005, 106) concludes that "if the person we would like to become speaks an L2, the *ideal L2 self* is a powerful motivator to learn the L2 because of the desire to reduce the discrepancy between our actual and ideal selves". Thus, if in our students' image of the self they want to become, they include an aspect of successful language learning, this can provide strong support for the learning process. Teachers can help to develop this self-image by, on the one hand, helping to make being a L2 speaker seem attractive and, on the other, making it seem possible through their encouragement and by stressing that if learners are willing to work to learn the L2, they will be successful in doing so.

There is conclusive research evidence that self-concept determines behaviour. What students feel about themselves will affect the way they approach the learning experience and also their relationships with others. Connecting with many previous studies, the research of Brown and Smart (1991) with university students showed that subjects who conceived of themselves as kind and helpful exhibited prosocial behaviour. They also found that those with high self-esteem, even after failure, were more capable of maintaining a positive view of self. Subjects with low self-esteem not only had difficulty in reaffirming their self image after failure, they then showed a tendency to act in a selfish manner. They concluded that "self-representations appear to play a critical role in guiding and regulating behavior" (p. 373), an idea which has important implications beyond the individual and beyond the classroom given the possibility that "ultimately social change may be effected by affecting the self" (p. 375).

## 3. Enemies of a positive self-concept

In language learning, more than in most other areas of the curriculum, our self-concept can often be truly endangered. When we are trying to learn a second language, the self is especially vulnerable because it is deprived of its normal, familiar vehicle of expression. In fact, *language shock* may occur when learners "fear that their words in the target language do not reflect their ideas adequately, perhaps making them appear ridiculous or infantile" (Arnold and Brown 1999, 21-22).

When students are learning a foreign language, speaking in the language involves taking risks. In any situation we may be judged by what we say. Since we know that when we speak in the foreign language we cannot yet express ourselves fluently, we see the self that we present as a limited version of our real self. If the classroom atmosphere is not supportive, it will be that much more difficult for students to take the necessary risks involved in attempting to communicate. Teachers often underestimate the discomfort students experience when required to display their ability to speak in the language in front of their peers. Insistence by the teacher on unrealistic models of perfection will only increase their feeling of self-consciousness and inadequacy. In no way is this to say that we do not demand the best of our students, but we cannot get the best from them if there is affective interference in their cognitive processing. There are many enemies of self-esteem in the classroom. Hoffman (1999) discusses some of them: labelling, criticism, sarcasm, put downs, comparisons, and evaluating the person rather than the behaviour. If these are not avoided, learners' self-concept will not be protected in the classroom.

In language learning and use communication in the language is a vital factor, but oral communication in the foreign language has been shown to be especially anxiety provoking (Horwitz et al. 1991). In the field of communication studies oral communication apprehension has been shown to be associated with low self-esteem (McCroskey et al. 1977), and it is highly plausible that in the specific context of second language learning the relationship would be even stronger, given the added difficulty of formulating one's message in a language one does not totally control.

## 4. A realistic view of self-esteem for the language classroom

In the language classroom attention to self-esteem can help to direct learner energy which has been diverted from the learning task and focused on non-productive identity beliefs back to a state which is productive for acquisition. However, it is extremely important to make clear from the outset that work with self-esteem does not include empty praise, which may create unreasonable expectations and an inaccurate sense of reality. Confidence comes from competence. Realistic concern with learner self-esteem in the language classroom does not focus on creating false beliefs of a positive nature to replace the negative ones. Rather, it is a question of providing learners with the means to succeed in their language learning while at the same time reducing any limiting false beliefs about their worth and their abilities that keep them from reaching their potential. Learners must both *be* competent and *feel* competent. Similarly, we cannot lead students to expect the road toward language learning to be free of obstacles. Obstacles exist and they help us develop our muscles as we overcome them. Once again, effective work with self-esteem must be realistic.

Lozanov has pointed out that positive suggestion can be useful up to a point, as it can exercise a placebo effect on the learners, helping them to put any negative beliefs about themselves on hold. However, the placebo must then be supported by the feedback on the learners' ability that comes from real accomplishment (Hooper Hansen 1999). In Suggestopedia, for example, it is claimed that the real reinforcement for learners' self-esteem comes from the facilitation of more efficient learning. Learners need to be aware of their worthiness and capabilities, but more effective than telling them they are capable is helping them to experience how well they can learn.

Self-esteem is, we have seen, important for learning. But can we really do anything about it? Many, like Underhill (1989), feel that in doing work in areas of affect such as self-esteem lies the answer to the question of what makes teaching really effective. What we do with this or any other aspect of affect does not need to be heavy-handed and obvious; many times the greatest changes can come from very subtle actions. Perhaps the most important factor in promoting learners' self-esteem is a caring attitude on the part of the teacher. If we try to understand our students, to feel empathy for them, they will perceive this, and the classroom atmosphere can change quite radically. Studies done on teacher immediacy and learning have shown that affective learning "motivates students to engage in task-relevant behaviors" which then lead to cognitive learning (Rodriguez, Plax and Kearney 1996, 297). These studies conclude that "affect is a means to an end, or, said differently, affect is the mediator between a number of teacher communication variables and cognitive learning" (op cit. 303). The way the model they developed works is that when teachers create an affectively-based relationship which supports their students through immediacy behaviours such as interpersonal closeness, warmth, and friendliness, this predisposes the students to spend more time on learning, leading to cognitive payoffs in the classroom.

Similarly, teacher confirmation, or "the process by which teachers communicate to students that those students are valuable, significant individuals" (Ellis 2004, 2), has been shown to foster greater cognitive and affective learning. One particularly useful aspect of teacher confirmation studies and the development of teacher confirmation scales is that they specify concrete observable behaviours such as "smiles at students" or "answers students' questions fully" rather than abstract and unmeasurable concepts such as "respects students" (Elllis 2004, 7)[2].

To help students who exhibit very low self-esteem, there is a clear need for expert guidance, and as teachers we may quite rightly feel we lack proper training to deal competently with such a situation. However, all teachers can contribute to creating a more "self"-happy environment in the classroom. The following general suggestions may be helpful:

- Start from where the students are at and listen to them as they are, non-judgementally and empathetically.
- On exams try to find out what the students know rather than what they don't know.
- Use humour only "with" students, never "against" them.
- Find ways to correct spoken errors with tact.
- Remember that undesirable behaviour is generally rooted in low self-esteem. To improve this behaviour try to focus on the root, not the surface manifestation of the problem.

---

[2] León (2005 and this volume) has applied teacher confirmation to language teachers and has developed a teacher confirmation scale for the foreign language teaching context.

- Consider all students as worthwhile people and let them know this. If you accept and value them, this will facilitate their self-acceptance.
- Ask yourself if you were a student in your class, would you feel safe and supported? How easy would it be for you to take the risks inherent in language learning?

## 5. Reasoner's model of self-esteem applied to language learning

For specific applications of self-esteem research to the language classroom, it may be helpful to start from the model of Robert Reasoner (1982). He posits five components of self-esteem:

- Security – knowing that I am safe, physically and emotionally
- Identity – knowing who I am
- Belonging – knowing others accept me
- Purpose – knowing what I want to do and to achieve
- Competence – knowing I can

We can develop each of these in the language classroom at the same time as we work on language skills.

### 5.1. Security

Studies of teacher confirmation (Ellis 2000; León 2005 and this volume) point to the importance of establishing a secure environment to make risk-taking a reasonable venture. One way to do so has to do with the area of dealing with mistakes. Research shows that students want to get feedback about errors they make, but insensitive correction can lead to anxiety. Teachers can explain that mistakes are a normal, positive aspect of the learning process. To model learning to accept one's mistakes, Murphey (1998a) recommends teachers to tell "mistake stories" about times they have made funny little mistakes, and so in a sense they set an example for what they want students to do: feel at ease in the classroom and not be so afraid of making mistakes that they greatly reduce their opportunities for learning the language.

### 5.2. Identity

As Williams (1994) has said, language is part of a person's identity, and by means of language we communicate who we are to others. She stresses that when learning a new language, not only do we acquire skills and knowledge of the rules of the language, we also modify our idea of self.

We learn who we are through interaction with others. To reaffirm their identity, students can play the following version of a children's game. In groups of four, they complete statements such as the following for everyone in the group, including themselves.

Name ______________________

1. If I were an animal, I would be a ....
2. If I were a plant, I would be a ...
3. If I were a quality, I would be ....
4. If I were a famous person, I would be...
5. If I were a song, I would be....

(For the others they use their names: "If Pedro were an animal, he would be a...", "If Gina were a plant, she would be a…).

Focusing on one person in the group, the other members all read what they wrote about this person. S/he can choose one of the comments from each of the others and ask them to explain it. For example, if someone tells him/her "If you were a song, you would be *Imagine*", s/he can ask why and the classmate might say "Because you are very idealistic". In this way, students are being mirrors for others to see aspects of themselves and at the same time they are drilling the formation of the second conditional. Finally, the person reads his/her own sentences about herself. The process is repeated for each member of the group.

## 5.3. Belonging

Speaking of the question of classroom identity, Murphey (1998b, 15) contends that "students seek (unconsciously) an answer to the question "Who am I in this place with these people?" and that "the characteristics of this classroom identity will determine how much they invest themselves in the course". They will inevitably invest more if they have a sense of belonging.

To develop belonging in the classroom, students first of all need to know each other, and learning others' names at the beginning is an important step. One way to start is to give them a post-it the first day and have them write their name on it and draw four pictures of things that are related to themselves. They then walk around talking to their classmates, asking about their pictures and at the same time learning their names. The following class they can form two parallel lines and with others in their own line try to remember as many names of classmates in the other line as possible. Volunteers can be called on to try to name everyone in the other line.

Especially in a second language context where students may not have many groups they can feel a part of, a sense of belonging can be developed if teachers form groups of four or five students which will be maintained for a certain time (two weeks, a month, the whole course...). Each group can decide on a group name and prepare a collage of their photos, with texts about each member, pictures of things they like, etc. These will be displayed and can be the source of diverse activities. Some of the normal class activities can be done in these groups, and others from cooperative learning (Casal 2002) can be incorporated to give students a chance to get to know each other as they work together towards common language and personal goals.

## 5.4. Purpose

Learning a second language is a very long, complex process and it is helpful for learners to set short-term goals. Even for those who really want to learn the language, it is not always useful for them to consider that “learning the language” is their goal. Goals need to be more manageable. Dörnyei (2001, 82) suggests that “short-term goals can help the learner to structure the learning process... [and] might provide immediate extra incentives”.

Teachers can encourage students to set manageable, short-term goals to support their learning. As a checklist for effective goal setting we can use the following **7-P** scheme:

- **Positive**. A goal should lead to a positive outcome that the learner wants.
- **Possible**. The goal should be within the learner’s capabilities at the present moment.
- **Precise**. The goal should be expressed in very concrete terms.
- **Plan**. There should be a plan to follow, clear steps to take towards the goal.
- **Periods**. There should be time periods by which the different steps will be completed.
- **Problem-solving.** Learners need to foresee problems that might occur and have solutions ready to use when they do.
- **Progress.** Learners need to have ways to evaluate their progress

## 5.5. Competence

One specific way to work effectively with learners’ feelings about their competence is to focus on self-talk. Learners can be made aware of these continual inner monologues that we produce almost unconsciously throughout the day. Our self-talk is directly related to our self-esteem. If our self-esteem is healthy, our self-talk generally tends to be of a more positive nature; if it is low, the self-talk tends to be negative (*I'll never get this... I'm a real disaster...*). Learners can be made aware of self-talk, encouraged to observe it and to beware of negative comments to themselves.

Another way to develop a sense of competence is to teach learners to set short-term goals which they can readily achieve and recognize as successfully achieved. This can bring them a sense of competence, a sense of "can do".

Closely linked to the notion of competence is the concept of autonomy, which Little (1991, 4) defines as "capacity for detachment, critical reflection, decision-making and independent action". As autonomy grows, so does the sense of competence. To develop both, within the Common European Framework one of the most significant aspects for the classroom is the use of Portfolios (Kohonen 2001; McDonald 2004). The essence of the Portfolio is a record of experiences with language learning, and it is directly connected with reflection. Many coursebooks now provide sections where learners are guided in the process with checklists of skills ("I can introduce somebody... I can ask for things..."). Even on this very basic level of reflection, as McDonald affirms (2004, 12), "Ticking off little chunks of 'Can dos' in turn serves as a form of motivation". This motivation is directly related to the students' feeling of competence.

Many classroom activities can also lead students to a greater appreciation of their competence. One possibility is to have students prepare a short talk in English about something they are good at or something they enjoy doing. Then working in small groups, which makes speaking easier, they give their talks. Students should be encouraged to ask their classmates questions about their talks and to provide supportive comments (*That is really interesting. You must be pleased. I'd like to be able to do that*). An exercise like this can easily be related to language work on the level of pragmatics in the area of politeness, complimenting, etc.

In research in Thailand, Liu (1997) found that video recording students' performances of oral presentations and role-plays had positive effects on both their self-esteem and their oral proficiency. As they knew their work would be recorded, they made a great effort to do their best, and with the recordings they had concrete, tangible evidence of their competence, of how they were capable of using the foreign language.

It should be mentioned that, like any affect-based work, self-esteem activities are only truly effective when an atmosphere of trust and respect exists in the classroom. For Rogers (1983), this climate can be found when we develop our qualities of genuineness, unconditional acceptance and empathy.

## 6. Conclusion

If teachers are to enhance learners' self-concept, it is important for them to be first concerned with their own, to be aware of their needs and their capabilities, of themselves. As Palmer (1998, 8) says, "when I do not know myself, I cannot know who my students are... [and] I cannot teach them well... Whatever self-knowledge we attain as teachers will serve our students and our scholarship well. Good teaching requires self-knowledge". Self-knowledge is a vital first step towards self-esteem, whether that of teachers or of students.

After parents, teachers are quite possibly the people who have most influence on the development of one's self-esteem, especially in the stages before adolescence. At all ages, however, they can affect learners' self-concept in both positive and negative ways, but as Hadfield (1992, 86) points out, "Negativity has a very powerful attraction. For some reason, criticism is easier to voice than praise, dissatisfaction than satisfaction". It is very important, then, for teachers to be aware of the influence they have on students' self concept and of the importance of self concept for learning.

Canfield and Wells (1994, 5) stress that self-esteem activities in the classroom are not frills that can be dispensed with: "The research literature is filled with reports indicating that cognitive learning increases when self-concept increases. The data suggesting this conclusion is quite extensive and overwhelming". Yet, who has not heard teachers say that being concerned with matters such as self-esteem is not part of their job? These same teachers may then go on to complain about discipline problems, lack of student participation or any number of other impediments to successful learning, which in reality may be intimately related to matters of self-concept. Even when our students have healthy self-esteem, they can benefit from a confidence-encouraging atmosphere. Andrés (1999, 89) points out that "success in language learning is inextricably linked to the way in which learners experience the classroom: as a place where their weaknesses will be revealed or as a space for growth and development".

To those who claim that a concern with students' self-concept is not necessary for language teachers, we might stress that one basic reason that self-esteem is significant for us is that its absence can create a serious block to learning. Beyond this, however, if we agree with many educators that both we and our students are empowered by personal growth and that concern with growth factors can be useful in any curriculum, it seems quite reasonable to take self-concept into consideration. This may entail no more than developing a sensitive attitude towards students or it may include exercises that relate directly or indirectly to aspects of self-esteem such as identity or belonging. If we as teachers become fully aware of the importance for the learning process of students' self-concept, ways to enhance it that we are comfortable with in our classes will present themselves and, as an added benefit, our own self-concept will be strengthened in the process.

## Works Cited

Andrés, V. de. 1999. Self-esteem in the classroom or the metamorphosis of butterflies. In *Affect in Language Learning*, ed. J. Arnold. Cambridge: Cambridge University Press.

Arnold, J., and H.D. Brown. 1999. A map of the terrain. In *Affect in language learning*, ed. J. Arnold. Cambridge: Cambridge University Press.

Brown, H. D. 1991. *Breaking the language barrier.* Yarmouth: Intercultural Press.

Brown, J.D., and S.A. Smart. 1991. The self and social conduct: Linking self-representations to prosocial behavior. *Journal of Personality and Social Psychology* 60, (3): 368-375.

Canfield, J., and H.C. Wells. 1994. *100 ways to enhance self-concept in the classroom.* Boston: Allyn and Bacon.

Casal, S. 2002. El desarrollo de la inteligencia interpersonal mediante las técnicas del aprendizaje cooperativo. In *Inteligencias múltiples, múltiples formas de enseñar inglés*, ed. M. Fonseca. Seville: Mergablum.

Coopersmith, S. 1967. *The antecedents of self-Esteem.* San Francisco: Freeman & Co.

Deutsch, M., and L. Solomon 1959. Reactions to evaluations by others as influenced by self evaluations. *Sociometry* 22: 93-112.

Dörnyei, Z. 2001. *Motivational strategies in the language classroom.* Cambridge: Cambridge University Press.

—. 2005. *Psychology of the language learner: Individual differences in Second Language Acquisition.* Mahwah: Lawrence Erlbaum.

Ehrman, M., and Z. Dörnyei. 1998. *Interpersonal dynamics in second language education: The visible and invisible classroom.* Thousand Oaks: Sage.

Ellis, K. 2000. Perceived teacher confirmation: The development and validation of an instrument and two studies of the relationship to cognitive and affective learning. *Human Communication Research* 26: 254-291.

—. 2004. The impact of perceived teacher confirmation on receiver apprehension, motivation and learning. *Communication Education* 55, (1): 1-20.

Hadfield, J. 1992. *Classroom dynamics.* Oxford: Oxford University Press.

Hoffman, E. 1999. *The Learning adventure.* Middlewich: Learn to Learn.

Hooper Hansen, G. 1999. Learning by heart: A Lozanov perspective. In *Affect in Language Learning,* ed. J. Arnold. Cambridge: Cambridge University Press.

Horwitz, E.K, M.B. Horwitz, and J. A. Cope. 1991. In *Language anxiety: From theory and research to classroom implications*, ed. E.K. Horwitz and D.J. Young. Englewood Cliffs: Prentice Hall.

Kohonen, V. 2001. Developing the European language portfolio as a pedagogical tool for advancing student autonomy. In *All together now. Papers from the Nordic conference on autonomous language learning*, ed. L. Karlsson, F. Kjisik, and J. Nordlund. Helsinki: University of Helsinki Language Centre.

Krashen, S. 1982. *Principles and practice in Second Language Acquisition.* Oxford: Pergamon Press.

León, I. 2005. La confirmación del profesor de inglés percibida por el alumnado en educación secundaria. Unpublished MA thesis, University of Seville.

Little, D. 1991. *Learner autonomy: Definitions, issues and problems.* Dublin: Authentik.

Liu, Y. 1997. Video presentation: Using the camcorder to work miracles in the KEFL classroom. *ThaiTESOL Bulletin* 10: 2.

McCroskey, J., J. Daly, V. Richmond, and R. Falcione. 1977. Studies of the relationship between communication apprehension and self-esteem. *Human Communication Research* 3, (3): 269-277.

McDonald, A. 2004. A frame for learning. *English Teaching Professional* 35: 10-12.

Markus, H., and A. Ruvolo. 1989. Possible selves: Personalized representations of Goals. In *Goal Concepts in Personality and Social Psychology*, ed. L.A. Pervin. Hillsdale: Erlbaum.

Murphey, T. 1998a. *Language hungry. An introduction to language learning fun and self-esteem.* Tokyo: Macmillan Language House.

—. 1998b. Friends and classroom identity formation. *IATEFL Issues* 145: 15-16.

Palmer, P. 1998. *The Courage to teach.* San Francisco: Jossey and Bass.

Puchta, H. 1999a. Creating a learning culture to which students want to belong. In *Affect in Language Learning*, ed. J. Arnold. Cambridge: Cambridge University Press.

—. 1999b. Beyond materials, techniques and linguistic analyses: The role of motivation, beliefs and identity. *IATEFL 1999: Edinburgh Conference Selections.*

Reasoner, R. 1982. *Building self-esteem in secondary schools.* Palo Alto: Consulting Psychologists Press, Inc.

Rodríguez, J., T. Plax, and P. Kearney.1996. Clarifying the relationship between teacher nonverbal immediacy and student cognitive learning: Affective learning as the central causal mediator. *Communication Education* 45: 294-305.

Rogers, C. 1983. *Freedom to learn for the 80s.* Columbus: Charles E. Merrill.

Rosenberg, M. 1965. *Society and the adolescent self-image.* Princeton: Princeton University Press.

Secord, P. F., and C.W. Backman. 1964. *Social psychology.* New York: McGraw-Hill.

Stevick, E. 1980. *Teaching languages. A way and ways.* Rowley: Newbury House.
Underhill, A. 1989. Process in humanistic education. *ELT Journal* 43: 250-60.
Williams, M. 1994. Motivation in foreign and second language learning: An interactive perspective. *Educational and Child Psychology* 11: 77-84.

# PART II:

# THEORY AND RESEARCH

# CHAPTER THREE

# SELF-ESTEEM AND LANGUAGE LEARNING: BREAKING THE ICE

VERÓNICA DE ANDRÉS[1]
(UNIVERSIDAD DEL SALVADOR, ARGENTINA)

*This chapter is about a ground breaking experience linking self-esteem and language learning. It shows how self-esteem can affect language learning and how it can be used as a vehicle for improving language acquisition while fulfilling other educational goals such as personal development and social integration.*

## 1. Introduction

Juan: an eight year old boy with bright eyes and dark hair. With only a few years of formal schooling, he had managed to major with honours in disruptive behaviour. He was often in trouble at school and his academic performance was poor. Rejected by his classmates, feared by his teachers, he was labelled the "class bully" He became, however, the best teacher that I have ever found on my own pathway to learning.

Many times, as teachers, we feel that our lesson did not succeed in spite of careful planning, good preparation and knowledge of the subject. We know something went wrong, yet we cannot say why it did not go well. What we wanted to happen did not happen and we struggle to find better teaching methods in the pursuit of becoming effective teachers. Yet, despite all our efforts, it is often the case that we feel that there are some students we can never reach, no matter how hard we try. Now I realise Juan´s constant challenges were what led me to dive

---

[1] Verónica de Andrés teaches at the Universidad del Salvador (Buenos Aires). Educator, trainer and speaker on self-esteem in more than a dozen countries, she is founder of SEAL-Argentina and a member of the Executive Committee of the International Council for Self-Esteem. E-mail: veronicawings@fibertel.com.ar

heart-long into researching self-esteem and its role in education and specifically in language learning: I wondered if the answer to many puzzling questions about *effective* teaching might be found in *affective* learning.

Self-esteem? What's that? I asked myself. "Self-esteem in the Schools", an article written by Murray White and published in the journal of SEAL (Society for Effective Affective Learning), was the springboard for my journey into this subject, a subject which has occupied not only my mind but also my heart.

As soon as the seed was planted in me, I set out to learn as much as I could on the subject and soon I was in the middle of what was to become, as far as I know, the first research project linking self-esteem and language learning.

The place to carry it out was Juan´s class. Through songs and poems, stories and games we plunged into deep issues of acceptance, love, understanding, friendship, co-operation, uniqueness and talents and… language learning! The project was called "I'm glad I'm me" (Andrés 1993).

What happened to Juan? Children were asked to draw a picture of themselves at the beginning and at the end of the project and write or say comments about themselves. In his initial drawing Juan pictured himself all wrapped up: eyes with a mask, head with a helmet, hands with gloves, and his body under the water. And he wrote "I am in the sea".

"When he turned in his final picture, drawn only a few months after the implementation of the programme, I was moved by what I saw: uncovered face, smiling eyes and open arms with muscles. And I shall never forget what he wrote: "I discovered that I am *normal*".

Fig. 3-1. Pre and post tests “A picture of myself”.

Not only had his behaviour improved dramatically but also his English language skills. I observed changes in him as well as in all the other students in the class. Yet, it was through him that I discovered that teaching and healing can be two sides of the same coin, that no teaching is really effective unless it is affective. So I decided to go deeper into the subject and in 1996 I carried out the pilot study described below.

My first step was to review the available literature on the theories about self-esteem.

## 2. Theoretical background

### 2.1. What is self-esteem?

Self-esteem can be defined basically as confidence in our own potential. However in a comprehensive review of self-esteem literature, the concept of the "self" often appears ambiguous, vague, and problematic, as many terms are used to refer to the same thing. A historical overview of the term and its use is therefore necessary to clarify the concept of self-esteem.

### 2.2. The Antecedents of the Concept of Self-Esteem

#### The self (James 1890)

The complexity of the nature of the "self" was for centuries left to the realms of philosophy until William James restructured the concept from the perspective of psychology. James concluded that it is possible to study the nature of the self, wrestling with the objective and subjective nature of the self: the "me" and the "I". His view of the self is the result of the process of an infant **developing** from a state of confusion to an eventual adult state of self-consciousness. James underlined the discrepancy between the ideal self and the perceived self or self-image; the gap between them can be considered as a measure of a person's self-esteem. Subsumed under the self, there are three aspects: the self-image (how the person sees him/herself), the ideal self (what the person would like to be) and self-esteem (what the person feels about the discrepancy between these two aspects) (Lawrence 1988).

## The looking-glass theory of self (Cooley 1902)

According to Cooley (1902) the individual forms his/her self-image as a result of a reflection of the environment-as he/she receives feedback from others-and also as a "bouncing off the environment" (Lawrence 1988). Earliest concepts of self-image are related to body-image. Sex-role and identity also begin at an early stage in the family. This is followed by a perception of refined physical and mental skills, the awareness of which mainly develops at school through the interaction with teachers and peers. Mruk (2006, 170) points out that the latency period (from 7 to 11) is extremely important "for the development of self-esteem because this is when children discover, become know by, and eventually identify with, their abilities and characteristics". As young children gather information about their value as persons through interactions with significant others (Coopersmith 1967), teachers act as mirrors through which children see themselves. If this image is poor or negative, they see themselves as worthless and they act in consequence. Young children are highly sensitive to the opinions teachers have of them and the main risk is that they often adopt these opinions as their own (Kostelink et al. 1988).

## The phenomenological approach of self (Carl Rogers 1951)

Humanistic psychologist Carl Rogers introduced the concept of a three-fold self: the ideal self, the perceived self, and the real self, which is very similar to James′ formulation. Rogers stated that the child's interpretation of the life experience determines self-esteem levels. This "phenomenological approach" is based on the concept that it is the person's interpretation of the events which determines emotions and not the events themselves. Rogers has greatly contributed to our knowledge of the self as object: I-subject-know about me-object. The self as object is the aspect we can know about, explore and attempt to change in desirable directions. Furthermore Rogers' theory is related to the concept of the organism, the self and congruence. The organism is the total person, including our basic inborn needs (e.g. food, shelter), our feelings and our social needs. In Rogers' view the most important social need is for *positive regard,* which he considered the main socialising force behind behaviour. If the various needs of the organism are met, then the individual develops a self which is in congruence with it. If not, there is a degree of incongruence that may lead to psychological ill health. In my experience as an educator I have seen that the need for positive regard is often neglected in the classroom; moreover, it is sometimes totally ignored in the search for high standards, achievement and controlled behaviour. Unfortunately, the outcome of such an attitude is the reverse of what is intended: we tend to point out the negative behaviour, ignoring that we reinforce what we pay attention to.

## Self-concept and motivation (Maslow 1954)

Maslow's general dynamic theory of motivation focused on a hierarchy of five levels of needs which represent driving forces behind behaviour: basic physiological needs, need for security, need to belong, need for self-esteem, and need for self-actualisation. Maslow claimed that the apex of his famous pyramid -the need for self-actualisation-cannot be reached unless all other needs are satisfied roughly in order, beginning with the physiological needs (e.g. air, food, shelter and clothing) which he placed at the bottom of the pyramid. Purkey (1970) argued that the importance of self-concept in motivation is that the motive behind all behaviour is the maintenance and enhancement of the perceived self. In other words, both children and adults behave in ways which are consistent with how they view themselves. Given the importance of the teacher's role in the consolidation of a child's self-image (Coopersmith 1967), one of the goals of my action research project (Andrés 1997) was to explore ways of enhancing a child's self-esteem developing first and foremost the necessary conditions to develop a sense of security, identity and belonging in the classroom.

## Self-confidence and Second Language Acquisition (Krashen 1985)

Krashen argued that language acquisition can only occur in a non-threatening atmosphere fostering self-confidence and high motivation. He described acquisition as a question of attitude rather than aptitude, basically as a subconscious process that takes place when the acquirer is so involved in the message that he temporarily "forgets" he is hearing or reading another language. Moreover, comprehensible input or a meaningful message is necessary but not enough: the learner needs to be open to that input. This will not be possible if the affective filter is up and the acquirer is unmotivated, lacking self-confidence, feeling afraid of making mistakes or being humiliated in front of others; in short when he considers that the language class is a place where his weaknesses will be revealed. Krashen's theory was highly significant in the context of my first research project about language learning and self-esteem; as the subjects of that study where young children learning English as a foreign language. The interpretation of this theory led me to reflect with the teachers involved in the project on the importance of creating an environment where the teachers and the classrooms could be experienced by the children as relaxed, non-threatening, supportive and stimulating.

## 2.3. Research on Self-Esteem

### Coopersmith's seminal work (1967)

Coopersmith, an important pioneer in the field of research on self-esteem, reported in 1967 that children's self-concept was a predictor of their ability to read in first grade. He defined self-esteem in terms of how we evaluate ourselves and our characteristics, the personal judgement of worthiness that is expressed in attitudes we hold toward ourselves. In his book *The Antecedents of Self-Esteem* (1967), Coopersmith states that a child's self-image is formed by the repeated responses received from the significant others: parents first, teachers next and peers later on. As an outcome of his research, he developed a list of "warning signals" considered as indicators of low self-esteem: when a person is fearful and timid; bullying and arrogant; indecisive; pessimistic (expecting failure), and reluctant to express opinions.

### Self-esteem and academic achievement

It was not until the late seventies and eighties that self-esteem became an issue of consistent study and research. The interest grew mainly among educators who began to investigate the link between self-esteem and failure or success at school. During these decades a large number of articles appeared in professional journals and books in the United States. Many studies establishing correlations between self-esteem and academic achievement are found in the literature of this period: e.g. Scheirer and Krant (1979), Wylie (1979). Correlation was shown but causation remained a matter of debate. Holly (1987) compiled a summary of the current studies and pointed out that most indicated that self-esteem is the result rather than the cause of academic achievement, though he acknowledged that a certain level of self-esteem is necessary for a student to achieve.

In 1989 Dr Martin Covington, from the University of California, carried out an extensive study of the research on the relationship of self-esteem to academic achievement. He reported:

> ...a review of the correlational studies report a positive association between achievement and indices of self-esteem: as the level of self-esteem increases, so do achievement scores... perhaps most important, self-esteem can be modified through direct instruction and such instruction can lead to achievement gains.

While the interest in self-esteem and achievement originated in the United States, a review of the British literature indicates that the issue was also considered important in the UK. The correlation between self-concept and persistent school absenteeism was explored by Reid (1982); results showed that persistent absentees had low self-concepts. A study conducted by Carson and Wooster (1982) "Improving reading and self-concept through communication and social skills" at the University of Nottingham showed that dramatic improvement in reading and self-concept can be achieved through the implementation of a Communication and Social Skills Programme. Some of the techniques described in Wooster's and Carson's programme, such as Circle-time were used in this project. In 1990, the First International Conference on Self-Esteem was held in Oslo, Norway. This event drew educators from the United States, Great Britain and various countries in Europe. In 1995, the Second International Conference on Self-Esteem was organised in Cambridge, UK. And the movement has continued growing; an international conference was held in 2005 in Liverpool with speakers coming from the North America, Asia, Africa, South America and Europe.

## Self-Esteem and social relationships

Harter (1999) has pointed out the importance of the development of self-esteem for both cognitive and social growth. A crucial factor of self-concept is seen in developing positive social relationships. In an early study Mead (1934) reviewed this area and concluded that school becomes an environmental extension which continues and enhances the processes begun at home in the development of the self-picture, providing the individual with new evaluative contexts. The importance of pupil-teacher interactions for self-esteem is well documented in several studies: Hargreaves (1967), Rosenthal and Jacobson (1968), Douglas (1968), Pidgeon (1970). Richmond's study (1984) pointed out that that self-picture can be changed in the classroom. Along these lines, Mruk (2006) comments on the evolutionary nature of self-esteem, that there are opportunities to increase–or decrease–it throughout our life.

Teacher verbalisations are a key factor in determining the degree to which children perceive themselves as worthy and competent or the opposite (Kostelnik et al. 1988). As Lowenstein (1983, 231) has shown "Prolonged deprivation and lack of exposure to the positive emotions of love, concern, tenderness, verbal and physical affection result in poor self-control and low self-esteem".

A **positive verbal environment** is essential to develop harmonic relationships in the classroom, both for students and teachers. This positive climate enhances their self-perceptions and competence and worth (Openshaw 1978). In addition, children's self-awareness increases as they have opportunity to express themselves, explore ideas and interact spontaneously with other children (Kostlenik et al. 1988). Baurmind (1977) indicates that as an outcome of such an environment, teachers find it easier to establish rapport with children. Several authors such as Rogers (1961), Coletta (1977), and Gazda (1977) point out that a positive verbal environment is synonymous with warmth, acceptance, respect and empathy. These four conditions constitute the foundation for constructive child growth and development (Kostelnik et al. 1988).

## 2.4. Criticisms of the self-esteem work in education

Should schools try to help students feel better about themselves? Educators are divided on this issue. Kohn's (1994) research led him to conclude that most discussions of theory and practice of self-esteem are unsatisfactory, that there is no evidence that shows self-esteem as a key causal variable and finally that the intrinsic value of the concept of self-esteem is subject to controversy.

One clear weakness of self-esteem research is related to the measurement of self-esteem; in many cases how the concept has been measured appears unclear. "What have most researchers done to measure people's self-esteem? Simply asked experimental subjects how favourably they regard themselves" (Kohn 1994). Thus the ratings are exclusively based on what subjects wish to say about themselves. Self-report measures are seen as problematic because they depend on how much or how little people wants to tell about themselves and how they want to appear in front of others. In addition, although at present there are more than 200 instruments in use, most of them have not been appropriately validated. Wiley's (1974) extensive review of research showed that there are few criteria for determining whether a measure is valid or not. Even Robert Reasoner (1992), leader of the self-esteem movement in the USA, stated that definitive research on self-esteem has been difficult due to the variety of definitions, to the many self-esteem measures used, and to the multiple factors influencing it.

The second point that Kohn discussed is related to the intrinsic value of the concept of self-esteem. He discusses the *desirability* of focusing on this issue on the grounds that if children's attention is trained primarily on themselves, the whole educational enterprise could be said to encourage self-absorption bordering on narcissism. However, as it has been pointed out in the first chapter of this book, Reasoner (1992) made the point that if we limit the concept to "happy feelings", "feeling good", or "confidence boosting", as Kohn seems to do, we are missing the depth of the issue.

Kohn´s interpretation of self-esteem is one of the most common misinterpretations on the issue, which consists in taking self-esteem nearly as a synonym of narcissism. Self-esteem has nothing to do with an inflated ego. Quite the contrary, a trait of egotism and self-centredness is an indication of low self-esteem, a need to cover up deep wounds by pretending to be what we are not. Self-esteem has to do with having a realistic appreciation of who we are; and of the impact that we have on others. Self-esteem has to do with learning to set up rules and healthy limits in a democratic way, with knowing both our light and our shadows, with seeing our potential in our shadow, with knowing when to act as individuals and when to act as part of a group, with finding meaning and purpose in our actions. Finally, it has to do with developing a feeling of achievement and success, and also of celebration, realizing that no-one is a success alone.

Even if there is no conclusive research that proves that self-esteem is the most important factor that affects academic achievement or social behaviour, studies done in the nineties have clearly shown that self-esteem programmes can make a difference in education.

Robert Reasoner′s Building Self-Esteem Programme, which was the basis of the action-research project described in this chapter, was used for conducting a three year research control study. Many positive changes were shown, such as less antisocial behaviour among students, less absenteeism, more positive leadership and higher academic motivation (Reasoner 1992).

Similarly, in 1992 Michele Borba′s programme was used for a control study over 1000 students to look into the effectiveness of a school wide self-esteem programme for elementary students; the results showed, for example, that the number of students who were considered at risk of school failure was reduced by 66% when they participated in these programmes that focused on security, identity, affiliation or belonging, a sense of purpose and a sense of competence.

An article published in the New York Times 1999 about a 12 year study done by Hawkins and reported on in the Archives of Pediatrics and Adolescent Medicine states that enhancing self-esteem through grades 1 to 6 improved behaviour, school performance and attendance.

There is no question that self-esteem can be nurtured through **successful learning experiences that enable the learners to experience themselves as competent**–and a student that feels this way is likely to take the risks and challenges involved in the learning process and enjoy the outcomes. This is coherent with the most widely accepted definition for self-esteem, that of Nathaniel Branden who defines healthy self-esteem as “the disposition to experience oneself as competent to cope with life’s challenges and being worthy of happiness” (1994).

## 3. Action-research project

Considering the strong relationship between self-esteem and learning, in 1993 I had decided to explore possible connections between self-esteem and language learning by adapting self-esteem activities for the EFL classroom and putting them in practice in a primary school English class. This very successful experience led me to continue my research by carrying out a pilot study (1996), in order to build the framework for the future development of a programme for language learning.

This pilot study was conducted by the teachers of English in a private school in Buenos Aires; all students were Spanish speakers who were taught the Argentine National Curriculum in the morning shift and English as a Foreign Language in the afternoon shift.

Children in Grades 1 and 2 were the subjects of the study. The success criterion was measured from two different perspectives: that of individual case-study children and that of the whole class. Data were gathered from samples of children's work, projective tests, class and individual observations, teachers' diaries, the researcher's diary, photographs, questionnaires administered to teachers, students and parents and a semi-structured interview with the teachers.

The aims of the study were to see:

1. if through the implementation of a self-esteem pilot programme children's self-esteem could be enhanced in a foreign language environment
2. if this would positively affect children's social relationships
3 if this would have a positive effect in their academic performance

The method used was "collaborative action research", which Cohen and Manion define as an on-the-spot procedure, pursued by a group of teachers that work alongside a researcher in a sustained relationship, designed to deal with concrete problems, located in an immediate situation, whose emphasis is on obtaining knowledge for a particular situation and purpose. Furthermore, this method was considered appropriate since self-esteem can be linked to the development of attitudes and values, a process which implies "encouraging more positive attitudes to work or modifying pupils' value systems" (Cohen and Manion 1994).

## 3.1. Procedures

Cohen and Manion's eight stage model was followed to reach the objectives of the intervention study. This framework was deemed flexible enough to be adjusted to this particular project.

The first stage involved identification, formulation and evaluation of the problem. The main challenges identified were the following: the need to set a pilot study to determine the usefulness of self-esteem activities; the need to find positive ways to deal with social relationships in the classroom, the need to enhance children's self-confidence as a prerequisite to improving their academic performance.

The second stage included discussion and negotiation, and formulation of purposes and assumptions. After a meeting with the heads of the school together with the English primary teachers, as the researcher, I was encouraged to conduct the intervention study with first and second forms (six to eight year old students) in cooperation with the teachers of English. An initial questionnaire was administered to the teachers and several group discussions were held at the beginning of the project to consider purposes and assumptions of the study.

The third stage involved a review of the research literature. The researcher provided input to the teachers in two formal workshops, and current research findings on the topic of self-esteem were discussed and commented in several meetings.

In the fourth stage a set of guiding objectives were stated. As an outcome of the previous stages the following guiding objectives were projected for the intervention study:

- **To develop children's understanding of themselves**
  - to learn about their individuality and uniqueness.
  - to enhance their ability to express feelings.
  - to encourage them to think positively about themselves.
- **To develop understanding of others**
  - to be respectful of others.
  - to increase awareness of and skills in friendship making.
- **To communicate more effectively**
  - to listen while others are speaking.
  - to wait for their turn.
  - to improve English language skills.

The fifth stage was concerned with selection of research procedures. The process would include a variety of sources of data to ensure triangulation (Cohen and Manion 1994): initial questionnaire to teachers, questionnaires to students and parents at the end of the project, final interview with teachers. In addition, three children with indications of low self-esteem would be selected to build case studies. Data collection for case studies would be provided by teachers' and researcher's diaries, field notes, classroom observations, and projective tests.

The sixth stage was concerned with choice of evaluation procedures for continuous evaluation. Evaluation of case studies would involve enhancement of children's social relationships (attitude towards peers and adults) and enhancement of self-image. It was expected that the latter would be reflected in academic achievement: since the teachers involved in the project were the teachers of English, children's attitude towards the learning of English was considered relevant. The success of the whole project would be evaluated through triangulation: questionnaire administered to teachers, parents and children at the end of the project.

The seventh stage encompassed the implementation of the project itself. The time limit for implementation of the programme was 10 weeks. The study would be carried out during one forty minute session three times a week for three months. In these months the following concepts were explored: uniqueness, growth and change, feelings, talents and abilities, co-operation, friendship and communication techniques. Most activities were based on the work of Murray White (1992), Robert Reasoner (1982) and Michele Borba (1989), and were adapted by the researcher to fit the foreign language classroom. The methods used to teach these concepts were a mixture of brainstorming, feelings circles, activity sheets, arts and crafts, reading and singing.

The eight and last stage involved the interpretation of data: inferences to be drawn and overall evaluation of the project would be carried out by the teachers and the researcher. This stage would be reached at the end of school term, the first two weeks of the month of December.

## 3.2. Research tools and results

### Projective tests

One of the most powerful research tools used was children's drawings.

A "Picture of Me" and a "Picture of the Group" were used as pre and post tests. An activity such as drawing, which is so natural and spontaneous in young children, was chosen as it could provide an insight into a child's general and basic nature (Cox 1992). These pictures were used together with other available data; they were used as a rough screening device for understanding a child's initial and final level of self-esteem and social relationships and as an evidence of change after ten weeks of implementation of a self-esteem programme.

### Questionnaire to parents

At the end of the ten-week programme, parents from Grades 1 and 2 were invited to open classes to observe and share self-esteem activities with their children. After this, 31 questionnaires were sent out. Parents' opinions on the project were considered essential to measure the effectiveness of the programme, since they could provide information of behaviours displayed at home.

Out of the 31 questionnaires that were distributed among parents–19 for Grade 2 and 12 for Grade 1–a total of 22 were returned (71%). In view of the time of the year, nearly the end of school term, the response to this questionnaire was considered very good, 83.3% responded from Grade 1 and 63.2% from Grade 2. The large percentage of respondents suggested an interest in the project. Although questionnaires were anonymous, most parents returned them with their names.

Question 1 asked for parents' opinions about the relevance of the project. Figures 3 and 4 show how parents from Grade 1 and 2 respectively responded. The answers were most encouraging: all parents except one answered that the project had responded to their child's needs and interests.

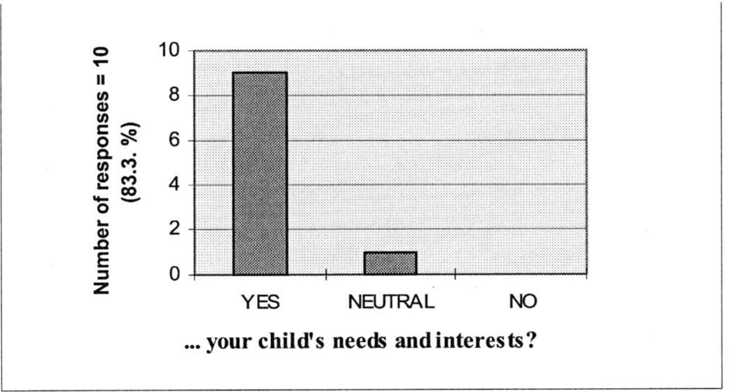


Fig. 3-2. Grade 1. Parents' Questionnaire-Parents' answer to the question: "Did the project respond to your child's needs and interests?"

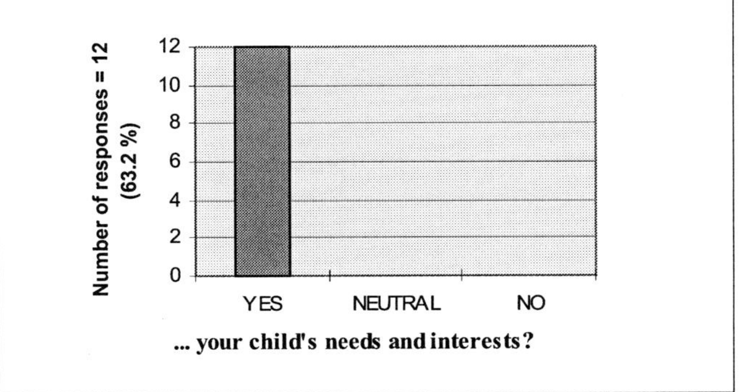


Fig. 3-3. Grade 2-Parents' Questionnaire-Parents' answer to the question: "Did the project respond to your child's needs and interests?"

It is not easy to respond to questions about learners′ self-esteem, particularly for parents. Therefore, although all the questions were cautiously devised and piloted, an open ended item was included for parents to indicate other possible areas of progress ("others"), as it was considered that this would be less threatening. Ten families answered this question, indicating some aspects that, interestingly, were very similar to the objectives that the teachers and the researcher had devised for the programme: *"to feel more confident, to increase English vocabulary, to improve communication with classmates, to discover their strengths, to promote reflection and understanding, to develop enthusiasm for learning"*. Perhaps the most significant answer was the one from one mother whose husband had died from cancer a few weeks before the questionnaire was sent. She wrote *"The project helped my child to express how he felt, to understand others and himself too. My suggestion would be to continue with this project because promoting self-esteem is to give our children a firm base to stand on for the rest of their lives. This project helped my child in a very difficult time of his life"*.

The final question was also open-ended to allow for comments and suggestions. All comments were very encouraging; some parents indicated that they would want more information on the subject, others asked for workshops for parents and suggestions about activities to be carried out at home and some requested a follow up of the project for the following year. These answers pointed out the need to work very closely with the families.

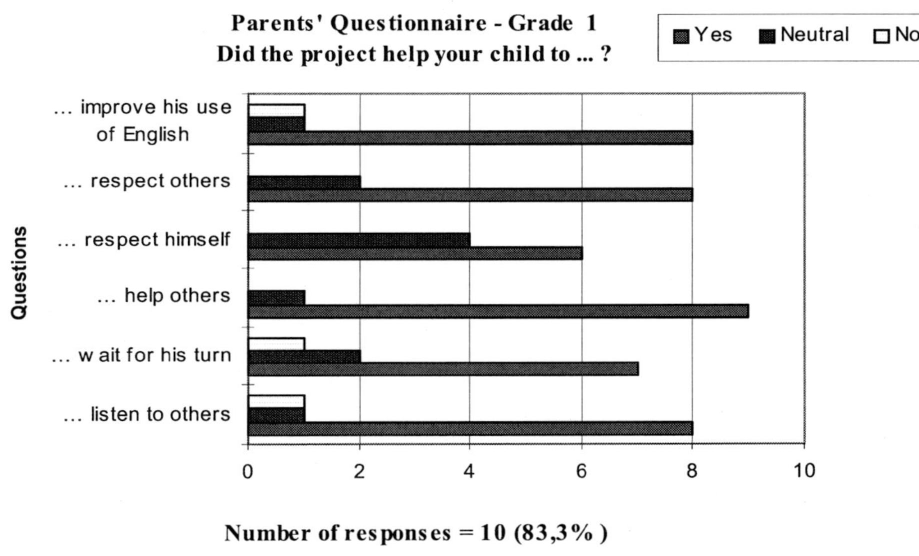


Fig. 3-4. Grade 1-Parents' Questionnaire-Parents' answer to the question: "Did the project help your child to...?"

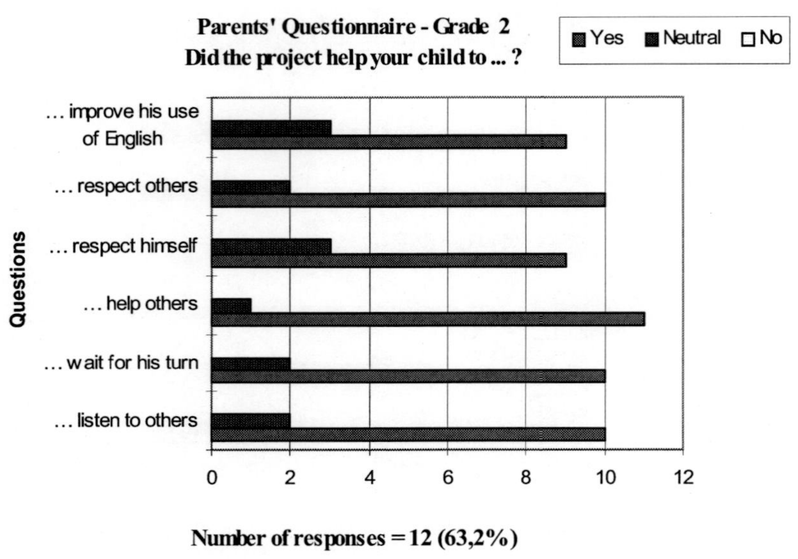


Fig. 3-5. Grade 2-Parents' Questionnaire-Parents' answer to the question: "Did the project help your child to...?"

## Questionnaire to children

As the children were the subjects of the action-research, their opinion of the project was crucial. Thus the questions to be included were carefully devised and piloted by the researcher in collaboration with the teachers in order to find out children's overall appreciation of the project, determine which activities were most successful and evaluate the achievement of objectives set for the programme.

In November a survey was administered to the children. A number of aspects had to be taken into consideration in order to design this instrument. Given the age of the children, mostly 6 to 8 year olds, their knowledge of English as a foreign language as well as their limited reading and writing skills, it was considered of the utmost importance that the instructions should be concisely and clearly written, in plain English, orally explained and discussed and finally translated into Spanish, to ensure complete understanding on the part of these young subjects. Thirty-one questionnaires were distributed among children-19 for Grade 2 and 12 for Grade 1. The number of responses was 19 for Grade 2 (100%) and 11 for Grade 1 (91,7%). Question 1 asked for children's opinion on the project. The results shown in figures 7 and 8 indicate a high level of acceptance of the project: 91% "yes" answers from Grade 1 and 95% "yes" answers from Grade 2.

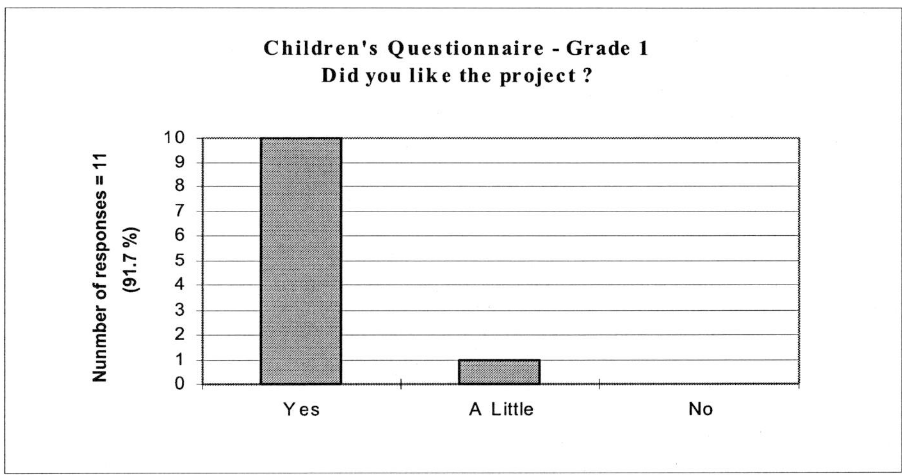


Fig. 3-6. Grade 1-Children's Questionnaire-Children's answer to the question: "Did you like the project?"

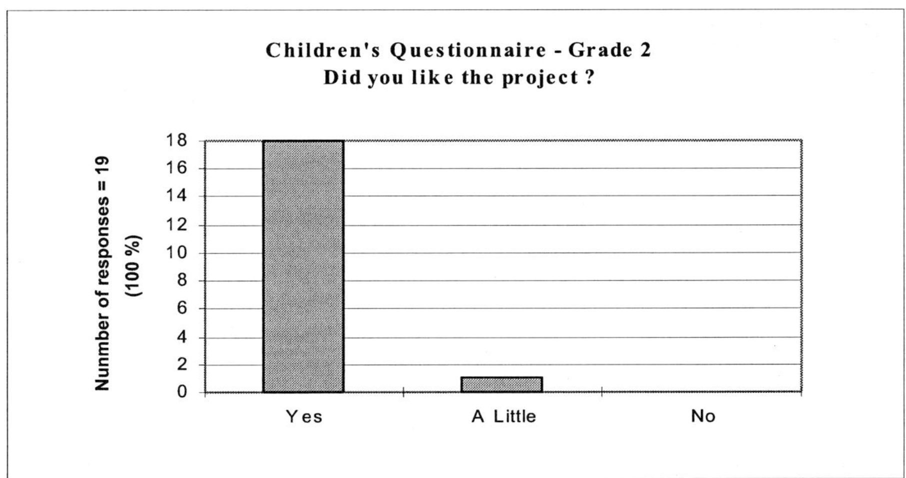


Fig. 3-7. Grade 2-Children's Questionnaire-Children's answer to the question: "Did you like the project?"

Question 2 was designed to elicit children's evaluation of the activities. Their answers showed a very positive attitude towards the activities (see Appendix 1 for a brief description). Percentages of "yes" answers were high in both grades. In Grade 1, Paper Chain was the most popular activity, in Grade 2: Special Day. The results for each grade displayed in figures 9 and 10 suggest that Special Day was a significant activity for both grades. As Murray White (1992) stated "I believe that the first reason for the success of the Special Day procedure is that the children know they will be appreciated and affirmed".

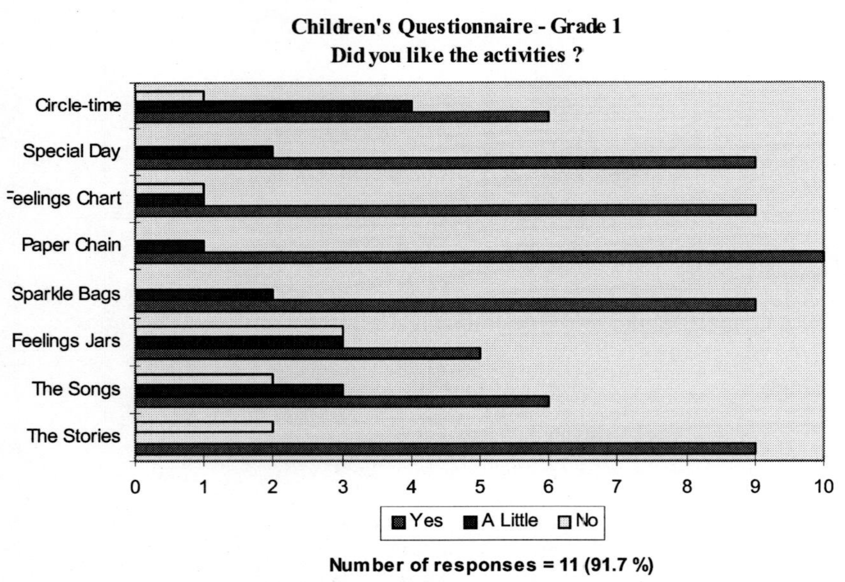


Fig. 3-8. Grade 1-Children's Questionnaire-Children's answer to the question: "Did you like the activities?"

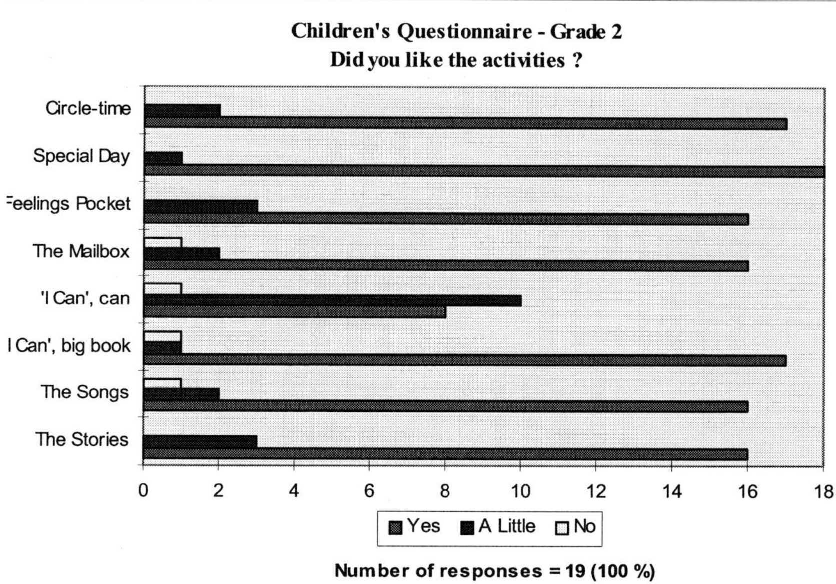


Fig. 3-9. Grade 2-Children's Questionnaire-Children's answer to the question: "Did you like the activities?"

In question 3 the children were required to evaluate the skills and attitudes that they may have developed throughout the project. The question was presented as "What do you think that you have learned in this project?" Children's answers from Grades 1 and 2 are shown in figures 11 and 12 respectively. It was interesting to see that the answers of these young subjects were very positive. In Grade 1 the areas with most "yes" answers were "to wait for your turn" and "respect others" (91%). The other areas to be evaluated also had high positive answers: "improve English", "respect yourself" and "help others" (82%). The ability to "listen while others are speaking" got a 73% of yes answers. In Grade 2 the most successful areas were: "help others" and "listen when others are speaking (95%), "communicate in English" and "respect yourself" (89%), "respect others" and "wait for your turn" (84%). Question 4 was open-ended; children could draw or write comments on the project: all responses indicate a high level of acceptance of the programme. Summarising, these high percentages of positive answers suggest achievement of the objectives of the programme.

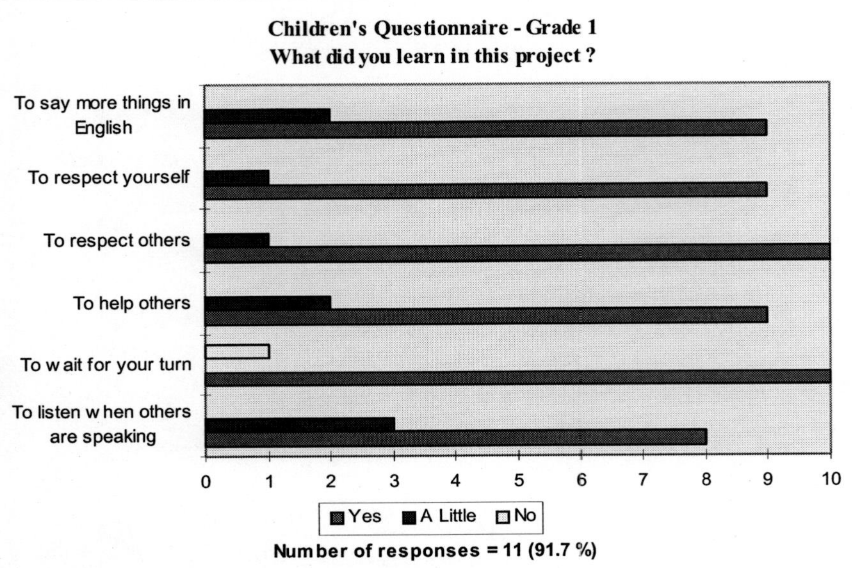


Fig. 3-10. Grade 1-Children's Questionnaire-Children's answer to the question: "What did you learn in this project?"

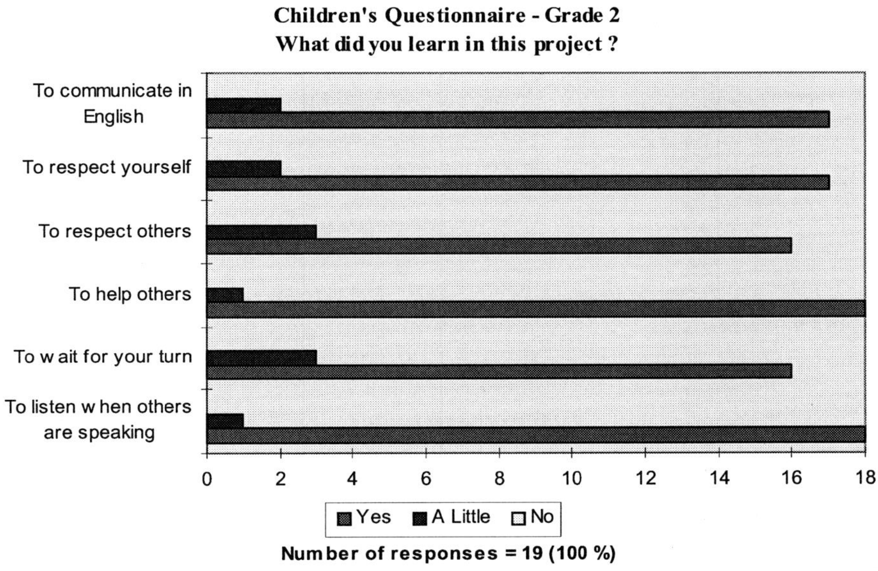


Fig. 3-11. Grade 2-Children's Questionnaire-Children's answer to the question: "What did you learn in this project?"

## Interview with teachers

Both teachers that participated in the project were dynamic and supportive and both showed a true caring attitude for their students. It is important to note that their openness and interest was very important to be able to conduct this research.

In December, four months after beginning the project, a semi-structured interview was conducted with the teachers. Questions were designed to allow them to express in depth their opinion on: the role of the teacher in the consolidation of a child's self-image, benefit of the programme for the class as a whole, aspects improved, evaluation of the activities, difficulties encountered, comments on case-study children, support they received from school and researcher, feedback received from parents and an evaluation of their own learning. It was most encouraging to observe that both teachers considered their role in the formation of a child's self-image of the utmost importance, that they clearly stated that the programme had been beneficial not only for case-study children but for the whole class, that salient aspects improved were related both to social and academic skills (especially oral and reading skills) and that the difficulties encountered were overcome by implementing a whole language programme which implied reading meaningful literature. Both teachers expressed having received enough support from the school and the researcher and positive feedback from parents. Perhaps the teachers' evaluation of the project could be summarised in their own words. The Grade 1 teacher said "*...this project has made me a better teacher...I think that other teachers in the world should try it because it is great*".

The Grade 2 teacher concluded by saying "*...I think that this aspect of teaching is very important and it will definitely be included in my way of teaching. I found it very useful and I think it's impossible to teach without it now that I have used it... I feel lucky to have been part of this project and to have learned so much from it*".

## 4. Conclusion

We can conclude that self-esteem work can be a vehicle for improving language acquisition while we are working in our particular area of the curriculum, in this case foreign language learning, and we can be also fulfilling broader educational goals. Children live in an extremely complex and changing world. Even very young children, such as the subjects of this intervention, have to learn how to cope with academic challenges as well as issues such as a lack of belonging in a group, lack of nurturing time with parents, and sometimes death, separation and divorce of parents. So should self-esteem be taught in the classroom? Perhaps, as Reasoner (1992, 30) says,

> The question should be do we have a choice? Self-esteem cannot be considered the panacea to all problems in the classroom, yet it may well be our hope for a better world.

## Works Cited

Andres, V. de. 1993. *Self-esteem in the classroom.* Unpublished small scale classroom research, College of Preceptors, UK.

—. 1997. *Developing self-esteem in the primary school: A pilot study.* Unpublished intervention study. Oxford: Oxford Brookes University.

Baurmind, D. 1977. *Some thoughts about child-rearing.* In M. Kostelnik, L. Stein and A. Whiren. 1988. Children's self-esteem. The verbal environment. *Childhood Education*, Fall: 29-32.

Borba, M. 1989. *Esteem builders. A K-8 self-esteem curriculum for improving student achievement, behaviour and school climate.* California: Jalmar Press.

Carson, A., and A. Wooster. 1982. Improving reading and self-concept through communication and social skills. *British Journal of Guidance and Counselling* 10, (1): 83-87.

Cohen, L., and L. Manion. 1994. *Research methods in education.* London: Routledge.

Coletta, A. 1977. *Working together: A guide to parental involvement.* In M. Kostelnik, L. Stein and A. Whiren. 1988. Children's self-esteem. The verbal environment. *Childhood Education*, Fall: 29-32.

Cooley, C. H. 1988. Human nature and social order. In *Enhancing self-esteem in the classroom*, ed. D. Lawrence. London: Paul Chapman Publishing Ltd.

Coopersmith, S. 1967. *The antecedents of self-esteem.* San Francisco: Freeman and Co.

Covington, M. 1989. *The social importance of self-esteem.* Berkeley: U.C. Press.

Cox, M. 1992. *Children's drawings*. London: Penguin Books.

Douglas, J. 1968. *The home and the school.* In M. Richmond. 1984. The self-concept of academically able and less-able children in a comprehensive school-a comparative study. *Remedial Education* 19, (2): 57-58.

Gazda, G. 1977. Children's self-esteem. The verbal environment. *Childhood Education*, Fall: 29-32.

Hargreaves, D. 1967. *Social relations in a secondary school.* In M. Richmond. 1984. The self-concept of academically able and less-able children in a comprehensive school-a comparative study. *Remedial Education* 19, (2): 57-58.

Harter, S. 1999. *The construction of the self: A developmental perspective.* New York: Guilford.

Holly, W. 1987. *Self-esteem: Does it contribute to students' academic success?*. Eugene: Oregon School Study Council, University of Oregon.

James, W. 1890. *Principles of psychology.* In D. Lawrence. 1988. *Enhancing self-esteem in the classroom.* London: Paul Chapman Publishing Ltd.

Jenkins, H. 1991. *Getting it right: A handbook for successful school leadership.* Oxford: Blackwell.

Kohn, A. 1994. The truth about self-esteem. *Phi Delta Kappa*, Dec: 272-283.

Kostelink, M., L. Stein, and A. Whiren. 1988. Children's self-esteem. The verbal environment. *Childhood Education*, Fall: 29-32.

Krashen, S. 1985. *The input hypothesis: Issues and implications.* New York: Longman.

Lawrence, D. 1988. *Enhancing self-esteem in the classroom.* London: Paul Chapman Publishing Ltd.

Lowenstein, L. 1983. Developing self-control and self-esteem in disturbed children. *School Psychology International* 4, (4): 229-235.

Maslow, A. 1954. *Motivation and personality*. In B. Noad. 1979. Maslow's needs hierarchy related to educational attitudes and self-concepts of elementary student teachers. *Educational Review* 31, (1): 51-57.

—. 1968. *Towards a psychology of being*. New York: Van Nostrand Reinhold.

Mead, G. 1934. *Mind, self and society*. In M. Richmond. 1984. The self-concept of academically able and less-able children in a comprehensive school-a comparative study. *Remedial Education* 19, (2): 57-58.

Mruk, C. J. 2006. *Self-Esteem research, theory and practice*. New York: Springer Publishing Company.

Openshaw, D. 1978. *The development of self-esteem in the child: Model interaction*. In M. Kostelnik, L. Stein and A. Whiren. 1988. Children's self-esteem. The verbal environment. *Childhood Education*, Fall: 29-32.

Pidgeon, D. 1970. *Expectations and pupil performance*. In M. Richmond. 1984. The self-concept of academically able and less-able children in a comprehensive school-a comparative study. *Remedial Education* 19, (2): 57-58.

Purkey, W. 1970. *Self-concept and school achievement*. Englewood Cliffs: Prentice Hall.

Reasoner, R. 1982. *Building self-esteem: A comprehensive program*. Palo Alto: Consulting Psychologists Press.

—. 1992. What's behind self-esteem: You can bring hope to failing students. *School Administrator* 49, (4): 23-30.

Reid, K. 1982. The self-concept and persistent school absenteeism. *British Journal of Educational Psychology* 52: 179-187.

Rogers, C. 1951. *Client-centred therapy*. Boston: Houghton-Mifflin.

—. 1961. *On becoming a person*. In M. Kostelnik, L. Stein and A. Whiren. 1988. Children's self-esteem. The verbal environment. *Childhood Education*, Fall: 29-32.

Rosenthal, M., and L. Jacobson. 1968. *Pygmalion in the classroom*. In M. Richmond. 1984. The self-concept of academically able and less-able children in a comprehensive school-a comparative study. *Remedial Education* 19, (2): 57-58.

Scheirer, M., and R. Krant. 1979. Increasing educational achievement via self-concept change. *Review of Educational Research* 49: 131-150.

White, M. 1992. *Self-Esteem: Its meaning and value in the schools*. Cambridge: Daniels Publishing.

Wooster, A., and N. Leech. 1985. *Personal and social education for slow learning children: A research and development project*. In C. Hall and J. Delaney. 1992. How a personal and social education programme can promote friendship in the infant class. *Research in Education* 47: 29-39.

Wylie, R. 1974. *The self-concepts: A review of methodological considerations and measuring instruments. Vol. 1.* Lincoln: University of Nebraska Press.

—. 1979. *The self-concept: Theory and research on selected topics. Vol. 2.* Lincoln: University of Nebraska Press.

# Appendix A

## The Activities

Some of the most significant activities are described below:

**Circle-time**: This is a group activity that uses strategies aimed at helping children develop skills to understand themselves and to express their individuality and to appreciate others and the value of friendship. It contributed to their communication skills as the rules of the "game" are: "talk only when it is your turn, you can only speak when it is your turn, and you can say 'I pass' if you want". Children sat on the floor in a circle, the teacher said an incomplete sentence and gave an example to finish it off, the child next to her repeated the phrase and added his or her own ending and so on. Children could pass if they wished and were allowed to use their mother tongue if necessary. As children said their thoughts (mostly in Spanish in the beginning) the teacher translated what they had said into English and registered their comments in order to make a mind-map, that was later used as a vocabulary bank. Some of the topics discussed during Circle-time were: "I feel sad when…", "I'm good at…", "I feel angry when…", "When I grow up I..." "A friend is...". Comments from case study children were all written down for further analysis. Circle-time was also helpful for the development of speaking and listening skills. It was observed that gradually listening became part of their normal attitude and fluency in speaking was improved.

**Special Day:** This was another significant activity used to promote a sense of security, identity and belonging at the same time. The activity was aimed at helping children listen to each other, wait for their turn and above all **get them to appreciate others**, as this is one of the most effective ways of enhancing children's self-esteem. One child was selected in a random way, by pulling names out of a "magic" box. Every child knew they would have a Special Day. When the child was selected, s/he was invited to leave the room, while the rest of the children brainstormed positive things about him/her. These comments were registered by the teacher on a Special Day Certificate. The child was invited to come back into the classroom and sit in the middle of the circle and he/she was given a badge that said "I'm special!" and the Certificate. His/her classmates took turns saying thing like "I think you are a good friend", "I believe you are a good football-player", "I think you are strong, capable, intelligent...". The remarks were prefaced with the statements "I think" or "I believe" to indicate that it was the speaker's opinion because it stopped the child receiving the compliments from denying them either at conscious or sub-conscious level. Of course, sincerity was the keynote; no-one was forced to say anything they did not mean. The adjectives that children could use were displayed on the walls as reminders of compliments to consider and most of them were "acquired" from the songs they had learned throughout the project. At the end of each Special Day, the child was given another sheet that said "The reasons my class like me are..." where s/he was asked to "copy" the adjectives from the certificate. Many times we found that the children wanted to do so immediately, they just couldn't wait to go home to do this "homework". One mother said that her child had put the Special Day Certificate on the refrigerator door so everyone could see it.

**Paper Chain:** Grade 1 used this activity which consisted in writing the name of the person that made a positive comment or caring gesture on one side of a coloured strip of paper, and then the ends were stuck together forming a link. The next strip was passed through the link to begin a chain. The paper chain was displayed at a height easily accessible to the children. As the chain grew children had a concrete evidence of all the positive attitudes they had shown throughout the project. The paper chain grew so much that it went all around the classroom. It was interesting to observe that, although in the beginning the names that were written were mainly the same, towards the end all the names were on the chain. Perhaps even more important was to see that the children did not compete among themselves: they never compared which names had more links; instead they counted the number of links that were on the chain to see the progress of the whole class.

**Sparkle Bags:** in order to practice giving and receiving positive statements, Grade 1 used the Sparkle Bags Centre. Each child decorated his/her own paper bag which was put near the window at their eye level. Each day the children wrote a "Sparkle Message" to others and put them inside the appropriate bag(s). Every day there was a special moment when children looked inside their bags and read aloud the messages they received. Some children needed a lot of help to read out their messages. The teacher encouraged them to help each other, so the ones that could read "more", helped the others. In the beginning this activity presented some problems: as the teacher was concerned that not all the children might receive a message, each child had to take a name out of a box to see who they would write a comment for in order to ensure that everybody would get a message.

**The Mail Box**: Grade 2 used this activity as a daily routine. A "greeting cards centre" was set up where children could create cards for their classmates and others who were important to them. The teacher introduced the mail-box by giving one card to each child. They discussed the meaning of the messages and the purpose of sending cards to each other. Ideas for writing messages were displayed on the walls and were also kept inside a box near the activity centre. Not all the children used this "vocabulary bank", many wrote their cards spontaneously and thus made many mistakes. These were not "corrected" but rather they helped the teacher to find out their most common difficulties and create language charts with high frequency words they needed to communicate the feelings and ideas in writing.

**Literature:** the use of literature was a very important part of the project, as it covered two main functions. One was to build vocabulary and develop English language skills, fundamental needs of these young children, for whom English was a foreign language. The other one, and perhaps even more important, was to encourage self-acceptance and self-understanding since the subjects discussed in these books reflected children's most common difficulties: anger, isolation, lies and rejection. The books were read to enable discussions of the topics that were later on discussed in Circle-time.

The books used in the classroom were:

- *Do You Want to be my Friend?* by Eric Carle (Friendship)
- *The Very Hungry Caterpillar* by Eric Carle (Growth and Change)
- *Ernie's little lie* by Elliot Dam (Lies)
- *Nobody Cares About Me* by Roberts Sara (Isolation)
- *Where the Butterflies grow* by J. Ryder (Growth and Change)
- *Where the Wild Things are* by M. Sendak (Anger)

**Arts and Crafts:** In view of the age of the children "hands-on activities" were necessary. Some of the activities were the following:

To discover their uniqueness the children took their own **fingerprints** and observed them with a magnifying glass. They looked excited when they noticed that they were all different.

To explore the concept of growth and change Grade 1 made a small science project on butterflies and prepared a **life-cycle mobile.** The teacher gave them pre-cut shapes of butterflies that they had to decorate, when they finished this activity one child said: "they all have the same shape but they are all different!"

Grade 1 made a big book, illustrating the story "Do you want to be my Friend?" and second grade made a big book titled "I Can Book", illustrating and writing about their talents and abilities. Grade 2 made an individual collage after reading and discussing the book *Where the Wild Things Are.*

**The Love Walk:** The children formed two lines facing each other. One child had to walk slowly in between the two lines. As the child walked the others gave him or her "high 5" or a pat on the back, sharing kind words. We encouraged the child to walk really slowly to feel the love in the gestures and words expressed. This was repeated until all children had finished their walk through the lines.

**Songs:** We used the songs from the cassette "Special as I can Be" by Anne Infante, with amazing results. These songs are basically positive affirmations, which we found very useful for language learning, and also for dissolving negative beliefs that children might hold about themselves. We experienced that these songs were a powerful tool to break habitual negative thinking as when children say to themselves "I am not good enough", "I can´t do it", "I am stupid". Singing affirmations was an excellent way to record over these destructive statements and replace them with healthy, self-enhancing messages. We sang these songs and we danced while we sang them; this added emotion and energy, building in the classroom a happy "can-do-spirit".

# Appendix B

## The Questionnaires

### Questionnaire to Teachers

Self-esteem can be defined as:
*confidence in our ability to think,*
*confidence in our ability to cope with challenges of life and,*
*confidence in our right to be happy.*
*It is the feeling of being worthy, deserving to assert our needs and wants. It allows us to experience satisfaction (Coopersmith 1967).*

Research has shown that children who feel good about themselves learn more rapidly and behave better.

1.- Do you agree with this definition of self-esteem? **YES / NO**

2.- If you don't agree, what would you change?
..........................................................................................
..........................................................................................
..........................................................................................
...........

3.- In your opinion, what is your role in the consolidation of a child's self-image?
..........................................................................................
..........................................................................................
............

4.- Do you believe that children in your class benefit from
the implementation of a self-esteem programme? **YES / NO**

If your answer is "YES" :
A) Who? All the children or some of them?
..........................................................................................
..........................................................................................
..........................................................................................
.............

B) How? What aspects would change or improve?
........................................................................................................
........................................................................................................
........................................................................................................
.............

C) When? How often should activities be implemented?
........................................................................................................
........................................................................................................
........................................................................................................
.............

5.- Are there children in your class that show indications of lack of confidence?
**YES / NO**

6.- Do you think a self-esteem programme would help them?
**YES / NO**

7.- Are there children in your class that show problems in their social relationships?
**YES / NO**

8.- Would a self-esteem programme help them?
**YES / NO**

9.- Are you satisfied with the way behaviour problems are dealt with?
**YES / NO**

10.- Do you think a self-esteem programme would help?
**YES/ NO**

11.- What topics do you consider more relevant in a self-esteem programme?
(body, feelings, family, friendship, talents, abilities)
........................................................................................................
........................................................................................................
........................................................................................................
.................

12.- Of the five basic characteristics of self-esteem: security, identity, belonging, purpose and competence, which are the ones you prefer to develop and work on in this project?
Choose two and state why.
.............................................................................................................
.............................................................................................................
.............................................................................................................
................

13.- Do you feel confident to implement a self-esteem project in your classroom?
**YES / NO**

14.- What suggestions would you like to add (e.g. need for more input, guidelines, resources)
.............................................................................................................
.............................................................................................................
.............................................................................................................
................

15.- In this project how do you picture yourself in terms of planning, delivery and evaluation of the same?
.............................................................................................................
.............................................................................................................
.............................................................................................................
.................

16.- How do you picture the researcher, in terms of planning, delivery and evaluation of the project?
.............................................................................................................
.............................................................................................................
.............................................................................................................
.................

THANK YOU VERY MUCH !

## Children's Questionnaire - Grade 2

| | | YES | A LITTLE | NO |
|---|---|---|---|---|
| 1) **DID YOU LIKE THE PROJECT?** | | ☺ | 😐 | ☹ |
| 2) **DID YOU LIKE THE ACTIVITIES?** | | | | |
| 2.1 | CIRCLE TIME | ☺ | 😐 | ☹ |
| 2.2 | SPECIAL DAY | ☺ | 😐 | ☹ |
| 2.3 | FEELINGS POCKET | ☺ | 😐 | ☹ |
| 2.4 | THE MAIL-BOX | ☺ | 😐 | ☹ |
| 2.5 | ' I CAN ' CAN | ☺ | 😐 | ☹ |
| 2.6 | ' I CAN ' BIG BOOK | ☺ | 😐 | ☹ |
| 2.7 | THE SONGS | ☺ | 😐 | ☹ |
| 2.8 | THE STORIES | ☺ | 😐 | ☹ |

3) **WHAT DO YOU THINK THAT YOU HAVE LEARNED IN THIS PROJECT?**

| | | | | |
|---|---|---|---|---|
| 3.1 | TO LISTEN WHEN OTHERS ARE SPEAKING | ☺ | 😐 | ☹ |
| 3.2 | TO WAIT FOR YOUR TURN | ☺ | 😐 | ☹ |
| 3.3 | TO HELP OTHERS | ☺ | 😐 | ☹ |
| 3.4 | TO RESPECT OTHERS | ☺ | 😐 | ☹ |
| 3.5 | TO RESPECT YOURSELF | ☺ | 😐 | ☹ |
| 3.6 | TO COMMUNICATE IN ENGLISH | ☺ | 😐 | ☹ |

4) **WOULD YOU LIKE TO WRITE OR DRAW SOMETHING ABOUT THE PROJECT?**

THANK YOU VERY MUCH !

## Parents' Questionnaire

Throughout this year we have implemented a self-esteem project which was intensified during the months of September, October and November. We are now at the stage of evaluation. We would be grateful for your comments, your responses will remain anonymous and will be used to improve the project. Please return this questionnaire by November 25th. Thank you very much.

Please answer all the questions by putting a check in the appropriate box.

1) Do you think that the self-esteem project has responded to your child's interests and needs?

Yes ☐ No ☐ Neutral ☐

2) Do you think that the project has helped your child to make progress in:

| | Yes | No | Neutral |
|---|---|---|---|
| • Listening when others are speaking | ☐ | ☐ | ☐ |
| • Waiting for his/her turn | ☐ | ☐ | ☐ |
| • Helping othersRespecting himself | ☐ | ☐ | ☐ |
| • Respecting others | ☐ | ☐ | ☐ |
| • Improve his/her use of English | ☐ | ☐ | ☐ |
| • Others | | | |

..........................................................................................................
..........................................................................................................
..........................................................................................................
...............................................................................

3) We would be grateful for any further suggestions or comments that you might have with reference to this project

..........................................................................................................
..........................................................................................................
..........................................................................................................
...............................................................................

Thank you very much for your co-operation!

# Appendix C

## The Interview Schedule

### Interview Questions with Individual Class Teachers Regarding Pilot Project on Self-Esteem

1- Having implemented a self-esteem project in your class, do you think that:

your role in the consolidation of a child's self-image is important?

-Why?

2- Do you think that **the children in your class** benefited from the programme?

- Who? All the children, most of them, a few or no-one?
- If yes, what aspects changed or improved?
    - classroom atmosphere
    - behaviour
    - language learning
    - others

3- With reference to **the activities**:

- were they suitable to your class needs and interests?
- which were the most successful ones? Why?
- which were the least successful ones? Why?
- did you encounter any difficulties in the implementation of the activities?
    - If your answer is yes, were they due to:
    - language difficulties
    - children's cultural background
    - others

4- Based on your observations, pre and post tests and other records such as report cards, do you consider that the programme helped the **individual case study children**

- to improve their self-confidence?
- to improve their social-relationships?
- to develop English language skills?
- to improve their communication skills?

(Please answer these questions considering each individual case study)

5- How did you feel throughout the programme?

6- Where the workshops useful to you?

7- Did you have enough support?

8- Did you get any feedback from parents?

9- What did you learn about:

- the children?
- the subject?
- yourselves?

10- Is there anything else you would like to add with reference to the project?

# CHAPTER FOUR

# SELF-ESTEEM AND SECOND LANGUAGE LEARNING: THE ESSENTIAL COLOUR IN THE PALETTE

FRANCISCO J. ÁVILA[1]
(UNIVERSITY OF CORDOBA, SPAIN)

*This chapter attempts to provide new insights into the role of self-esteem in language learning through a diachronic analysis of the term and its relationship with different factors of language learning. While there is abundant literature on the importance of self-esteem for living and learning in general, few studies have dealt with the effect of self-esteem on the learning of languages in particular. In light of this, the analysis and inferences made in this chapter aim to settle the question of self-esteem as a key factor in foreign language learning.*

## 1. Introduction

Every field of science is involved in its own quest for the philosopher's stone to solve each and every foundational problem. Since its conception, pedagogy, too, has sought its corner stone to facilitate the process of learning and the teaching of languages is no exception. Translations, phrase-books, tailor-made courses, cassette activities, language, video and computer labs are but a few of the many tools that have been developed in the pursuit of this particular *El Dorado*. However, it is hard to understand how in such a selfish

[1] F. Javier Ávila López divides his time between teaching English at a secondary school and giving courses in English and English literature at the University of Cordoba. He has taught English and Spanish in various countries including the former Czechoslovakia and England. His research areas range from the use of mental imagery and inner speech in language learning to motivation and the role of affective factors in language learning. E-mail: ff1avlof@uco.es

world as ours, it took so great an effort for people in the field to turn the look to themselves in the pursuit of the path to learning.

> Man struggles to find life outside himself, unaware that the life he is seeking is within him.
> —Kahlil Gibran

The term self-esteem originated from a Greek word meaning "reverence for self". In this twofold term, "self" stands for the values, beliefs and attitudes that we hold about ourselves, while "esteem" refers to the importance and worth that one confers upon oneself. As we can infer from this definition, acceptance of ourselves is central to the concept of self-esteem.

| First maxim: People need to accept themselves to achieve a proper level of self-esteem. |
|---|

Over the last century, the concept of self-esteem has evolved notably from a mere notion in the early stages of psychology to an integral part of human experience and motivation. Reich (1986) used Edith Jacobson's definition of self-esteem as "the expression of discrepancy or harmony between self-representation and the wishful concept of the self". William James (1890) provided a similar definition, formulating an equation that was key to understanding the term: "Self-esteem = Success / Pretensions".

People's need for self-esteem is underlined by the vast amount of both classical and contemporary literature that accounts for different types of behaviour related to that need. Indeed, over 10.000 studies have been published on self-esteem and its correlates (Scheff 1990). The basic assumption shared by this literature is that people need self-esteem for living. Greenberg et al. (1992, 2) state that people are motivated to maintain a positive self-image because self-esteem protects them from anxiety. High levels of self-esteem have been shown to produce a great number of valuable bonuses in almost every aspect of life. In the educational realm we achieve good academic performance (Dukes and Lorch 1989) or well-adjusted children (Buri, Kirchner and Walsh 1987). On the other hand, lack of self-esteem has been found to generate an incredible number of problems that range from lack of performance in learning to criminal records. The issue has gained so much attention that certain voices have risen against considering self-esteem the cornerstone of every success and its neglect as the origin of all the evils of society (see Ecclestone 2004; Cigman 2004). While the issue clearly merits thorough consideration across educational disciplines, the aim of this chapter is to provide a comprehensive view of the role of self-esteem in language learning.

Second maxim: Human beings need an adequate level of self-esteem to live.

Self-esteem has been a subject of primary importance since classical times. Plato, Aristotle and Socrates alike took into account the concept of self-awareness as part of the learner's environment. Steinem (1992, 31) traces the concept of self-esteem back to the seventeenth century, but it was not until the last century and a half that it became particularly relevant. W. James, C.H. Cooley, and G.H. Mead undertook to attach to the concept the importance it enjoys nowadays (see Coppersmith 1967, 29-31; Wells and Marwell 1976, 15-18). James, Vygotsky, and Piaget sought to move self-concept and awareness of self from the realm of philosophy to psychology, and tried to measure its impact. James (1890) centred his studies of self-esteem on introspection, viewing self-esteem as an evaluative process where pretensions are viewed as goals, purposes or aims and where successes are the perception that these goals have been attained. The more successful people think they are, the stronger self-esteem grows. Establishing the goal is an especially delicate process since it is here where the individual is at risk. If an individual perceives a lack of success because of mismatched goals and achievements or as compared to others, his self-esteem may be in danger. Yet lack of success is only dangerous if the subject perceives the area as important (Bernet et al. 1993, 141).

One school of thought that acknowledges the importance of self-esteem is that of Humanism, which believes human beings to be different from other species and possess capacities not found in animals, therefore attaching prime importance to the study of human needs and interests (Edwords 1989a,b). Contrary to operant conditioning theorists, who believe that all behaviour is the result of the application of consequences; or cognitive psychologists, who postulate the making of meaning as a primary factor in human learning which is isolated from the affective component, a central assumption of humanism is that human beings behave out of intentionality and values (Kurtz 2000; 2001). Humanists also believe that it is necessary to study the person as a whole, taking into account the burden the individual accumulates over her lifespan as determinant in the final product. The self, motivation, and goal-setting are also areas of special interest to this system of thought. Humanistic psychologists focus on the structure and organization of what a person knows and how his thoughts, beliefs, expectations and interpretations affect behaviour. They believe the concept of "self" held by individuals influences their behaviour and is related to their emotional state, well-being and judgment.

As regards pedagogy in particular, the implications of this humanistic concept is that self-actualization is a basic need of the learner (see Maslow 1954, Andrés in this volume). People who are self-actualized are also self-directed, confident, mature, realistic about their goals, and flexible. They are able to accept themselves, their feelings, and others around them. The human brain needs to have the feeling of being in control, to be able to take decisions (see Punset 2005, 80). Seemingly, the learning experience should foster in the learner the feeling that he is the controlling pivot of the whole process (see Seligman 2002 for a psychological explanation on the importance of being in control). Being in control of your own learning experience has nothing to do with choral repetition, closed-ended questions on intensive reading / listening or fill in the gap exercises, but is instead related to learning activities where the learner can project his own self, his opinions and his voice and process the information in his own way. Fostering learners' creative side and allowing them an increasingly greater degree of freedom to choose might be an interesting working procedure. Freedom to be creative in the learning process seems to be a central component to the self-actualization of learners. Teachers should therefore work as the conductors of the learning orchestras, creating the necessary conditions for students to be involved in the process of *finding out-wishing-creating-hoping to master-growing-learning* (see Rogers 1969).

The extraordinarily active pendulum of language teaching literature more often than not discards quite valuable approaches in favour of what is fashionable or new at the time. The studies in this book on the role of self-esteem in second language learning will show how that practice proves itself wrong. Humanistic principles and the importance attached to affect are still very important to second language learning. Given that this is a process that ultimately implies communication between *human beings*, participants' nature cannot be but determinant to the learning process.

When the pendulum swung towards the behaviourist realm, the constraints of the approach as a learning theory did not allow room for self-esteem in its description of the learning process beyond the notion that learning is the result of environmental conditions. Behaviourism views the mind as a "black box" where response to stimuli can be observed quantitatively, leaving aside the possibility of thought processes occurring in the mind.

Rosenberg (1965; 1979) proposes a socio-cultural approach in which self-esteem is conceived of as either a positive or a negative attitude that we have about ourselves (see also Rosenberg and Turner 1981). In this approach, self-esteem is viewed as a product of the influences of culture, society, family and interpersonal relationships. Feelings or beliefs about worthiness are key factors, with self-esteem related to anxiety or depression. Like Rosenberg's, Coopersmith's approach (Coopersmith 1967) views self-esteem as an attitude and an expression of worthiness where success as well as self-worth are indicators of self-esteem. Self-esteem is thus a construct or an *acquired* trait. While parents unquestionably play a crucial role in how individuals consider themselves worthy, this process is further reinforced by others.

Epstein (1985) maintains that self-esteem is a basic human need and that worthiness motivates people both consciously and unconsciously. Self-esteem is viewed as a consequence of our understanding of our environment and ultimately of the world. People continuously attempt to balance their own selves and their environment. According to Epstein, there exist different levels of self-esteem: *global* (general overall self-esteem), *intermediate*, which is specific to certain domains (competence, likeability of personal power), and *situational* (everyday, specific manifestations of self-esteem). All these levels are interrelated insofar as global and intermediate self-esteem affect situational self-esteem.

If we relate these three levels to the language learning environment, situational self-esteem in the resulting self-esteem triangle (see Figure 4-1 below) should work as the springboard to elaborate on the other two levels. If the appropriate learning conditions are given, the learner may achieve an adequate conception/perception of his own linguistic competence, thereby affecting his global self-esteem.

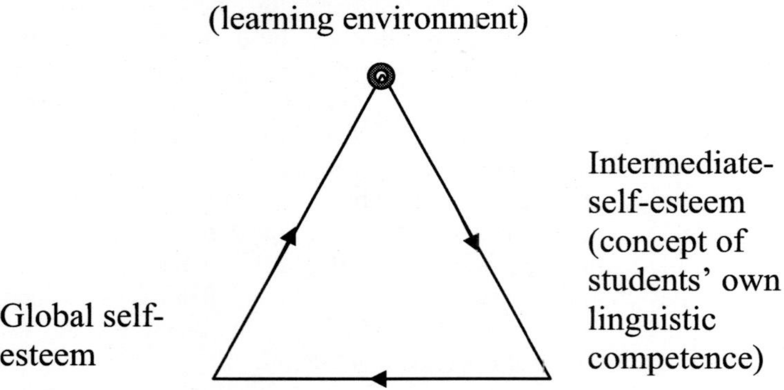


Fig. 4-1. The self-esteem triangle in the educational environment.

## 2. Self-esteem and second language learning

The incredibly vast realm of language learning and the multiplicity of factors that take place in every single act of learning a second language require the informed reader to consider the issue of language learning as a whole. It can be viewed as an impressionist landscape, where the real beauty of the picture can only be appreciated holistically, without attempting to focus on particular details that might prevent us from experiencing the "real thing". When any of the factors involved in second language learning are modified, the other elements involved and indeed the whole process may be substantially affected. Let us take the issue of anxiety, for example. If learners feel anxious about their learning experience, this fact will ineludibly affect their motivation to face the task, their affective engagement, their ability to process information and all the cognitive processes involved in learning. The real scope of self-esteem regarding the learning of a second language can best be understood by analyzing its relationship with diverse factors that work together towards achieving an affective and effective learning experience. Evans (2001) states that every decision starts with an emotion, therefore, the affective component of learning can no longer be considered a secondary colour in the learning palette, but is instead the essential one. Self-esteem or the feeling that one is an object of primary value in a meaningful universe (Greenberg et al. 1992) has been shown to be at the central core of human beings' emotional framework. This concept is especially relevant to second language learning of where the learner is faced with a new universe and has to manipulate it to be meaningful through complex processes of transference from the L1 and construction of meaning. When facing this new reality, the learner gains information regarding his own vulnerability. Self-esteem is his naturally endorsed defence system to deal with this defencelessness; it is a prerequisite for feeling loved, safe and secure– factors which are decisive in affective and effective learning.

Over the last three decades, researchers have defined constructs including self-efficacy, self-regulation, self-concept and locus of self to expand upon the realm of social cognitive theory and have investigated a wide range of variables, stages and settings. Part of this research makes reference to the learning of first and second languages. Although a number of studies have analysed the importance of self-esteem to other fields of learning, few have examined the direct influence of self-esteem on the learning of second languages. This chapter therefore aims to provide a general and integrated view of the issue. Like those *magic eye* posters or screensavers where you can only see the whole picture by not focusing on any specific part, the real scope of self-esteem in the process of learning a second language is best viewed holistically by considering its relationship to the cognitive and affective factors involved in the learning process.

## 3. Anxiety and self-esteem

The above considerations regarding the importance of self-esteem to life can clearly be extrapolated to the realm of foreign language learning-one of the most anxiety-ridden endeavours a human being can embark upon due to its unstable and ever-changing nature. As von Worde (1998, 3) explains:

> Anxiety is a serious problem in foreign and second language classrooms, experienced by perhaps one third to one half of students. Foreign language classroom anxiety has been identified as distinguished from other forms of anxiety and has been shown to have deleterious effects on the acquisition of and performance in a foreign language.

When dealing with self-esteem in the foreign language learning scenario, we find the learner trying to manage two unstable systems: a) his own self-esteem (which is highly dependant on the social milieu (see Avia 1995, 103) and b) the language learning process itself. If the subject seeks refuge in his self-esteem defence system when learning a foreign language and cannot find protection there, his performance will be poor, thus creating a vicious circle of unsuccessful learning. Foreign language anxiety has been identified as one of the factors that may inhibit language learning. One of the sources of this anxiety may be low self-esteem (von Worde 1998). It is therefore important that the learner maintain self-esteem at an adequate level for an affective and effective learning experience to take place. Onwuegwuzie et. al (1997) found that 14 variables significantly contributed to predicting foreign language anxiety, among them perceived intellectual ability, perceived appearance and perceived self-worth.

In his pentadimensional perspective of symptoms of anxiety, Rubio (2004) points out that in the psychological domain of language learning, self-esteem, rather than other external factors, is a major factor in activating foreign language anxiety.

Richmond and McCroskey (1989, 52-59) found a correlation between low self-esteem and high levels of communicative apprehension (see also McCroskey, Daly, Richmond and Falcione 1977, 269). Therefore, if we take into account Horwitz's (1986) conceptualisation of language learning anxiety where communicative apprehension is one of the three main factors of this process, a low level of self-esteem in the learner will generate language anxiety and thus prevent effective language learning from occurring.

Wozniewicz (1995) also lists low self-esteem as one of the causes that leads to the fear of communicating in the target language. Wozniewicz warns against the risk of making unfounded conclusions about *lack of communicative competence* when psychological, social, or personal factors may be responsible rather than scholastic inaptitude.

| Third maxim: A low level of self-esteem is related to communicative apprehension; one of the main factors of language learning anxiety which hinders language acquisition |
|---|

On the other hand, perhaps it is not anxiety as such that is detrimental to language learning, but the *type* or *level* of anxiety experienced by the student. As Oxford (1990, 142) argues, "a certain amount of anxiety sometimes helps learners to reach their peak performance levels, but too much anxiety blocks language learning. Harmful anxiety presents itself in many guises: worry, self-doubt, frustration, helplessness, insecurity, fear and physical symptoms". Since language learning seems to be an anxious endeavour, the problem therefore lies in controlling the level of anxiety in order to transform what could be considered a harmful factor into a useful tool that will foster the learning process.

It is therefore our task as language teachers to control the level of anxiety in our students. Anxiety must be redirected onto the right track to keep learners going instead of letting it "short-circuit" the learning process. By pursuing the right level of self-esteem in the language learning environment, the threat of harmful anxiety can be kept at bay. As Dörnyei (2001, 92) points out, cooperative instead of competitive learning might just be the natural solution to that threat:

> Few things are more detrimental to one's self-esteem than the constant threat of social comparison hanging over one's head like a sword of Damocles. This involves an excessive emphasis in comparing successful and unsuccessful learners and can be imposed in a variety of ways in the classroom, some more subtle than others.

Language anxiety also seems to be correlated with students' attitude towards the foreign language. Pudjiati (1996) points towards anxiety as one of the most important variables affecting attitude, attaching primary importance to *self-confidence* (Gardner et al. 1987; Gardner and Lambert 1972; Gardner et al. 1976) and *self-interest* in the FL. Those variables together with students' own background and classroom issues provide a general view of students' attitudes towards the target language. As Pudjiati (1996) stresses, all of these factors are related to self-esteem.

In Seyhan (2001) study of German and Japanese adult ESL students in the U.S.A., the author found a correlation between students' self-esteem, anxiety and motivation, where self-esteem is a predictor of students' eagerness to participate in oral interaction. This would seem to suggest that learners with a high sense of self-esteem might be better able to control their anxiety, thereby encouraging motivation and facilitating their involvement in communication (see Fonseca and Toscano in this volume for the interrelation between self-esteem and willingness to communicate).

The following analysis of the motivational factor in the language learning process will provide us with yet another primary colour to paint the whole language learning picture.

## 4. Self-esteem and motivation

FLL literature regards motivation as a key factor in language learning. Since the *affective revolution*[2], affective and cognitive factors are considered to be on an equivalent par with one another. Whether or not they are taken into account will be decisive to the effectiveness of a method or technique (see Arnold 1999).

As Scarcella and Oxford (1992, 51) assert: "Unquestionably motivation and attitude are very important in language learning success". Rubin (1975, 42) states: "Good language learning is said to depend on at least three variables: motivation, aptitude, and opportunity".

Gardner's (1983) equation on motivation holds sway in spite of the ebb and flow of the profession. He states that motivation is "[…] the combination of effort plus desire to achieve the goal of learning the language plus favourable attitudes toward learning the language" (Gardner 1985, 10).

Dörnyei (2001) attaches prime importance to the building-up of self-confidence in the motivation of FL learners (see Figure 4-2 below). As Brown (2001, 62) states: "Self-confidence: another way of phrasing this one is the *'I can do it!' principle* or the *self-esteem principle*. At the heart of all learning is a person's belief in his or her ability to accomplish the task".

---

[2] The Affective Revolution involves not only the realm of language learning. Other research fields such as psychology, neuropsychology and neurobiology have also been shaken up by the knowledge gained from new research techniques on the working of the brain. One of these is the PET technique (positron emission tomography, which has shown the crucial role that emotions play in every act of knowledge and ultimately of thought.

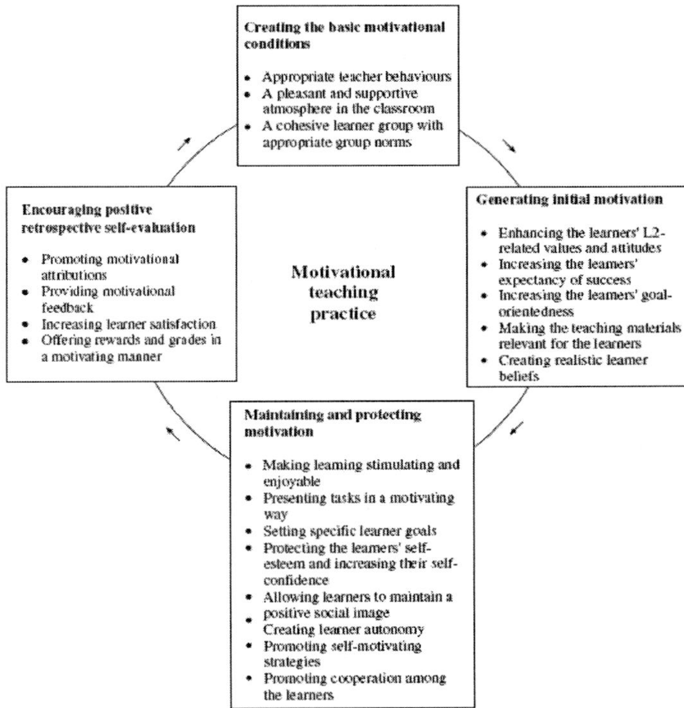


Fig. 4-2. The Components of Motivational Teaching Practice in the L2 Classroom (Dörnyei 2001, 29).

When referring to Reasoner's model of self-esteem (Reasoner 1982, 1991, 1994), Littlejohn (2001, 4) argues that "for the failing student in particular it is important that we try to develop their sense of success and their feeling that they can do something rather than a feeling that they can't".

Fig. 4-3. (Littlejohn 2001, 4).

As stated above, the notion of interrelatedness seems to be key to measuring the scope of self-esteem in language learning. So far we have considered the strong link between self-esteem, anxiety and motivation-three key factors in the affective component of learning. We need to consider the domino effect when modifying any one factor, in other words, if a student's self-esteem is not high, his anxiety will be detrimental to achieving effective performance.

Fourth maxim: Self-esteem, anxiety and motivation work together in the pursuit of an optimal learning experience.

## 5. Self-esteem and student autonomy

Language learning requires a high degree of personal involvement in the learning process. There is no such thing as a language-learning-passive-gymnastics where one can obtain the benefits of the activity without interacting with the linguistic data (at least in a foreign language environment). Any of the different skills involved in using language will require the learner to take an active role in the process. Clearly, self-determined learners (see Deci and Ryan 1985; 1987) enjoy the benefits of greater motivation since more motivation translates into more effective learning.

As pointed out above, the feeling of being in control is regarded as an important motivational factor in any endeavour (in fact, making your own decisions is considered one of the main factors of happiness; see Punset 2006). The challenging features of language learning make responsibility for our own demeanour a crucial factor in either the virtuous or the vicious circle of the learning process (see Dörnyei 2001, 137-144). As Oxford (1990, 11) states: "When learners take more responsibility more learning occurs, and both teachers and learners feel more successful". Consequently, those approaches that are centred around the learner's ability to take decisions in the continuous problem-solving process of learning are more likely to be successful. For instance, the use of a content-based syllabus requires that learners focus on meaning rather than form; additionally, learners find this type of activity more challenging and are thus more active in the learning process. This involvement, which is present in a content-based methodology, enjoys an intrinsically motivating potential (see Brown 1990; 2001).

Allowing students to take decisions on learning also helps them to be more committed to the selected tasks (Littlejohn 2001, 6). It brings the activity closer to the "I" of the learner, providing the feeling that he is the centre of the process. However, this whole process may turn out to be too challenging if the student feels he is unable to perform the task. In other words, if the success/pretensions quotient is not perceived as worthy, the learner will not be ready to take on the effort component of the motivation equation. It is very difficult to assume an autonomous learning demeanour if one does not feel capable of taking the necessary steps.

Cotterall (1995) and Wenden (1987) provide scientific data to demonstrate the correlation between learners' beliefs (see Arnold in this book) and learners' ability to learn autonomously. In line with this, Carter (1999, 17) points out in her study of beliefs and learner autonomy that "helping learners to reject their ill-founded beliefs about language and language learning and helping them not only to learn the target language but also to learn how to learn their L2–in short, helping them to become autonomous language learners-are fitting objectives at any level of instruction". Obviously, learners need to have a positive image of themselves, a high expectation that they will succeed in their endeavour to become autonomous language learners.

In a study of learners' belief systems, Tumposky (1991, 52) concludes that "learners' beliefs are influenced by the social context of learning and can influence both their attitude towards the language itself as well as toward language learning in general". Recall that in Gardner's (1985) equation attitudes are key factors in students' motivation. Therefore, if their beliefs about themselves and the learning process do not match up with the proper level of self-esteem, the learning experience will be seriously threatened.

> Fifth maxim: The affective pack (proper levels of self-esteem + motivation + anxiety) is determinant to achieving autonomous learners who can self-regulate their own language learning process.

## 6. Self-esteem and information processing

Learning is rooted in communication. Accordingly, improving the way information is processed by the participants in the communication process will result in better learning conditions. Let us try an introspective exercise to view the way we communicate when feeling anxious and demotivated. Take for example an oral exam in your mother tongue. Even now anxiety exerts a detrimental effect on your communication skills-you go blank, you cannot find the words to express your thoughts, you do not understand the questions. What about your processing skills at a boring presentation? Even if you want to absorb the information, it is an overwhelming task not to short-circuit in that situation. Finally, try to remember a communicative experience when you felt beforehand that you were not going to succeed (public speaking is usually regarded as one of these). Can you remember the physical symptoms, the escapist effect (*why on earth did I have to accept?)*, your lack of interest and motivation to perform the task? Can you still feel how your communication skills and even of your senses were hampered? Now do the opposite. Try to recall experiences when you were free of anxiety, interested in the task at hand and sure of your potential. You were probably communicative, loquacious, and quick to react and respond.

One of the most widely-accepted theories in this regard is that of Schema Theory (Anderson 1977; 1978; Carrell and Eisterhold 1988; Houston et al. 1989), which conceptualises the self as a set of schemata or organized body of propositions and descriptions that guides the selection and interpretation of new information. The schema is a template against which information is compared and information is interpreted to fit the person's schemata. For example, a learner's schema may include the belief that he is unable to speak fluently and it is therefore important for him to interact with a native speaker in order to feel good about himself. If his partners decide not to talk to him for any reason, he may interpret it as verifying that he is unable, and he will not probably achieve the proper fluency and will fail in his attempt to learn the language. Self-schemas act upon information, and construct and transform it to be meaningful to the self.

Dual Coding Theory, or DCT, is a complementary approach to Schema Theory. Originally proposed by Paivio (1986; 1990; 1991) and his colleagues (Sadoski, Goetz and Fritz 1993; Sadoski et al. 1990; Sadoski, Paivio and Goetz 1991; Sadoski and Paivio 1994), the DCT holds that there are two independent but interconnected systems: the verbal system and the non-verbal or imagery system. For meaning to be constructed, both systems of thought must be activated. While the verbal system operates in a sequential way, the imagery system functions in a simultaneous and global way. A clear advantage to the DCT is that it accounts for affective responses to the text; a factor that is not easily explained by semantic network theories that assume knowledge to be abstract. DCT considers that affection, which is non-verbal by definition, triggers non-verbal responses such as mental imagery (see Paivio 1986). Thus, mental imagery is our naturally allotted tool to bypass the traditional domains of cognition and affection.

Mental imagery seems to be an essential condition of thinking (see Damasio 1994) that is closely linked to the affective component of learning. Since self-esteem is an integral part of the affective domain it is easy to consider the importance of self-esteem when processing information. Our emotions play a crucial role in the way we process new information and integrate it into the general framework of knowledge. In fact, exposure to linguistic data in the target language will have completely different outcomes depending on our mood. Likewise, any new information will affect our state of mind and so close the affective circle. Take for instance the reading of a fairy tale in the L2. Our ability to interact with the information will no doubt depend on how we feel when reading it and the other way round. Anxious, demotivated, uninterested learners find it highly challenging to operate in the target language just as poor performance when trying to use the language may generate anxiety and lack of motivation. Stevick (1986) also points out the need to modify mental images in the mind of the participants for communication to take place.

Sixth maxim: Self-esteem has a direct incidence on the quality and quantity of our intake when learning a foreign language.

## 7. Self-esteem and the good language learner

Thus far we have seen how self-esteem and the affective and cognitive variables of second language learning are interconnected. We have also discussed how the quality of our L2 learning will be related to the way we feel whilst involved in the process and to our concept of ourselves. Kohonen's (1993; 1994) view of language learning as learner's growth is at the core of social cognitive theory. Let us examine Fig. 4-4:

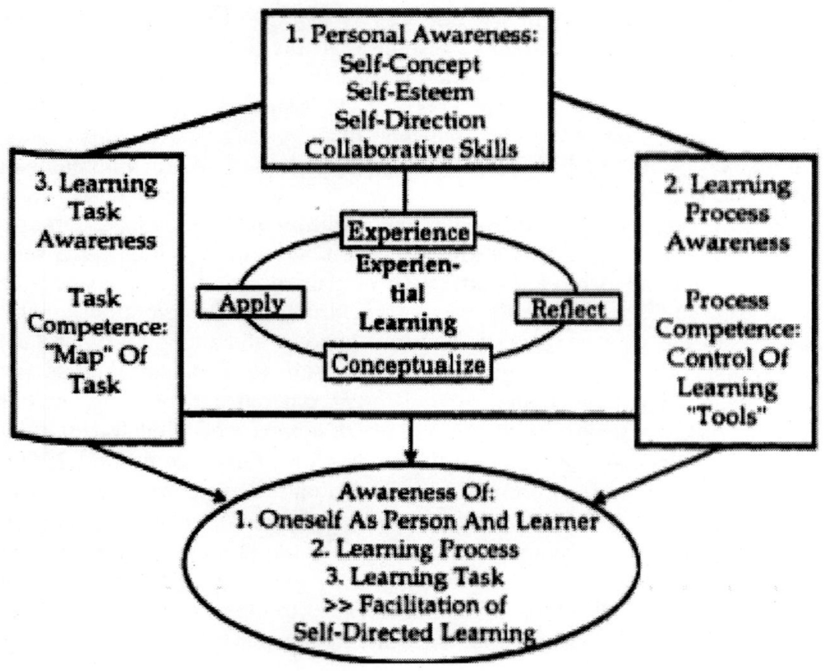


Fig. 4-4. Kohonen (1994, 61).

He attaches central importance to self-esteem, one of the components of the upper angle of the learning triangle, that of *personal awareness*. As we pointed out above, given that the process of learning a language is an extremely complex one, meeting tasks with success will have an obvious positive effect on learners' self-esteem. Sánchez-Herrero (1992) found an interrelation between cognitive and non-cognitive variables in English achievement tests with Spanish speakers. The affective variables that worked as predictors of the anxiety level were self-esteem, attitudes and motivation. Rouse (1988) also underlines the virtuous effect of language learning on self-esteem, stating that the learning of a second language may help to improve students' self-esteem (see also Anderson 1982, and Cohen and Norst 1989). This can be explained by students' need to perceive themselves as able communicators in the target language and the close relationship between language and self-identity.

Developing competent language learners while we develop competent people may seem to be an ambitious project, but we should aim high because there is always plenty of time to be second best.

The learner's self-esteem and his view of himself as a person and language learner are important factors that correlate with successful language learning. Language learning requires persistent effort, the ability and courage to cope with the unknown, tolerate ambiguity and accept mistakes. A person who is ready to accept with tolerance and patience the frustrations of ambiguity is in a better position to cope with these minor hurdles than a learner who feels frustrated in ambiguous situations. New learning and understanding are always potentially threatening (Kohonen 1994, 63).

An adequate level of self-esteem is thus correlated with intrinsic motivation where both forces interact to achieve affective-effective language learning. We, as teachers, need to take into account not only the advantages of properly fostering the development of such forces, but also the potential risks of *not* doing so. We have the palette; our task is to make sure the essential colour is on it. Dourado and Wolmer (2002) found evidence in their study that participants' high level of self-esteem and good learning performance feed on each other in the process of learning and highlighted the role of educators in building and maintaining their students' high self-esteem.

Also, in his review of the characteristics of the good language learner, Brown (1977, 134) regards self-esteem as a fundamental element of the successful learner and highlights the positive correlation between global self-esteem and the learner's oral production performance.

> Recent research that has attempted to define the good language learner can also yield information about the good language teacher. While it remains clear that there is much variation among learners, the following characteristics have been distinguished as identifying the good language learner: (1) field independence in classroom or tutored learning; (2) field dependence or empathy; (3) meaningful communication; (4) use of feedback; (5) optimal social distance with regard to the native and target cultures; and **(6) self-esteem[3].** By implication, the good

---

[3] Emphasis added.

> language teacher can be said to: (1) be able to deal with field independence; (2) respond to the student with empathy; (3) ensure the presence of meaningful communicative contexts in the classroom; (4) provide optimal feedback; (5) be sensitive to sociocultural alienation; and (6) **encourage self-esteem in the student**[4]**.**

Oxford (1992) and Oxford and Ehrman (1993) included students' self-esteem as one of the most important factors teachers should be able to understand in order to favour effective second language learning. Clearly, this is a relevant factor in second language learning instruction and students that manage their self-esteem appropriately are better language learners (see Seebauer 1997).

As mentioned above, language learning implies communication, and for communication to take place we need to be prepared to process information. Proposals such as Stern's (1980) on the potential of drama to foster the operation of some factors that serve to improve communication may be especially helpful for the language teacher and researcher. As Stern confirms, heightened self-esteem, motivation, spontaneity, increased capacity for empathy and lowered sensitivity to rejection are attributes more commonly found in language learners with a high level of self-esteem.

| Seventh maxim: Language teachers need to promote students' self esteem in the pursuit of good language learners |
|---|

## 8. Conclusion

Teaching experience reveals that the role of self-esteem in teaching praxis is more often than not left aside in favour of fashionable approaches, techniques and even materials and tools. Research and teaching praxis are traditionally separated by a gap that studies such as the present one have attempted to bridge. The aim of this chapter has been to provide a clear view of the scope of importance of self-esteem in second language learning; a specially demanding process which requires that each and every factor involved be optimized. As we have seen, affective factors are a key element in language learning since it is the learning person who is at the core of the process. It does not matter how innovative, avant-garde, comprehensive and technologically advanced an approach is if the subject is not affectively ready to learn. The different maxims postulated in this chapter, which are based on the pertinent literature and my

[4] Emphasis added.

own reflections, show how self-esteem is a key factor affecting the whole learning process. In turn, self-esteem has a direct and significant impact on other factors such as motivation, learning anxiety, learner autonomy and information processing. The final outcome in the SL classroom can again be attributed to the master painter who includes all of the colours on his palette. Thus, we as teachers should do our best to improve our students' self-esteem by fostering the virtuous-and not the vicious-circle of language learning. As Wolfe (1973) proposes, we need to redirect teacher-training programs towards a confluent training that includes not only cognitive but also affective skills. Awareness of these needs is essential to developing good teaching, a good learning environment, and good human relations.

In conclusion, when dealing with the importance of affective factors in learning I cannot help but feeling that we are simply elaborating on common sense and contributing little to the state of the question. While there exists abundant literature on the importance of self-esteem for learning and ultimately for living, little research is available on the role that self-esteem plays in language learning. Thus, a detailed study of that importance with special attention to affective variables might contribute notably to the language learning realm.

## Works Cited

Anderson, P. 1982. Self-esteem in the foreign language: A preliminary investigation. *Foreign Language Annals* 15, (2): 109-114.

Anderson, R.C. 1977. The notion of schemata and the educational enterprise. In *Schooling and the acquisition of knowledge*, ed. Anderson R. C. and R. J. Spiro. Hillsdale: Erlbaum.

—. 1978. Schema-directed processes in language comprehension. In *Cognitive Psychology and Instruction,* ed. Lesgold, A., J. Pelligreno, S. Fokkema and R. Glaser. New York: Plenum.

Arnold, J. 1999. *Affect in language learning*. Cambridge: Cambridge University Press.

Avia, M. 1995. El self. In *Personalidad: aspectos cognitivos y sociales, ed.* Avia, M., and M.L. Sánchez. Madrid: Pirámide.

Bernet, C., R. E. Ingram, and B. R. Johnson. 1993. Self-esteem. In *Symptoms of depression,* ed. Ch. G. Costello. New York: Addison Wesley Longman.

Branden, N. 1969. *The psychology of self-esteem: A New Concept of Man's Nature.* Los Angeles: Nash Publishing.

Brown, H.D. 1977. Cognitive and affective characteristics of good language learners. Paper presented at Los Angeles Second Language Research Forum, 1st, February 11-13, in Los Angeles, USA.

—. 1978. The good language teacher: Coping with the effect of affect. *CATESOL Occasional Papers* 4.

—. 1987. *Principles of language learning and teaching*. Englewood Cliffs: Prentice Hall.

—. 1990. M & Ms for language classrooms? Another look at motivation. In *Georgetown University Round Table on Languages and Linguistics*, ed. J.E. Alatis. Washington DC: Georgetown University Press.

—. 2001. *Teaching by principles: An interactive pedagogy to language learning*. Englewood Cliffs: Prentice Hall Regents.

Buri, J., P. Kirchner, and J. Walsh. 1987. Familial correlates of self-esteem in young american adults. *Journal of Social Psychology* 127: 583-588.

Canfield, J. 1993. *101 ways to develop student self-esteem and responsibility.* Boston: Allyn and Bacon.

Carrell, P., and J.C. Eisterhold. 1988. Schema theory and ESL reading pedagogy. In *Interactive approaches to second language reading*, ed. Carrell, P. L., J. Devine and D. Eskey. New York: Cambridge University Press.

Carter, B. 1999. Begin with beliefs. Exploring the relationship between beliefs and autonomy among advanced students. *Texas Papers in Foreign Language Education: Contemporary Issues in Foreign Language Learning and Teaching* 4, (1): 1-20.

Cigman, R. 2004. Situated self-esteem. *Journal of Philosophy of Education* 38, (1): 91-105.

Cohen, Y., and M. J. Norst. 1989. Fear, dependence and loss of self-esteem: Affective barriers in second language learning among Adults. *RELC Journal* 20, (2): 61-77.

Coopersmith, S. 1967. *The antecedents of self-esteem.* San Francisco: W.H. Freeman and Company.

Cotterall, S. 1995. Readiness for autonomy: Investigating learner's belief. *System* 23: 195-205.

Damasio, A. 1994. *Descartes' error: Emotion, reason and the human brain.* New York: Avon.

Deci, E.L., and R.M. Ryan. 1985. *Intrinsic motivation and self-determination in human behavior.* New York: Plenum Press.

—. 1987. The support of autonomy and the control of behavior. *Journal of Personality and Social Psychology* 40: 1-10.

Dörnyei, Z. 2001. *Motivational strategies in the language classroom.* Cambridge: Cambridge University Press.

Dourado, M.R., and L. Wolmer. 2002. Auto-estima e aprendizagem de linguas estrangeiras. *Trabalhos em Linguistica Aplicada* 39: 81-94.

Dukes, R., and B. Lorch. 1989. Concept of self, mediating factors, and adolescent deviance. *Sociological Spectrum* 9: 301-319.

Ecclestone, K. 2004. Learning or therapy? The demoralisation of education. *British Journal of Educational Studies* 52, (2): 112-137.

Edwords, F. 1989a. The promise of humanism. [Document available in http://www.americanhumanist.org/humanism/promise.html].

—. 1989b. What is humanism? [Document available in: http://www.americanhumanist.org/humanism/whatishtml.html].

Epstein, H. 1985. Review of the Piers-Harris Children's Self-Concept Scale (The way I feel about myself). *Ninth mental measurements yearbook*, ed. J.V. Mitchell, Vol.1: 1168-1169. Lincoln: University of Nebraska, Buros Institute of Mental Measurement.

Erika B. E. 1995. Behaviorism as a learning theory. [Document available in http://129.7.160.115/inst5931/Behaviorism.html].

Evans, D. 2001. *Emotions, the science of sentiment.* New York: OUP.

Gardner, R. 1983. Learning another language: A true social psychological experiment. *Journal of Language and Social Psychology* 2: 219-239.

Gardner, R. 1985. *Social psychology and second language learning: The role of attitudes and motivation.* London: Edward Arnold.

Gardner, R., and W. Lambert. 1972. *Attitudes and motivation in second language learning.* Rowley: Newbury House.

Gardner, R., P. Smythe, R. Clement, and L. Gliksman. 1976. Second language learning: A social-psychological perspective. *Canadian Modern Language Review* 32: 198-213.

Gardner, R., R. N. Lalonde, R. Moorcroft, and F.T. Evers. 1987. Second language attrition: The role of motivation and use. *Journal of Language and Social Psychology* 6: 29-47.

Greenberg, J., S. Solomon, T. Pyszczynski, A. Rosenblatt, J. Burling, D. Lyon, and L. Simon. 1992. Assessing the terror management analysis of self-esteem: Converging evidence of an anxiety-buffering function. *Journal of Personality and Social Psychology* 63: 913-922.

Houston, J. P., C. Hammer, A. Padilla, and H. Bee. 1989. *Invitation to psychology.* San Diego: Harcourt Brace Jovanovich Publishers.

Huitt, W. 2001. Humanism and open education. Valdosta: Valdosta State University.

James, W. 1890. *The principles of psychology.* Cambridge: Harvard University Press.

Kohonen, V. 1994. Teaching content through a foreign language is a matter of school development. ERIC Document Reproduction Service No. FL022997.

Kohonen, V., T. Folland, and L. Taivalsaari. 1993. Towards foreign language learning as personal growth: Supporting self-esteem and collaborative skills in foreign language learning. Paper presented at the Council of Europe Symposium, Heinola.

Kurtz, P. 2000. *Humanist manifesto 2000: A call for a new planetary humanism.* Amherst: Prometheus Books.

—. 2001. *Skepticism and humanism: The new paradigm.* New Brunswick: Transaction Books.

Littlejohn, A. 2001. Motivation where does it come from, where does it go? *English Teaching Professional* 19: 5-8. [Article also available at www.AndrewLittlejohn.net].

Luk, C. 1997. The role of self-concepts of technical school students in their learning of a second language. *Psychologia: An International Journal of Psychology in the Orient* 40, (4): 227-232.

McCroskey, J.C., J.A. Daly, V.P. Richmond, and R.L. Falcione. 1977. Studies of the relationship between communication apprehension and self-esteem. *Human communication research* 3, (3): 269-277.

Onwuegwuzie, A.J., P. Bailey, and C. Daley. 1997. Foreign language anxiety among college students. Paper presented at the Annual Meeting of the Mid-South Educational Research Association. Memphis.

Oxford, R. L. 1990. *Language learning strategies: What every teacher should know.* Boston: Heinle & Heinle.

—. 1992. Who are our students? A synthesis of foreign and second language research on individual differences with implications for instructional practice. *TESL Canada Journal/Revue TESL du Canada* 9, (2), spring : 30-49.

—. 1996. When emotion meets (meta)cognition in language learning histories. *International Journal of Educational Research* 23, (7): 581-594.

Oxford, R.L., and M. Ehrman. 1993. Second language research on individual differences. *Annual Review of Applied Linguistics* 13, 188-205.

Paivio, A. 1986. *Mental representations: A dual coding approach.* New York: Oxford University Press.

—. 1989. Basic puzzles in imagery research. In *cognitive and neuropsychological approaches to mental imagery*, ed. Denis, M., J. Engelkamp, and J.T.E. Richardson. Boston: Martinus Nijhoff.

—. 1990. *Mental representations: A dual coding approach (2nd ed.).* New York: Oxford University Press.

—. 1991. Dual Coding Theory: Retrospect and current status. *Canadian Journal of Psychology* 45: 255-287.

Pudjiati, S. 1996. Students attitudes toward foreign language. Annual Meeting of the Mid-South Educational Research Association. Tuscaloosa.

Punset, E. 2005. *El viaje a la felicidad. Las nuevas claves científicas.* Barcelona: Destino.

Reasoner, R. 1982. *Building self-esteem.* Palo Alto: Consulting Psychologists Press.

—. 1991. *Building self-esteem in the secondary schools: Teacher's manual and instructional materials*. Palo Alto: Consulting Psychologists Press.

—.1994. *Building self-Esteem in elementary schools. Administrators guide*. Palo Alto: Consulting Psychologists Press.

Reich, A. 1986. Pathological forms of self-esteem regulation. *Essential Papers on Narcissism*, ed. A.P. Morrison, 44-60. Originally published in *Psychoanalytic Study of the Child* 15: 205-32, 1960.

Richmond, V.P., and J.C. McCroskey. 1989. *Communication apprehension, avoidance and effectiveness*. Scottsdale: Gorsuch Scarisbrick Publishers.

Rogers, C. 1969. *Freedom to learn: A view of what education might become.* Columbus: Charles Merrill.

Rosenberg, M. 1965. *Society and the adolescent self-image.* Princeton: Princeton University Press.

—. 1979. *Conceiving the self.* New York: Basic Books, Inc. Publishers.

Rosenberg, M., and R. H. Turner, ed. 1981. *Social psychology: Sociological perspectives*. New York: Basic.

Rouse, J. 1988. Language learning and identity. *The English Journal* 77, (2): 22-28.

Rubin, J. 1975. What the good language learner can teach us. *TESOL Quarterly*, 9, (1): 41-51.

Sadoski, M., and, A. Paivio. 1994. A dual coding view of imagery and verbal processes in reading comprehension. In *Theoretical Models and Processes of Reading*, ed. Ruddell, R. B., M. R. Ruddell, and H. Singer (4th ed.). Newark: International Reading Association.

Sadoski, M., A. Paivio, and E.T. Goetz. 1991. A critique of schema theory in reading and a dual coding alternative. *Reading Research Quarterly* 26: 463-484.

Sadoski, M., E.T. Goetz, and J. B. Fritz. 1993. Impact of concreteness on comprehensibility, interest, and memory for text: Implications for dual coding theory and text design. *Journal of Educational Psychology* 85: 291-304.

Sadoski, M., E.T., Goetz, A. Olivarez, S. Lee, and N.M. Roberts. 1990. Imagination in story reading: The role of imagery in reading and a dual coding alternative. *Reading Research Quarterly* 26: 463-484.

Sánchez-Herrero, S. 1992. The predictive validation of an instrument designed to measure student anxiety in learning a foreign language. *Educational & Psychological Measurement* 52, (4): 961-966.

Scarcella, R.C., and R. Oxford. 1992. *The tapestry of language learning.* Boston: Heinle & Heinle.

Seebauer, R. 1997. Self-concept research as a basis for early second-language instruction. *Praxis des Neusprachlichen Unterrichts* 44, (1): 6-12.

Seligman, M. 2002. *Authentic happiness*. New York: Free Press.

Seyhan, S. 2001. The impact of anxiety, self-esteem and motivation on the oral communication of German and Japanese adult ESL students. Dissertation Abstracts International, Section A: The Humanities and Social Sciences, 61:10. 2001 Apr, 3930. U.S.A.

Steinem, G. 1992 *Revolution from within: A book of self-esteem.* Boston: Little, Brown and Company.

Stern, S. 1980. Drama in second language learning from a psycholinguistic perspective. *Language Learning* 30, (1): 77-100.

Stevick, E. 1986. *Images and options in the language classroom*. Cambridge: Cambridge University Press.

—. 1990. *Humanism in language teaching*. Oxford: Oxford University Press.

Tumposky, N. 1991. Students' beliefs about language learning: A cross-cultural study. *Carleton Papers in Applied Language Studies* 8: 50-65.

Von Worde, R. 1998. An investigation of students' perpectives on foreign language anxiety. PhD diss., George Manson University.

Wells, E., and G. Marwell. 1976. *Self-esteem: Its conceptualization and measurement.* Beverly Hills: Sage.

Wenden, A. 1987. How to be a successful language learner: Insights and prescriptions from L2 learners. In *Learner strategies in language learning*, ed. A. Wenden, and J. Rubin, 103-117. London: Prentice Hall.

Wolfe, D. E. 1973. Student teaching: Toward a confluent approach. *The Modern Language Journal* 57, (3): 113-119.

Wozniewicz, W. 1995. On Therapy for and Neutralization of the "Fear to Communicate". *Glottodidactica* 23: 167-172.

# CHAPTER FIVE

# THE SOCIAL DIMENSION OF IDENTITY AND SELF-ESTEEM IN THE FOREIGN LANGUAGE CLASSROOM

SONIA CASAL[1]
(PABLO DE OLAVIDE UNIVERSITY, SPAIN)

*The foreign language classroom represents a natural setting for socialization and learning. Groups provide the means to develop cognitive skills, constituting at the same time the context where human social needs can be fulfilled. In this chapter, it is claimed that identity and self-esteem work at a personal and a social level and the distinction is drawn between personal and social identity on the one hand and personal and collective self-esteem on the other. Belonging to a group and identifying with it provides the individual with a social identity and enhances their self-esteem, two key elements in personal well-being. However, Social Identity Theory, developed by Tajfel and Turner (1979), has consistently shown that loving one's group leads to hating other groups, creating stereotypes and prejudice and hampering work with those who are perceived as different. Minimizing the effects of Social Identity Theory in the classroom may be achieved by creating heterogeneous, non-stable groups, discovering each other's personality and above all, promoting positive interdependence, a social situation which makes learning and interpersonal relationships more effective.*

## 1. Introduction

The term "self-esteem" usually refers to the individual evaluation a person makes of their personal attributes (his/her identity) and is related to personal well-being. A safe environment, where individuals feel supported, allows them to reach self-discovery, self-esteem and self-directed learning (Rogers and

[1] Sonia Casal teaches at the Universidad Pablo de Olavide (Seville). Her interests are centred on the study of the different factors that facilitate language learning, especially cooperative learning. E-mail: scasmad@upo.es

Freiberg 1994, quoted in Lefrançois 1997, 316). Marzano, Pickering and Brandt (1990) have demonstrated the link between the level of students' self-esteem and academic achievement, showing that children and adolescents with a high level of self-esteem get better results at school. Rogers (1994) claims that our self-esteem can be worked out by comparing the idea we hold about ourselves and our ideal view. The closer these two are, the higher our self-esteem.

The definition of self-esteem at the beginning of this section, however, needs some specification. Part of the information we gather in order to evaluate our identity is not just a consequence of personal thoughts, but is rather the result of our membership within groups and social categories (Tajfel 1984, 292). The sense of belonging to groups and social categories relates to a basic human need and is a source of high or low self-esteem. Individuals need to develop at an individual level, but also at an interpersonal and a collective level. (Smith, Coats and Murphy 2001, 120).

Groups fulfil a number of personal and interpersonal needs for their members and are, therefore, a vital part of a person's life. Forsyth (1993) states that group benefits can be divided into five basic categories: 1) Groups provide the opportunity for contact and relationships with other individuals, promoting general communication and social interaction among people; 2) they contribute to creating warm, supportive and loving relationships with others; 3) they provide the opportunity for productivity, achievement, success and control of resources; 4) they supply the means to increase stability and decrease anxiety, minimizing self-doubt, tension, vulnerability, insecurity and self-pity while increasing self-esteem, relaxation, safety, and self- satisfaction; and finally, 5) they provide the opportunity for creativity, refinement of ideas, self-improvement and increased understanding of oneself and others.

The importance of groups in the individual's life is also observed in their influential correlations with learning. At school, personal features such as behaviour, gender, achievement or attractiveness tend to divide students into groups making socialization and learning intertwined processes. An individual's behaviour is determined by the interaction between their personality and that of the other group members, and this interaction will be decisive in learning processes. Johnson (1972, 256) argues that at both secondary and university levels the most important influences upon students' values and behaviour come from their peers. Aron and McLaughlin-Volpe (2001, 93) present evidence that supports the idea that peers with close relationships tend to include the perspectives and identities of their partners in their identities. The group is an extremely important influence on students' motivation and achievement and at times, it may be the group itself which praises or punishes certain behaviour.

Education and learning in their broadest sense, then, aim to create the bases upon which the individual will develop their identity at a personal and a social level, contributing to their global well-being. Groups in the classroom can help enormously to enhance socialization, and therefore self-esteem, by building a sense of "we" rather than "I" in supportive relationships; by developing critical thinking; by teaching and learning in a cooperative way; by implementing cooperation skills as well as personal values such as responsibility, autonomy, security and creativity.

## 2. Identity dimensions: Personal and social identity

The identity of a person corresponds to the attributes they have that make them unique as individuals and distinguish them from others (e.g. personality, beliefs, needs, motivations or skills). Miller and Harrington (1995, 204-206) point out that identity has four important features: relational, interactive, situational and affective.

Firstly, identity is relational: our self is partly defined by comparison with others. Many traits are clearly interpersonal such as, friendliness or humour. A second characteristic of identity is that it is interactive. Relationships with members of our environment form the basis upon which we build the view we hold of ourselves. Solé (1999, 34) comments that you will consider yourself friendly, clumsy or intelligent because others transmit this idea unconsciously.

A third feature of identity is that it is situational, that is, identity is not a fixed or stable concept. Depending on the context, individuals can be friendly while in a different context their attitude can change considerably. The fourth and final characteristic Miller and Harrington (1995) observe in personal identity is that it is affective. Identity has an emotional dimension and threats of any kind may cause anxiety and insecurity in individuals. Learning a foreign language involves tension that may result in anxiety and learning difficulties.

The relational, interactive, situational and affective components of personal identity show the relevance of social interactions when trying to understand the overall concept of personal identity. Together with social interactions, a person's identity is also shaped by their membership within groups, that is, by social identity. Social identity refers to the individual's knowledge that they belong to a social group: family, nationality, race, gender, religion, social class, sexual orientation or occupation. Our lives are full of examples of our belonging to different groups which do not stand in isolation: the positive aspects of social identity become meaningful only when compared with other groups.

According to Bergami and Bagozzi (2000, 556) there are three distinctive components involved in social identity: 1) a cognitive component, that is, the awareness that we belong to a group from which we can recognize our role in society; 2) an evaluative component which involves comparing our own group to other groups and usually leads to our portraying our own group in a positive light; and 3) an emotional component where those within the same group are viewed as similar (in-group), while those in other groups are looked upon as different (out-group). Group members differ in the degree to which they identify with the in-group. While low group identifiers are members who identify weakly with the group, high group identifiers empathise strongly.

Personal and social identity are interrelated concepts: we sometimes think of ourselves as unique individuals ("I") while at other times we think of ourselves as members of a social class or category ("we"). While our uniqueness influences the way we interact with others, the social and cultural context surrounding us significantly influences our feelings about an evaluation of ourselves. Culture can be related to high or low levels of self-esteem. Research has consistently shown, for example, that East Asian cultures and East Asian minority groups tend to report lower levels of self-esteem than Western cultures. (Spencer-Rodgers et al. 2004).

## 3. The social dimension of self-esteem in the foreign language classroom

In the previous sections, the social dimension of identity and the importance of groups in an individual's life have been stressed. At this point, it must be added that learning a foreign language is an interactive process, involving a cooperative effort to learn, understand and solve problems. Learning a foreign language does not only mean the study of structures and vocabulary but also the construction of a new social identity. Factors involved in learning a language, such as class participation, pair and group interactions, can pose threats to our students' identity and self-esteem. Therefore, the view of self-esteem as an evaluative component of identity where interpersonal and group behaviour play an important role cannot be disregarded. While personal self-esteem refers to the individual evaluation a person makes of their personal attributes, collective self-esteem describes their feelings or evaluation regarding the groups they belong to.

In most cases, the need to enhance personal self-esteem and collective self-esteem are complementary, since our personal self-esteem is usually boosted when our collective self-esteem increases. Luhtanen and Crocker (1992) argue that the more positive the feelings about a group (collective self-esteem), the higher one's personal self-esteem. However, when a collective effort ends in failure, members may protect their personal self-esteem by blaming other group members for the failure. Collective self-esteem, therefore, seems to serve the needs of personal self-esteem. Tajfel (1984, 293) claims that individuals stay in a group as long as the group fulfils their need to enhance the positive aspects of their social identity. When their needs are not met, individuals tend to abandon the group.

Group member evaluations also play a critical role in personal self-esteem. Forsyth (1993) claims that when students think that fellow group members evaluate them positively, their own personal self-esteem tends to become more positive. Hornsey, Trembath and Gunthorpe (2004) argue that even criticism coming from in-group members is taken more positively than criticism coming from outsiders. "It's OK if *we* say it, but *you* can't" (Hornsey, Trembath and Gunthorpe 2004, 500). This is what they call the *intergroup sensitivity effect*.

The importance attributed to identity and self-esteem as a phenomenon affected by social and cultural variables is shown further by Luhtanen and Crocker (1992), designers of a model of social identity and a collective self-esteem scale (see Appendix A) which is used as an indicator of individuals' positive evaluation of their social identity. The scale includes the following aspects: 1) membership collective social esteem, or a person's sense of how well they function as a member of a given social group; 2) private collective social esteem: a person's private evaluation of the social group; 3) public collective social esteem: the extent to which a person believes that the social group is valued by others; and 4) identity collective social esteem: the extent to which group membership is important to a person's individual self-concept.

Rahimi and Fisher (1999, quoted in Rahimi 1999, 11) demonstrated that individuals with lower collective self-esteem are more likely to interpret behaviour directed to their group in negative terms and this same low collective self-esteem may lead to negative evaluation of the out-group in an effort to enhance one's personal self-esteem. Due to the close link between personal and collective self-esteem, low collective self-esteem may indicate low personal self-esteem (Rahimi and Fisher 1997). Following Tice and Baumeister (2001), who state that personality changes seem to proceed from the outer self to the inner self, we argue that understanding how an individual reacts at a social level will allow us to analyse the details of their personal self-esteem.

## 3.1. Social Identity Theory

Social Identity Theory was developed by Henri Tajfel and John Turner in 1979 in order to explain relationships between large groups such as social classes and categories. In order to carry out experiments which have had enormous relevance in the field of social psychology, Tajfel and Turner formed minimal groups, that is, groups created according to a number of minimal conditions. In doing so, they tried to eliminate all the possible variables that are usually linked with favouritism among members of a same group (in-group favouritism) and discrimination against those who do not belong to their group (out-group discrimination). These minimal conditions included the following (Shiffman and Wicklund 1992): members in the group had no face-to-face interaction and the personal identity of group members was not known, there was no particular advantage of belonging to a particular group, nor a logical reason for holding a negative attitude against the group and, finally, there was no advantage or gain for the individual as a result of their making a particular response.

Their experiments showed that, despite the minimal group conditions, when randomly assigned to a group, individuals appeared automatically to think of that group as better for them than any alternative out-group and perceived themselves as similar to the members of their groups and different from the other out-groups. Their results led them to reach two main conclusions: Firstly, individuals have a tendency to sort people into social categories or groups. Once their social world is divided, individuals tend to enhance intergroup boundaries by accentuating similarities within groups and differences between these same categories (Aron and McLaughlin 2001, 95). According to this finding, students would be generally predisposed to cooperate with peers who they perceive as similar to themselves and would be likely to reject peers who they regard as different (Levy, Kaplan and Patrick 2004, 130).

Secondly, Tajfel and Turner found that group members enhanced their self-esteem and evaluated in-group members more favourably (Tajfel and Turner 1986). They claim that the reason for this may lie in the basic need human beings have to establish and maintain a positive identity by preserving positive self-esteem. Martinot et al. (2002, 1586) found that people belonging to stigmatised groups (African American, women, homosexuals) tend to compare themselves with other in-group members in order to protect their self-esteem, avoiding comparison with out-group members who may be seen as more fortunate.

These two findings have an important consequence in the intergroup relationship. By identifying with a group and observing others as members of a particular team, individuals tend to depersonalise them, being considered people who react as group members and not as individuals with personal traits or differences with their group. In other words, following Social Identity Theory, stereotypes and prejudices tend to arise among groups due to the division drawn between in-groups and out-groups. While a stereotype is a simplified mental image of a group shared by a number of people, a prejudice is an antipathy based on faulty and inflexible generalizations (Allport 1954, quoted in Ruggiero 1999).

Stereotypes and prejudices are the consequence of complex circumstances including the natural human inclination to form prejudgments, the manner children are raised at home, fears, sex conflicts, feelings of guilt and the social patterns in society and culture. Prejudice seems to be intimately connected with group membership and group interaction in the sense that group members often display prejudice and hostility against members of another group because they believe this group threatens their own group position and interests. Bobo (1999) shows that racial prejudice is not simply a collection of negative beliefs and feelings that result from an individual's egocentric concerns, but also involves a commitment to a preferred group position in society.

## 3.2. Minimizing the effects of Social Identity Theory in the foreign language classroom

Students in the classroom bring with them social attitudes and prejudices from the culture they live in. As Social Identity Theory shows, differences among social groups are exaggerated and stereotypes are used to illustrate these differences. Common traits among group members in the classroom are magnified in comparison to other out-group members, the evaluation of in-group members being more positive and resulting in a preference to stay and work with them. Traditionally, the development of positive interpersonal relationships and skills has had a secondary role in most classrooms. However, achieving these objectives is as important as the acquisition of information. Intergroup attitudes may be improved if the social organization process underlying the division into in-groups and out-groups is modified.

Deutsch (1949) described three social situations that can be found in a classroom: a competitive situation, where goals are in negative correlation; an individualistic situation, where students' goals are independent and a cooperative situation, where students cannot reach their objectives unless the other students do too. Later studies (Tjosvold and Johnson 1977; Johnson and Johnson 1979; Johnson, Johnson and Smith 1990; Johnson, Johnson and Holubec 1999) have indicated that competition among groups, where there is a negative correlation among students' goals, tends to accentuate boundaries among students, creating a stressful and tense atmosphere.

On the other hand, a positive and cooperative social situation (where positive social comparison is present) may reduce individual differences, enhancing both collective and personal self-esteem, improving students' willingness to learn and, therefore, their chances to develop at an individual and a social level. As students feel more comfortable sharing, helping, asking and answering questions, they are able to identify the individual natures of their classmates. When the uniqueness of each individual is internalised, students are able to start relationships more easily with a variety of groups, even with those with whom they have had no previous experience.

The creation of heterogeneous groups can be the first step to minimize categories in the classroom. Criteria such as gender, level of achievement, character or hobbies may help us to create groups with boys and girls, high-achievers and low-achievers, shy and more extroverted students as well as students from different racial backgrounds. Changing groups from time to time will give everybody in the classroom the chance to work with everybody else and build a feeling of class, rather than that of a sum of unconnected groups.

Minimization of threats to identity and self-esteem can be achieved by creating a relaxed classroom atmosphere where students feel free to ask and be asked, where everyone is at the same time an individual ("I") and a group member ("we"). The provision of opportunities for the personalization of group members offers students the opportunity to know each other more deeply, avoiding stereotypes and prejudice and enhancing interpersonal skills.

### 3.2.1. Positive interdependence

Positive interdependence describes a social situation where group members need each other to succeed using interpersonal skills. Face-to-face promotional interactions between group members help to ensure this. Johnson, Johnson and Maruyama (1983) argue that among social processes, positive interdependence is observed as that which creates more interpersonal attraction among the members of a group, as opposed to individualistic or competitive structures. This interpersonal attraction promotes group cohesion, that is, it provides its members with a shared basis of similarity, creating more possibilities of enhancing self-esteem and simultaneously satisfying the need to belong, one of the basic human motivations.

There are different ways of structuring positive interdependence in groups. Learning goal interdependence, for example, can be ensured if the group goals include that all group members must understand a specific concept well enough to explain it to another group. This is the basis of Jigsaw (Aronson 1978), a cooperative way of structuring the information to be learnt.

Grammar points can also be learnt following Aronson's technique. Here is an example: imagine the grammar point to be learnt or reviewed is the use of present simple versus present continuous. We will divide the class into five groups that we will call "expert" groups. In order to do this, we will prepare five different sets of cards (set 1: five verbs in 3rd person present simple; set 2: five verbs in present continuous; set 3: five sentences using present simple; set 4: five sentences using present continuous; set 5: five frequency adverbs). We will divide the cards among students and tell them that they must find students with a related card and sit and work with them.

These expert groups have the responsibility to learn/review five main grammar points related to present simple and continuous (group 1: present tense forms, especially 3rd person, negative and question forms; group 2: present continuous form, paying attention to *–ing* forms and their rules; group 3: when to use present simple; group 4: when to use present continuous; group 5: where frequency adverbs should be placed in present simple sentences). The information can be provided through the textbook or through a handout.

Once they have finished, each student in each group will be given a number so that all those with number 1 go to one group, all number 2 to another group, etc. A student from a different expert group will be now a member of each new group. Now, each student will be allotted five minutes to explain their grammar point, asking and answering questions. Having done this, the teacher will give students a handout with gapped sentences that students must complete individually using the correct form of present simple or continuous. Students must remember what their team-mates have explained in order to do the exercise correctly.

Another way to insure interdependence and the building of personal relationships is resource interdependence. This kind of interdependence relies on the fact that individuals possess specific resources needed for the group as a whole to succeed. No one can do all the work alone because they need the help of others (their resources). Any exercise can be modified to require students to cooperate and rely on each other. Correction, for example, can be carried out through resource interdependence in pairs. In order to do this, two handouts will be designed: Student A will have the answers for odd-numbered items and will have to complete even-numbered ones. Student B will have the opposite.

Role interdependence occurs when specific roles are assigned to group members. Among these are secretary, time keeper, language controller or quiet captain. Each role has its function: the secretary, for example, writes the final version of the activity or acts as spokesperson; the language controller must make sure that everybody speaks English; the quiet captain is responsible for the level of noise. These roles can rotate to give all team members experience.

Not only can tasks improve interpersonal relationships through positive interdependence: marks can also be dealt with in an interdependent manner. For example, besides students' individual scores on an exam, they may receive a certain number of points if all group members score at or above a certain mark.

In sum, positive interdependence makes the most of group and intergroup relationships, enhancing a positive social identity where, if students work with all the others throughout the year and depend on them in a positive manner, the division in-group/out-group disappears.

## 4. Conclusion

This chapter has stressed the viewpoint that identity and self-esteem are concepts not only derived from personal reflections but also from the individual's membership within groups. Groups provide the individual with a number of advantages and are an important source of learning, influencing students' behaviour at secondary and university levels.

Identity has been depicted as having a personal component with four main features (relational, interactive, situational and affective) and a social component: social identity or the knowledge that we belong to a group. Three conditions have been described as necessary to maintain a social identity: a cognitive, an evaluative and an emotional component. The interconnectivity of personal and social identity has been stressed.

Self-esteem has been considered as structured upon two bases: personal self-esteem and collective self-esteem. Luhtanen and Crocker (1992), designers of a social identity and a collective self-esteem scale, show the importance of identity and self-esteem as a social and cultural phenomenon. Rahimi (1999) has demonstrated the link between low collective self-esteem and low personal self-esteem.

Minimization of the effects of Social Identity Theory in the foreign language classroom may be achieved if the marked division between in-groups and out-groups is modified. A cooperative social situation may reduce individual differences and promote collective and personal self-esteem by the creation of heterogeneous groups, the personalization of group members and the promotion of interpersonal skills.

Positive interdependence through learning goals, resources or roles can be implemented in the classroom to promote learning, socialization and self-esteem.

## Works Cited

Ames, C. 1990. Effective motivation: The contribution of the learning environment. In *The social psychology of education. Current research and theory*, ed. R. S. Feldman, 235-256. Cambridge: Cambridge University Press.

Aron, A., and T. McLaughlin-Volpe. 2001. Including others in the self. Extensions to own and partner's group memberships. In *Individual self, relational self, collective self*, ed. C. Sedikides and M. B. Brewer, 89-108. Philadelphia: Psychology Press.

Aronson, E. 1978. *The jigsaw classroom*. Beverly Hills: Sage.

Bergami, M., and R. P. Bagozzi. 2000. Self-categorization, affective commitment and group self-esteem as distinct aspects of social identity in the organization. *British Journal of Social Psychology* 39: 555-577.

Bobo, L. 1999. Prejudice as group position: Microfoundations of a sociological approach to racism and race relations. *Journal of Social Issues*, http://www.findarticles.com/p/articles/mi_m0341/is_3_55.htm

Deutsch, M. 1949. A theory of cooperation and competition. *Human Relations* 2: 129-152.

Forsyth, D. R. 1993. Why so social an animal? The utility of interdependence. Richmond: Virginia Commonwealth University. Also available at [http://www.has.vcu.edu/psy/faculty/fors/rgroup.html].

Hornsey, M. J. , M. Trembath, and S. Gunthorpe. 2004. "You can criticize because you care": Identity attachment, constructiveness, and the intergroup sensitivity effect. *European Journal of Social Psychology* 34: 499-518.

Johnson, D. W. 1972. *Psicología social de la educación*. Buenos Aires: Kapelusz.

Johnson, D. W., and R. T. Johnson. 1979. Conflict in the classroom: Controversy and learning. *Review of Educational Research* 49, (1): 51-70.

Johnson, D. W., R. T. Johnson, and J. H. Edithe. 1999. *El aprendizaje cooperativo en el aula.* Barcelona: Paidós.

Johnson, D. W., R. T. Johnson, and G. Maruyama. 1983. Interdependence and interpersonal attraction among heterogeneous and homogeneous individuals: A theoretical formulation and a meta-analysis of the research. *Review of Educational Research* 53, (1): 5-54.

Johnson, D. W., R. T. Johnson, and K. A. Smith. 1990. Academic conflict among students: Controversy and learning. In *The social psychology of education. Current research and theory*, ed. R. S. Feldman, 199-231. Cambridge: Cambridge University Press.

Lefrançois, G. R. 1997. *Psychology for teaching*. Belmont: Wadsworth Publishing Company.

Levy, I., A. Kaplan, and H. Patrick. 2004. Early adolescents' achievement goals, social status, and attitudes towards cooperation with peers. *Social Psychology of Education* 7: 127-159.

Luhtanen, R., and J. Crocker. 1992. A collective self-esteem scale: Self-evaluation of one's identity. *Personality and Social Psychology Bulletin* 18, (3): 302-318.

Martinot, D., S. Redersdorff, S. Guimond, and S. Dif. 2002. Ingroup versus outgroup comparisons and self-esteem: The role of group status and ingroup identification. *Personality and Social Psychology Bulletin* 28, (11): 1586-1600.

Marzano, R. J., D. J. Pickering, and R. S. Brandt. 1990. Integrating instructional programs through dimensions of learning. *Educational Leadership* 47, (5): 17-24.

Miller, N., and H. J. Harrington. 1995. Social categorization and intergroup acceptance: Principles for the design and development of cooperative learning teams. In *Interaction in cooperative groups. The theoretical anatomy of group learning*, ed. R. Hertz-Lazarowitz and N. Miller, 203-227. New York: Cambridge University Press.

Rahimi, S. 1999. Collective self-esteem and shared identities: A comparative transcultural study. Mc Gill University: Canada. [http: //www.cs.mcgill.ca/~rahimi/texts/chap2.html].

Rahimi, S., and R. Fisher. 1997. Collective self-esteem and the construal of racism. McGill University: Canada. [http:// www.cs.mcgill.ca/~rahimi/texts/cse_cr.html].

Rogers, C. R. 1994. *Freedom to learn*. New York: Merrel.

Ruggiero, K. M. 1999. Introduction to the issue. *Journal of Social Issues,* [http://www.findarticles.com/p/articles/mi_m0341/is_3_55/ai_58549252.html].

Sedikides, C., and M. B. Brewer, eds. 2001. *Individual self, relational self, collective self.* Philadelphia: Psychology Press.

Shiffman, R., and R. A. Wicklund. 1992. The minimal group paradigm and its minimal psychology. *Theory and Psychology* 2: 29-50.

Smith, E. R., S. Coats, and J. Murphy. 2001. The self and attachment to relationship partners and groups. Theoretical parallels and new insights. In *Individual self, relational self, collective self*, ed. C. Sedikides, and M. B. Brewer, 109-122. Philadelphia: Psychology Press.

Solé, I. 1999. Disponibilidad para el aprendizaje y sentido del aprendizaje. In *El constructivismo en el aula*, ed. C. Coll, E. Martín, T. Mauri, M. Miras, J. Onrubia, I. Solé, and A. Zabala, 25-46. Barcelona: Graó.

Spencer-Rodgers, J. K. Peng, L. Wang, and Y. Hou. 2004. Dialectal self-esteem and East-West differences in psychological well-being. *Personality and Social Psychology Bulletin* 30, (11): 1416-1432.

Tajfel, H. 1984. *Grupos humanos y categorías sociales*. Barcelona: Herder.

Tajfel, H., and J. C. Turner. 1986. The social identity theory of inter-group behavior. In *Psychology of Intergroup Relations*, ed. S. Worchel and W. G. Austin, 33-47. Chicago: Nelson-Hall.

Tice, D. M., and Roy F. B. 2001. The primacy of the interpersonal self. In *Individual self, relational self, collective self*, ed. C. Sedikides and M. B. Brewer, 71-88. Philadelphia: Psychology Press.

Tjosvold, D., and D. W. Johnson. 1977. Effects of controversy on cognitive perspective taking. *Journal of Educational Psychology* 69, (6): 679-685.

# Appendix A

## Collective Self-Esteem Scale

Luhtanen, R. and J. Crocker (1992)

**INSTRUCTIONS:** We are all members of different social groups or social categories. Some of such social groups or categories pertain to gender, race, religion, nationality, ethnicity, and socioeconomic class. We would like you to consider your memberships in those particular groups or categories, and respond to the following statements on the basis of how you feel about those groups and your memberships in them. There are no right or wrong answers to any of these statements; we are interested in your honest reactions and opinions. Please read each statement carefully, and respond by using the following scale from 1 to 7:

| 1 | 2 | 3 | 4 | 5 | 6 | 7 |
|---|---|---|---|---|---|---|
| **Strongly disagree** | **Disagree** | **Disagree somewhat** | **Neutral** | **Agree somewhat** | **Agree** | **Strongly agree** |

____ 1. I am a worthy member of the social groups I belong to.

____ 2. I often regret that I belong to some of the social groups I do.

____ 3. Overall, my social groups are considered good by others.

____ 4. Overall, my group memberships have very little to do with how I feel about myself.

____ 5. I feel I don't have much to offer to the social groups I belong to.

____ 6. In general, I'm glad to be a member of the social groups I belong to.

____ 7. Most people consider my social groups, on the average, to be more ineffective than other social groups.

____ 8. The social groups I belong to are an important reflection of who I am.

____ 9. I am a cooperative participant in the social groups I belong to.

____ 10. Overall, I often feel that the social groups of which I am a member are not worthwhile.

____ 11. In general, others respect the social groups that I am a member of.

____ 12. The social groups I belong to are unimportant to my sense of what kind of a person I am.

____ 13. I often feel I'm a useless member of my social groups.

____ 14. I feel good about the social groups I belong to.

____ 15. In general, others think that the social groups I am a member of are unworthy.

____ 16. In general, belonging to social groups is an important part of my self-image.

The four subscales are as follows:

- Items 1, 5, 9 and 13 = Membership self-esteem.
- Items 2, 6, 10 and 14 = Private collective self-esteem.
- Items 3, 7, 11, and 15 = Public collective self-esteem.
- Items 4, 8, 12, and 16 = Importance to Identity.

First, reverse-score answers to items 2, 4, 5, 7, 10, 12, 13, and 15, such that (1 = 7), (2 = 6), (3 = 5), (4 = 4), (5 = 3), (6 = 2), (7 = 1).

Then sum the answers to the four items for each respective subscale score, and divide each by 4.

# CHAPTER SIX

# LANGUAGE ANXIETY AND SELF-ESTEEM

ANA M. ORTEGA[1] (UNIVERSITY OF JAÉN, SPAIN)

*This chapter discusses the role of self-esteem in the phenomenon of foreign language anxiety. Language anxiety has been a widely discussed and researched topic, particularly since the eighties. Even though there are very few research studies specifically focused on trying to clarify the relationships between anxiety and self-esteem in a systematic manner, self-esteem has often been considered to be in the heart of the language anxiety phenomenon. This chapter intends to offer a comprehensive view of how the individual's self-concept and self-esteem have been seen to relate to the foreign language anxiety experience in its formation process.*

## 1. Anxiety and self-esteem in Second Language Acquisition models

Language anxiety has been taken into consideration as an influential variable by a great number of the best known models of Second Language Acquisition (SLA) that have been proposed for the last thirty years, especially by those that have highlighted the importance of affective variables in the learning process. The observation that self-esteem also appears contemplated as a variable, often close to language anxiety, in many of these models, not only suggests the possibility of an existing relationship between language anxiety and self-esteem but can also give us some clues for the understanding of the interplay between these two variables in the process of second language learning.

Krashen's Monitor Model (1981, 1987) proposes a distinction between language acquisition, as a subconscious process that results from active use of the language, and language learning, as a conscious process of rule learning. In

---

[1] Ana María Ortega Cebreros (Ph.D.) teaches English and English Language Teaching Methodology in the English Language Department at the University of Jaén. Her main research interests are social and psychological factors in language learning and teaching. E-mail: amortega@ujaen.es

this model Krashen proposes that the attitudinal variables of anxiety and self-esteem, along with motivation, could affect language acquisition representing them as intervening parts of the proposed Affective Filter Hypothesis. The affective filter would be responsible for either blocking the input to which the learner is exposed to or letting this input go through the Language Acquisition Device (LAD).

Those whose attitudes are not optimal for second language acquisition will not only tend to seek less input, but they will also have a high or strong affective filter–even if they understand the message, the input will not reach that part of the brain responsible for language acquisition, or the LAD (Krashen 1987, 31). Even though Krashen's model does not give an explanation about the role of any of the affective variables in the Affective Filter Hypothesis or how they interact, other models have tried to account for the interplay between anxiety and self-esteem in different and probably complementary ways, sometimes on the basis of empirical research.

The Intergroup Model, proposed by Giles and Byrne (1982), which focuses on the language acquisition process of minority groups, shows how the variable of situational anxiety helps to determine the individual's success in acquiring the second language by having influence on the learners' self-confidence and in turn on their predisposition to participate in natural communicative encounters which allow them to improve their second language skills.

Clement's Social Context Model also provides important information about the relationship between self-esteem and language anxiety. According to this model, in multicultural settings, the self-confidence factor is responsible for a second motivational process that would operate along with the primary motivational process of integrativeness or fear of assimilation. Self-confidence appears constituted in this model by the second language use anxiety perceived by the learner and the learner's self-ratings of proficiency (Clément 1980; Clément and Kruidenier 1985; Clément 1986). These are variables that present high negative correlations with each other, that is to say, second language anxiety decreases when self-ratings of proficiency are high and viceversa. Besides, in this sociomotivational model self-confidence appears influenced by the frequency of contact of the individual with members of the target language community and the extent to which these contacts happen to be pleasant to the individual. Consequently, anxiety is considered in a way to be influenced by the learner's contact with speakers of the target language. In sum, putting together Giles and Clement's views on anxiety and self-esteem suggests that anxiety and self-esteem regarding language use can both affect and be affected by communicative interactions and that they should be negatively correlated.

Anxiety also plays a role in Schumann's Acculturation Model (Schumann 1986), but this time under the terms of language shock and culture shock.

According to this model, the affective variables that affect the acculturation process or social and psychological integration of a subject in the target language community are the following: language shock or perceived fear or apprehension about using a second and weaker (for the learner) language, culture shock or "the anxiety resulting from disorientation encountered upon entering a new culture" (Schumann 1978, 32), motivation or reasons for trying to acquire the second language, and ego permeability or degree of flexibility of ego boundaries, connected to the ability to empathize.

Some years later, following the model of the Affective Filter Hypothesis, Schumann (1994) would represent the importance of the affective variables by means of a memory system that would keep a record of all the emotional reactions (preferences and refusals) of the individual to different stimuli. According to Schumann, this memory device would serve to evaluate the target language, the target culture, and the target language community, according to the experience accumulated by the learner. In the case of classroom language learning, it would be used by learners to evaluate the materials, the activities and the teacher, trying to discern if they are pleasant, novel, relevant to the learner's aims and needs, compatible with their ability, and supportive of their own personal and social image. These two last features seem to evoke the variables of anxiety and self-esteem even though Schumann does not use these terms in this latest proposal.

Even though in his latest proposal Schumann was taking into account situations of foreign language learning in classroom contexts, in contrast to situations of contact between languages or second language acquisition, the model that most clearly took into account the anxiety variable with reference to the specific context of the language classroom was Gardner's Socio-Educational Model. In this model, "there are four different types of individual differences that will influence achievement directly, intelligence, language aptitude, motivation and situational anxiety", which is seen as important "because it would have an inhibiting effect on the individual's performance, thus interfering with acquisition" (Gardner 1985, 147-148).

After some experimental research, Gardner and his colleagues soon became aware of the need to use situationally-based measures of anxiety instead of general measures of anxiety when doing their research on the role of attitudes and motivation in language learning (Gliksman, Gardner and Smythe 1982; Gardner, Lalonde and Pierson 1983; Gardner and Clément 1990; Gardner and MacIntyre 1993). The Attitude and Motivation Battery would include then two different anxiety scales: a French Use Anxiety Scale, for measuring the anxiety perceived by the learner in real situations of second language use, and a French Classroom Anxiety Scale made up of five items that would be later used by Horwitz, Horwitz and Cope (1986) to design a much larger research instrument specifically focused on this topic, namely the Foreign Language Classroom Anxiety Scale (FLCAS). The items of Gardner's French Classroom Anxiety Scale would read as follows (Gardner 1985, 179):

> French class anxiety
>
> It embarrasses me to volunteer answers in our French class.
> I never feel quite sure of myself when I am speaking in our French class.
> I always feel that the other students speak French better than I do.
> I get nervous and confused when I am speaking in my French class.
> I am afraid the other students will laugh at me when I speak French.

As can be seen above, low self-confidence was taken into account in the formulation of some of the items of the language classroom anxiety scale as a predictor of anxiety. Low self-confidence is in fact a recurrent topic in any existing questionnaire devised for measuring language anxiety. As Gardner and MacIntyre (1993, 6) would later state, "in some ways, the antithesis of the anxious student is the self-confident one". Considering the amount of research that Clement and Gardner had done together (cf. Clément; Major, Gardner and Smythe 1977; Clément, Gardner and Smythe 1977, 1980), it seems natural that Gardner's explanations on the role of language anxiety in his Socio-Educational Model of Second Language Acquisition would contemplate to some extent the interplay between language anxiety and self-confidence represented in Clement's Social Context Model.

## 2. The problem of foreign language classroom anxiety

Language anxiety is one of the affective variables that have been traditionally considered as a matter of concern in communicative classrooms. For foreign language learners, it is very common to experience feelings of apprehension about communicating in a language that is not their own native language. When students experience foreign language anxiety in class, they can easily be afraid to speak the foreign language in front of other students and in front of the teacher. This is a problem that can hinder the attainment of two common aims of communicative classrooms: the use of the target language as a regular instrument of communication in the language classroom and, ultimately, the development of the student's oral competence.

There are at least three different types of manifestation (physiological, behavioural and/or cognitive) that appear to be associated with the presence of foreign language classroom anxiety among learners. As an emotional state, anxiety is associated to the excitement of the limbic system (Scovel 1978). The communication between the limbic system and the autonomous nervous system can make the learner perceive certain physiological manifestations such as a heart rate increase, mouth dryness, an altered breathing pace, excessive sweating or the opposite, feeling cold, among others. At other times, anxiety manifestations are more obtrusive and can be even noticed by the teacher in certain behaviours like nervous laughing, blushing, shivering, speaking with a low or trembling voice, repetitive nodding, avoiding eye-contact and participation, stuttering and stammering, nervous coughing, scratching movements, touching or playing with one's hair or manipulating other objects nervously (Scarcella and Oxford 1982, 56; Young 1991; Oxford 1999; Rubio 2004a; Rubio 2004b). At a deeper level, these physiological and behavioural manifestations are triggered by mental processes like too self-demanding or perfectionist thoughts, perceptions of incompetence, feelings of insecurity or inferiority characteristic of low self-esteem and other negative beliefs that are likely to interfere with the resolution of the task at hand.

Instead of as a manifestation of a trait of general anxiety, the experience of foreign language classroom anxiety has been considered as a situational type of anxiety intrinsically connected to the circumstances in which foreign language learning takes place. At first sight, there are certain circumstances surrounding the language learning experience that can make foreign language learning in a classroom context specially challenging, if not daunting, for the learner. On the one hand, students often get involved in a learning experience in which the knowledge of the object of study often seems to be imperfect or not sufficient to cope with classroom demands; on the other hand, there seems to be a continuous demand to use this imperfectly known object of study as an instrument to communicate in less than ideal conditions, that is, in front of a teacher who is always ready to correct and/or feeling observed or evaluated at the same time by a large number of students.

Part of the uniqueness of the foreign language classroom anxiety experience resides in the fact that it seems to relate to several kinds of anxiety at the same time. Firstly, feelings of incompetence or of not having enough skill or knowledge to cope with classroom demands can also be found when trying to learn other subjects, for instance in maths anxiety. Secondly, communicative interactions in the foreign language are likely to trigger the same feelings of social or interpersonal anxiety that characterize general communication apprehension in the native language. Thirdly, fears about being on the spot or feeling observed are connatural to the experience of stage fright. Last, but not least, communication events in the second language can be experienced by the learner as little trial situations where his/her competence is being tested, which can make foreign language classroom anxiety similar to test anxiety to some extent.

Comparing foreign language classroom anxiety to those other anxiety processes would not be possible without considering a common component that seems to be in the root of all of them, namely fear of negative evaluation. In fact, the possibility of finding similarities between foreign language anxiety and other types of anxiety, suggests that the foreign language classroom context probably presents a variety of factors that can be anxiety-inducing and that interact together making the fear of negative evaluation specially common and intense among language learners.

On the one hand, communicative language classrooms, because of their interest in developing the oral skills, have inevitably and paradoxically meant an important increase in the learner's exposure to situations that are likely to induce communication apprehension (Phillips 1989; Young 1990; Arnold and Brown 1999). Not in vain, even though anxiety has been studied in association with other language skills as well (Young 1999), speaking is considered by teachers, students and researchers as the foreign language skill that is most likely to induce anxiety in the student during the learning process (Horwitz, Horwitz and Cope 1986; Young 1992). This is so not only in oral tests, where speaking anxiety combines with the anxiety generated by test situations (Rubio 2004a), but also with reference to the normal dynamics of everyday lesson. The interactive dynamics of the foreign language class brings into play a number of situational factors which are very likely to be perceived as anxiety-inducing by the learner: listening comprehension problems, teachers' requests to participate, time-pressure, teachers' feedback and possible evaluation by the teacher and by other classroom mates (Ortega 2002).

Interactive language classrooms can easily make students feel on the spot. Perceptions of being constantly evaluated by the teacher and observed by other classroom mates can easily induce anxiety in the learner in any classroom context. Still, if the students have to understand and make themselves understood in a language they only know imperfectly, the situation can become extremely challenging for the learner's self-concept. Consequently, self-esteem can be of crucial importance for approaching the task of learning a foreign language and performing with relative success. As Young (1990, 541) says,

> Individuals with low self-esteem tend to have high levels of language anxiety, communication apprehension, and social anxiety. Low self-esteem can be particularly significant in a language class where students are expected to perform orally more often than in larger history, government or chemistry classes.

## 3. Is it really me when I speak the foreign language?

Communicating in a language that is not the first language and in which the learner does not feel confident enough can easily create discomfort and unrest in the students because learners approach communication with the constant fear that they will have difficulty both in understanding and in making themselves understood. Considering that speaking is a naturally spontaneous activity, part of the problem resides not only in the knowledge acquired, but also in the fact that it takes a long time for the learner to develop some automatism in the application of certain learnt rules to the spoken use of the language. During this period, the learner will be making mistakes in the oral use of forms that he knows how to construct perfectly if given enough time.

The immediacy required by spontaneous oral use of the language is therefore going to pose a constant challenge to the learners' perception of themselves as competent communicators even if the learners are supposed to have an acceptable writing and reading competence[2]. As a result of having their self-concept challenged, students may start to worry about their self-image and feel fear–even panic–or inhibition. If the students do not perceive their oral interaction to be satisfactory, this bad concept of themselves as communicators may affect their willingness to participate in future communicative events in the L2 and, ultimately, limit their possibilities to develop their communicative competence (Tsui 1996, 155).

However, there still exists a further problem connected to language anxiety that touches on the individual's self-concept at a deeper level. For Horwitz et al. (1986), one of the features that characterizes foreign language anxiety most is the lack of correspondence between the image the individual has of him/herself in his/her first language and the impaired self-image that he can project to others with his/her deficient knowledge of the L2. As Tsui (1996, 156) points out, when communicating in a language that is imperfectly mastered, the learner can easily feel that the image of him/herself that s/he is projecting to others does not show his/her real personality and intelligence. This is a problem that can be frequently noticed as a life experience in the diaries written by language learners. A corpus of testimonies gathered by Hilleson (1996, 255) by means of learner's diaries shows, for example, that learners can not only worry about not projecting their true personality but also question the permanence of it or even compare themselves with mentally handicapped children:

---

[2] This situation is very typical of European foreign language classroom contexts where the possibilities to learn the language by having natural exposure to it are quite limited in comparison with second language acquisition contexts.

> "Sometimes I sound ruder than I mean to in lessons. It sounds too frank –'that's wrong' for example".

> "I don't tell as many jokes or make fun because I am afraid that people don't understand. Therefore I have become much more serious".

> "I hope I have same character as before but till now I still can't find".

> "I went to social service today. The school is for children who have a mental problem. But still they can speak English".

These perceptions are more likely to be experienced in a second language acquisition context, where students need to manage using the L2 to deal with real life demands and socialize with native speakers, than in foreign language learning contexts. It seems relevant in this respect that when talking about the process of acculturation that a learner must undergo to acquire a language, Schumann (1975) had already pointed out the problem that the language learner can behave normally in his/her own native linguistic and cultural environment but is obliged by the circumstances to show a basically incompetent self in a foreign environment.

## 4. Self-esteem in the constitution and evolution of foreign language classroom anxiety

Considering that feelings of incompetence have often appeared associated to L2 language anxiety, it is not surprising that one of the factors that has received more attention in the studies on language anxiety is the possibility of finding correlations between anxiety and L2 proficiency measures. Apart from the fact that the results of some research studies have not been conclusive in this respect, those cases where positive correlations between both factors have been found have often posed problems of interpretation inasmuch as it seems difficult to determine whether lack of linguistic competence can be considered as a cause or as an effect of language anxiety: "Does anxiety interfere with pre-existing ability and therefore impair performance? Or does poor performance, based solely on ability, lead to anxiety as merely an effect?" (MacIntyre and Gardner 1991, 109). This type of question has also been formulated very often with reference to the studies on motivation and the correlations found between this factor and L2 proficiency. In both cases the answer to the egg-or-the-chicken question is found in a model of reciprocal causality, that is, in a model that allows for the possibility that both factors influence each other.

MacIntyre and Gardner (1989; 1991, 110) propose a model of constituting evolution of foreign language anxiety in which the anxiety experiences lived at the first stages of learning a language appear constituted by manifestations of communication apprehension, test anxiety or novelty anxiety (anxiety to new situations). As a result of having repeated negative experiences in the learning of a foreign language, the subject could then begin to develop certain negative attitudes more specific and inherent to the foreign language learning situation and these would start to constitute foreign language anxiety. As part of the process, learners would also develop a series of negative expectations that would result in their concern about their own self-image, which in turn would make it difficult for the learner to concentrate on the aim of the foreign language task in course. Failure at performing in the L2 would then strengthen negative expectations, helping thus to increase the learner's anxiety. As Mruk (1999, 85) points out, when discussing the relationship between self-esteem and success, "too many failures tend to engender a sense of interpersonal incompetence, learned helplessness, and perhaps even hopelessness, depending on how frequent and how severe the failures happen to be".

The model of constitution of foreign language anxiety proposed by MacIntyre and Gardner (1989; 1991) makes sense considering language anxiety on a longitudinal basis as a kind of trait anxiety that has formed in response to recurrent negative experiences lived in the foreign language learning situation. Still, considering foreign language anxiety as an evolving cycle must not distract our attention from the fact that it is a situational experience. Consequently, the negative expectations on the part of the learner that according to MacIntyre and Gardner (1991) characterise language anxiety can only be understood from a situational perspective, that is to say, having a closer look at what is going on in the students' mind in relation to the particular situation or context in which s/he is required to perform in the L2.

## 4.1. Language anxiety and self-esteem in context

To talk about anxiety in contextual terms requires a redefinition of the presumed relationship between language anxiety and the student's communicative competence, since it is not the student's competence but rather the student's perceived competence for coping with the contextual demands that determines the level of anxiety perceived by the individual and, ultimately, the individual's approach to the task or, on the contrary, his/her refusal to undertake it.

If there is a key that suggests why some people accept or perceive a language-learning situation as anxiety provoking and therefore manifest the [...] symptoms, it most likely is fear of failure (rejection) to meet the demands set in the external element plus the perceived self-perpetuating nature of this condition (Williams 1991, 24).

Attributing language anxiety to perceptions of incompetence to deal with situational demands allows for the possibility that even advanced learners of English can experience high levels of language anxiety, since language learning situations normally change and are perceived by students as more demanding as they progressively reach higher levels of competence (Ortega 2003). On the other hand, this perspective on language anxiety is consonant with the motivational theory of self-efficacy proposed by Bandura (1986), according to which transactions with the environment are mediated by feelings of self-efficacy or "people's judgments of their capabilities to organize and execute courses of action required to attain designated types of performances" (Bandura 1986, 391). Perceptions of lack of capability for coping with the demands of a particular situation can often result in anxiety reactions like avoidance, distress or self-concern that would interfere with the learner's concentration on the task.

The subject's self-esteem is involved in the process of facing a task by means of the subject's relative expectations of being successful after estimating his/her competence in relation to the environment demands. For Heyde (1977, 227), the feelings that individuals have about their own ability to confront a language learning task are expressions of their self-esteem and play a fundamental role motivating or hindering the application of the necessary cognitive processes.

> [...] if we feel that we can't speak a second language, or if we feel that we don't have the ability to learn a second language, our language behaviour will act accordingly. In short, the level of self-esteem may either block or facilitate the cognitive domain in its application of the rules and thereby affect the second language output.

Furthermore, taking into consideration the possibility of treating self-esteem as a global or as a situational phenomenon (cf. Mruk 1999), in Heyde-Parsons' research approach, the context would play a central role as the breeding ground of self-esteem. For her, self-esteem could be hierarchically represented in different levels that would proceed from the individual's general self-esteem to more specific levels of self-esteem related to specific activities. When studying the relations between the individual's self-esteem and second language acquisition, Heyde-Parsons (1983) found that the correlations between the individual's level of success at carrying out a foreign language activity and the individual's level of self-esteem became stronger as the self-esteem measures became more contextually specific or related to the task at hand.

According to Foss and Reitzel (1988), a step beyond in the contextual perception of competence is taken by Spitzberg and Cupach (1984) and their Relational Competence Model. In this model, "competence is assumed to be an interpersonal impression that depends on the individuals involved, their relationship, and the nature of the particular encounter", which suggests that "a communicator is competent if perceived so by self and/or others" (Foss and Reitzel 1988, 441).

In connection with the consideration of competence as an interpersonal perception, the processes of classroom competitiveness and risk-taking may help to exemplify how the learner's self-esteem and its influence on anxiety are configured in relation to contextual demands and, more specifically, in relation to the learner's perception of other people's perceptions about his/her own competence in the classroom.

### 4.1.1. Classroom competitiveness and self-esteem

The role of self-esteem in the phenomenology of foreign language classroom competitiveness and its relation to the classroom anxiety experience are depicted by Bailey (1983) in a qualitative study conducted by means of learner's diaries. According to the experiences recorded by subjects in this study, foreign language classroom anxiety may be induced and/or increased by the student's competitiveness if the learner feels inferior when comparing him/herself with other students, with what s/he estimates teachers expect of him/herself or with an ideal self-image. According to Bailey (1983, 96-97), competitiveness may result in different types of anxiety. If, as a result of the anxiety perceived, the subject develops a temporary or permanent tendency to avoid contact with the anxiety-inducing situation that generates the image of inferiority, the learner can be experiencing debilitating anxiety. If, on the contrary, the individual's feelings of inferiority result in their willingness to participate or study more, the anxiety perceived by the student can be considered as facilitating anxiety. From the previous observation we can infer that the individual's perception of his/her capacity or capability in relation to the perceived contextual demands plays a fundamental role in determining either the student's fear to approach the anxiety-inducing situation (debilitating anxiety) or the subject's motivation to face the challenging situation (facilitating anxiety).

With reference to this distinction between debilitating and facilitating anxiety, it is certainly not irrelevant that semantically we must differentiate between the person who feels anxious about speaking a L2 and the person who feels anxious to speak the L2. Considering the possibility of attributing a positive effect to anxiety, the evolution of anxiety has sometimes been represented along an inverted-U model (Williams 1991). This inverted-U model would show how a low level of excitement would result in little success in the task, while an increase in the level of excitement would yield an increase in the level of success up to a limit after which progressive increase in the degree of excitement would start to be associated with failure. But, according to Allwright and Bailey (1991, 98), what would really discriminate the type of anxiety perceived by the student are the expectations of success maintained by the learner:

> Knowing that success is not guaranteed, but that making a real effort might make all the difference between success and failure, we may do better precisely because our anxiety has spurred us on. If, on the other hand, we would really like to succeed but feel that, no matter how hard we try, we are most likely to fail, then our anxiety is likely to make it even more difficult for us to produce our best.

Williams and Burden (1997) also offer a clear description of how the perceived competence and the self-concept affect the language learning process. According to their socio-constructivist model of language learning, the students' perceptions of external contextual elements and, specially, of their interpersonal relations in the classroom context are considered as factors that help to shape the students' perceived competence. Williams and Burden's model of learning is based on the so-called social comparison theory. According to this theory, the student's perceived competence for learning is determined by a more or less accentuated tendency of the individual to compare him/herself with other people and, consequently, to develop his/her self-concept as a result of this comparison with others and of the information s/he receives about him/herself from others. The social comparison theory, along with the evidence provided by some studies that the most influential figures on the students' perceived competence are people who are perceived by the learner as similar or relevant for their life, makes Williams and Burden (1997) conclude that the teacher's or the classroom mates' positive or negative reactions are factors that influence the student's self-concept and motivation in the classroom context, which reminds us very much of the previous description of the competitiveness phenomenon provided by Bailey (1983).

### 4.1.2. Risk-taking and self-esteem

A related phenomenon in which the learner's perceptions of the external context can be seen to influence the learner's perceived competence is risk-taking. This is a process in which the learner becomes involved whenever s/he decides to approach a communicative task. According to Beebe (1983), if the learner desires to face a communicative situation, s/he needs to assume the risk of making errors/mistakes (risk-taking) having in mind the contextual presence of certain evaluative factors such as grades and/or the teacher's and the students' reactions.

Learning to speak a second or foreign language involves taking the risk of being wrong, with all its ramifications. In the classroom, these ramifications might include a bad grade in the course, a fail on the exam, a reproach from the teacher, a smirk from a classmate, punishment or embarrassment imposed by oneself (Beebe 1983, 39).

Decisions to take risks in relation to the context appear in turn determined by the balance made by the learner between the positive and the negative consequences of assuming such risks. For instance, the subject may make a balance between the risk of losing face when making errors and failing to communicate, on the one hand, and the gain of learning to communicate by taking risks, on the other hand.

If taking risks in the language constitutes the mediating process of facing and approaching a communicative task, it seems natural that having language anxiety and self-doubts will hinder the process of taking risks. Ely's research on discomfort, risk-taking and motivation has shown some evidence supporting this hypothesis. The instrument used by Ely (1986) to measure the individual's willingness to take risks in the foreign language class was designed taking into consideration indicators of the individual's predisposition to experiment with perceived difficult linguistic items and of the individual's tolerance of making mistakes or bad use of the language. After being applied to a group of first year university students, the scale yielded results that could be positively correlated with students' voluntary participation and negatively correlated with a measure of language class discomfort, which suggests that language anxiety and risk-taking are negatively related.

Ely's findings acquire a special importance in the light of Swain's Comprehensible Output Hypothesis (Swain 1985). This hypothesis states that, rather than the exposure to comprehensible input, what really promotes language learning is the comprehensible output produced by the learner at a level a bit beyond his/her own actual competence. This presupposition highlights the importance that the learning process takes place in a non-threatening environment where the learner can feel safe and willing to speak the L2 and to take risks with the language without being afraid of making mistakes. Moreover, the use or practice of the spoken language has been considered as a helpful process for learning to become acquisition (Bialystok 1981) or, what is the same, for the forms learnt by the student to become automatic or available for unconscious use of the language (McLaughlin 1978; Sharwood-Smith 1981). In other words, if we want the learner to become a fluent speaker of the L2, it is important to create a suitable affective environment where the learner can feel well predisposed to use and keep using the L2 for oral communication without worrying too much about making mistakes.

## 5. Language anxiety reduction measures and self-esteem

Acknowledging the influence of external factors on the experience of language anxiety allows for the possibility of manipulating the classroom environment in a number of ways in order to make the classroom more inviting to participate. Consequently, some of the techniques proposed to reduce language classroom anxiety seem to have been formulated taking into account particular contextual factors or certain elements of classroom dynamics that have been considered as anxiety-inducing for the learner (Lucas 1984; Price 1991; Young 1991; Ortega 2002): accommodating teacher's talk to students' competence level (i.e. repeating, paraphrasing, speaking more slowly or articulating better) has been considered helpful to reduce learners' perceived difficulties at listening comprehension; organizing group or pair-work and organizing activities to encourage learners to get to know each other can help students not to feel evaluated by other classroom mates; adopting a non-authoritarian role as a teacher and using positive feedback instead of attitudes of overcorrection can contribute to reduce learners' feelings of being evaluated by the teacher, help them not to feel afraid of making mistakes and encourage them to take risks with the language; giving students enough time to do the assigned language exercises and increasing wait-time or the time allowed for students to respond can help students not to feel anxious because of lack of preparation; using predictable patterns of participation or asking for volunteers to answer difficult questions can alleviate students' fears of being called to participate in class by reducing the element of surprise.

Learners' feelings of incompetence can be alleviated to some extent by the previous facilitating measures inasmuch as they can help to make classroom dynamics less threatening for the learner's self-esteem. Other teaching techniques that can help to protect learners' self-esteem and increase their self-confidence are providing experiences of success (for instance, adjusting the level of difficulty of the activities to the students' abilities), making learners feel better equipped for dealing with task difficulties by teaching learner strategies, particularly communication strategies, and reducing learners' anxiety by making use of cooperative work patterns and avoiding social comparison and competition in class (Phillips 1991; Dörnyei 2001).

Apart from the previous environmental measures, other anxiety-reducing measures that have been proposed seem to deal with perceived feelings of incompetence or lack of self-confidence in language learning tasks at a more perceptual or metacognitive level. The administration of questionnaires designed to elicit students' experiences with language anxiety or learners' beliefs about language learning in class has been considered as a helpful tool for the teacher to recognise the presence among students of language anxiety problems or of certain related perfectionist or self-demanding attitudes in language learning (Horwitz et al. 1986; Horwitz 1988). However, the possibility that learners themselves may obtain a direct benefit from the mere practice of answering these types of questionnaire must not be overlooked either. On the one hand, answering self-reports of this kind can be beneficial for the learners inasmuch as it can help them to develop some awareness about their anxiety problems and other language learning problems; on the other hand, by participating in this kind of practice, students have the opportunity to realise how the teacher is able to anticipate the student's anxiety feelings and, consequently, they could interpret the practice as a sign of the teacher's concern about the issue, which might, in turn, help learners perceive the teacher as an understanding figure and therefore contribute to improve classroom rapport.

If students' perceived incompetence to deal with the demands of the language learning situation is involved in feelings of language anxiety, it seems natural that unrealistic expectations about central issues such as the relative difficulty of language learning, the expected rate of progress or how languages should be learnt can result too self-demanding for the learner and therefore contribute to his/her experience of language anxiety. As Phillips (1991, 6) says, "it is understandable that students with a distorted view of language learning become anxious when the techniques they use and assumptions under which they operate fail to produce the expected results". That is why later common discussion on self-reports has been considered to help put things into perspective and have a reducing effect on learners' anxiety. For instance, discussing openly in class the results of self-reports on language anxiety and language learning beliefs can help to counteract the true value of certain irrational but very disempowering and self-limiting beliefs that can be in the root of students' reluctance to speak in class: the idea that making mistakes in class is terrible, that it is better not to speak if one cannot do it perfectly, or that there are always other people who are better at learning languages.

Making mistakes has been considered a natural and inescapable part of the process of learning a language, particularly of the process of learning to speak that language. Having a perfectionist attitude when approaching the process of L2 speaking is likely to be very self-demanding for the learner and, consequently, s/he may prefer to avoid involvement in this situation as a result of perceived lack of competence to deal with the task (Gregersen and Horwitz 2002). A belief that one is worse or inferior to others in learning or speaking a foreign language also reveals self-esteem problems. This kind of feeling promotes a self-defensive or face-saving kind of learning in which the learner prefers not to take risks in order save his/her own self-image. Discussing the true value of all these negative beliefs in class can help students change their views, having a cognitive restructuring effect that can help to reduce students' language anxiety.

Cognitive restructuring, learner's self-talk, rational emotive therapy, systematic desensitization and modelling and guided participation are other techniques that have been regarded as useful for helping learners to cope with language anxiety (Rubio 2004b). The way these activities seem to reduce language anxiety is trying to change initial feelings of incompetence into self-confident attitudes that allow learners to approach the learning task.

According to McCoy (1979, 187) cognitive restructuring is based on the assumption that "most anxieties are due to the irrational way in which people often construe their world, i.e., that their self-verbalizations lead to self-defeating statements". This technique involves a process of eliciting initial disempowering beliefs and transforming them later into related positive thoughts. It can be achieved by certain activities specifically designed for that aim although sometimes cognitive restructuring activities present the affective aim in combination with the goal of practising a particular language aspect. Some NLP activities based on attitudinal thinking and reframing of negative beliefs can be very useful in this regard (Revell and Norman 1997, 47-50).

Similarly, in the technique of rational emotive therapy proposed by Foss and Reitzel (1988), students would be asked to produce a list of their fears about speaking the new language. This activity would be also likely to elicit certain irrational beliefs about the nature of language learning that should be progressively refuted by involving the learner in the process of answering three consecutive questions: 1. What irrational belief do I want to dispute?; 2. What evidence exists of the falseness of this belief?; 3. Does evidence exist of the truth of this belief?

The techniques of cognitive restructuring and rational emotive therapy are similar inasmuch as they both want to develop students' awareness about his/her irrational beliefs and they both try to undermine the foundations of self-limiting beliefs. Another technique that tries to accomplish a change from negative anxiety-inducing thoughts to positive productive thoughts is self-talk. This technique gets the learner mentally involved in a prospective anxiety-inducing situation and encourages him/her to notice the difference between trying to deal with the situation using anxiety provoking self-talk ("I can't talk in public. I'll forget everything") and approaching the same situation with productive self-talk ("I can handle this…Just relax") (Young 1990). Cognitive restructuring, rational emotive therapy and self-talk are all techniques metacognitively oriented since they involve the learner in the process of reflecting on his/her own language learning beliefs.

Other techniques seem to be more oriented towards modifying learners' behaviour. This is the case of systematic desensitization, and modelling and guided participation. The technique of systematic desensitization has been successfully used with people who have problems of communication apprehension in situations of public speaking and therefore its effectiveness has been considered liable to be extrapolated to language learning situations. The final objective of this technique is to help the learner have a positive reaction to the anxiety-inducing situation by repeated exposure to it (McCoy 1991). There are two main processes involved in desensitization: 1. imagination of the situation and simulation of the response and 2. participation in real-life situations.

Modelling and guided participation have also been found useful for reducing language anxiety. These techniques are based on the assumption that successful performance is the most effective way of changing related anxieties. There are two main steps to follow when using these techniques: 1. modelling the performance activities and 2. encouraging and assisting the person in jointly performing different subtasks that appear progressively graded in terms of difficulty. The model or guide would gradually withdraw as the person starts to perform without experiencing anxiety (McCoy 1991, 187-188).

Taking into account that general self-esteem may also be involved in the process of language anxiety, other language learning activities that can be considered to reduce language anxiety are those that try to develop and foster students' self-confidence by involving the learner in a process of reflecting on his/her own strengths or getting some public recognition of his/her abilities or qualities, not necessarily connected with language learning (Moskowitz 1978; Davis and Rinvolucri 1991). These humanistic exercises try to combine linguistic aims with the creation of an appropriate or supportive socio-affective atmosphere that facilitates learners' oral production.

## 6. Language anxiety and self-esteem in the light of the socio-constructivist perspective

The discussion presented in this chapter on the constitution and development of language anxiety has shown that there is a complex variety of manifestations and factors involved in the process of foreign language classroom anxiety. Language anxiety is therefore an intricate phenomenon that can only be fully understood in the confluence between a world of external contextual factors that surround the learning process and the internal world of the learner. It is precisely in this interplay where the student's self-esteem and the learner's assessment of his/her own competence become relevant as intervening factors in the experience of language anxiety.

Taking into account the complexity of language anxiety as a socio-perceptual phenomenon, a comprehensive study of this process requires the use of a perspective able to account for the intervention of both social and individual factors. A socio-constructivist perspective of learning can therefore offer an appropriate framework to approach the study of language anxiety. If we take as a point of reference the socio-constructivist model of language learning that Williams and Burden (1997) proposed, we can observe that foreign language learning can be influenced by a series of external factors such as the students interact with (other students and teachers) and their reactions, the students' family context, their educational and cultural context and certain environmental factors such as classroom comfort, the resources available for teaching or classroom size. On the other hand, according to the same model, language learning can also be affected by internal factors of the learner such as students' interest, their perceived competence, their self-concept, their attitudes to languages and language learning and affective states such as confidence, fear and anxiety, among others.

If we focus our study on the processes involved in the experience of foreign language anxiety, the socio-constructivist perspective appears appropriate, as it allows us to study the convergence of social and affective factors in the student's spoken interaction. On the one hand, this perspective can be useful to account for the influence on language anxiety of all those contextual and environmental factors that have been considered as anxiety-inducing in the literature on language anxiety: exposure to a big audience, the novelty of the communicative situation, teacher's evaluation and correction, an authoritarian attitude on the part of the teacher, unpredictable participation requests or lack of preparation, time pressure, etc. (Horwitz et al. 1986; Daly 1991; Price 1991; Ortega 2002). On the other hand, the psychological side of the socio-constructivist perspective of language anxiety highlights the relevance in the language anxiety process of an internal factor, the individual's self-esteem, as a construct that results from the student's perception of his/her own abilities in relation to others and to his/her estimation of the task difficulty.

The same socio-constructivist perspective has shown to be fruitful when trying to draw certain pedagogical implications connected to the language anxiety problem. On the one hand, there is a long list of pedagogical implications that appear to be directly connected to the evaluation of the anxiety-inducing effect of the previous environmental factors (see section 5 of this chapter). This is the case of warnings about teaching attitudes of overcorrection or the recommendation to use reduced groups or pair-work for oral communication activities, in order to diminish students' perceptions of being evaluated by the teacher and the students respectively. All these environmental pedagogical implications, which highlight the social side of language anxiety, stress the teacher's role as facilitator or creator of favourable conditions for learning to take place.

Due to the singular interplay between both sides of the socio-perceptual world, the psychological side of learners' anxiety, constituted by learners' self-deprecating thoughts, perceived lack of competence, worry and apprehension can obviously be affected by environmental changes made in order to make language learning situations less challenging for the learner's self-concept. However, the psychological aspect of language anxiety can also be addressed metacognitively trying to change certain learners' preconceptions and self-limiting beliefs that may be deeply ingrained in the learner and can contribute to his/her anxiety. Discussion on self-reports, cognitive restructuring, rational emotive therapy and self-talk are anxiety-reduction techniques that operate at a metacognitive level in two ways: firstly, trying to detect the presence of irrational self-damaging beliefs and, secondly, restructuring these negative beliefs into more positive and productive ones for the learning process. In this case, the adoption of metacognitive anxiety-reduction strategies or other techniques oriented towards the aim of fostering the learner's confidence seem to assimilate more the teacher's role to that of a therapist.

Apart from being suitable for accounting for the complexity of manifestations, factors and pedagogical implications related to language anxiety, a socio-constructivist model of language learning facilitates the establishment of a line of continuity in the European context with the socio-psychological orientation which has been so commonly used for studying Second Language Acquisition in the American context. If American research studies on second language learning have traditionally paid more attention to situations of contact between languages than to the classroom context as influential social contexts (cf. Gardner and Lambert 1972; Clément 1980; Giles and Byrne 1982), the socio-constructivist perspective of foreign language classroom anxiety makes it possible to recover a social dimension of the anxiety problem even in environments where different language communities do not coexist, by paying attention the classroom itself as a social context that can be influential on the students' psychological experiences.

## Works Cited

Arnold, J., and H. D. Brown. 1999. A map of the terrain. In *Affect in language learning*, ed. J. Arnold, 1-24. Cambridge: Cambridge University Press.

Allwright, D., and K. M. Bailey. 1991. Focus on the language classroom. An introduction to classroom research for language teachers. Cambridge: Cambridge University Press.

Bailey, K. M. 1983. Competitiveness and anxiety in adult second language learning: looking at and through the diary studies. In *Classroom oriented research in Second Language Acquisition*, eds. H. W. Seliger and M. H. Long, 67-103. Rowley: Newbury House.

Bandura, A. 1986. *Social foundations of thought and action. A social cognitive theory*. Englewood Cliffs: Prentice-Hall.

Beebe, L. M. 1983. Risk-taking and the language learner. In *Classroom oriented research in second language acquisition*, eds. H. W. Seliger and M. H. Long, 39-65. Rowley: Newbury House.

Clément, R. 1980. Ethnicity, contact and communicative competence in a second language. In *Language: social psychological perspectives*, eds. H. Giles, W. P. Robinson and P. M. Smith, 147-154. Oxford: Pergamon.

—. 1986. Second language proficiency and acculturation: An investigation of the effects of language status and individual characteristics. *Journal of Language and Social Psychology* 5, (4): 271-290.

Clément, R., R. C. Gardner, and P. C. Smythe. 1977. Motivational variables in second language acquisition: A study of francophones learning English. *Canadian Journal of Behavioural Science* 9: 123-133.

—. 1980. Social and individual factors in Second Language Acquisition. *Canadian Journal of Behavioural Science* 12: 293-302.

Clément, R., L. J. Major, R. C. Gardner, and P. C. Smythe 1977. Attitudes and motivation in second language acquisition: An investigation of Ontario Francophones. *Working Papers on Bilingualism* 12: 1-20.

Clément, R., and B. G. Kruidenier. 1985. Aptitude, attitude and motivation in second language proficiency: A test of Clément's Model. *Journal of Language and Social Psychology* 4: 21-37.

Daly, J. 1991. Understanding communication apprehension: An introduction for language educators. In *Language anxiety. From theory and research to classroom implications*, eds. E. K. Horwitz and D. J. Young, 3-13. Englewood Cliffs: Prentice-Hall.

Davis, P., and M. Rinvolucri. 1991. *The confidence book*. London: Longman.

Dörnyei, Z. 2001. Motivational strategies in the language classroom. Cambridge: Cambridge University Press.

Ely, C. M. 1986. An analysis of discomfort, risktaking, and motivation in the L2 classroom. *Language Learning* 36, (1): 1-25.

Foss, K. A., and A. Reitzel. 1988. A relational model for managing second language anxiety. *TESOL Quarterly* 22: 437-454.

Gardner, R. C. 1985. *Social psychology and second language learning*. London: Edward Arnold.

Gardner, R. C., and R. Clement. 1990. Social psychological perspectives on Second Language Acquisition. In *Handbook of language and social psychology*, eds. H. Giles and P. Robinson, 495-518. West Sussex : John Wiley and Sons.

Gardner, R. C., R. N. Lalonde, and R. Pierson 1983. The Socio-Educational Model of Second Language Acquisition: An investigation using LISREL Causal Modeling. *Journal of Language and Social Psychology* 2: 1-15.

Gardner, R. C., and W. E. Lambert. 1972. Attitudes and motivation in second language learning. Rowley: Newbury House.

Gardner, R.C., and P. D. MacIntyre. 1993. A student's contributions to second language learning. Part II: Affective variables. *Language Teaching* 26: 1-11.

Giles, H., and J. L. Byrne. 1982. An intergroup approach to Second Language Acquisition. *Journal of Multingual and Multicultural Development* 1: 17-40.

Gliksman, L., R. C. Gardner, and P. C. Smythe. 1982. The role of the integrative motive on students' participation in the French classroom. *Canadian Modern Language Review* 38: 625-647.

Gregersen, T., and E. Horwitz. 2002. Language learning and perfectionism: Anxious and non-anxious language learners' reactions to their own oral performance. *The Modern Language Journal* 86: 562-570.

Heyde, A. W. 1977. The relationship between self-esteem and the oral production of a second language. In *Teaching and learning English as a second language: Trends in research and practice*, eds. H. D. Brown, C. A. Yorio and R. H. Crymes, 226-239. Washington, D.C.: TESOL '77.

Heyde-Parsons, A. W. 1983. Self-esteem and the acquisition of French. In *Studies in Second Language Acquisition*, eds. K. M. Bailey, M. H. Long and S. Peck, 175-187. Rowley: Newbury House Publishers.

Hilleson, M. 1996. "I want to talk with them, but I don't want them to hear": An introspective study of second language anxiety in an English-medium school. In *Voices from the language classroom. Qualitative research in second language education*, eds. K. M. Bailey and D. Nunan, 248-275. Cambridge: Cambridge University Press.

Horwitz, E. K., M. B. Horwitz, and J. A. Cope. 1986. Foreign language classroom anxiety. *The Modern Language Journal* 70: 125-132.

Horwitz, E. K. 1988. The beliefs about language learning of beginning University foreign language students. *The Modern Language Journal* 72: 283-294.

Krashen, S. D. 1981. *Second Language Acquisition and second language learning*. Oxford: Pergamon.

—. 1987. *Principles and practice in Second Language Acquisition*. Englewood-Cliffs: Prentice-Hall.

Lucas, J. 1984. Communication apprehension in the ESL classroom: Getting our students to talk. *Foreign Language Annals* 17: 593-598.

MacIntyre, P. D., and R. C. Gardner. 1989. Anxiety and second language learning: Toward a theoretical clarification. *Language Learning* 39: 251-275.

—. Methods and results in the study of anxiety and language learning: A review of the literature. *Language Learning* 41: 85-117.

McLaughlin, B. 1978. The Monitor Model: Some methodological considerations. *Language Learning* 28: 309-332.

Moskowitz, G. 1978. *Caring and sharing in the foreign language class. A sourcebook on humanistic techniques*. Boston: Heinle and Heinle.

Mruk, C. J. 1999. *Self-esteem. Research, theory and practice*. New York: Springer Publishing Company.

Oxford, R. 1999. Anxiety and the language learner. In *Affect in language Learning*, ed. J. Arnold, 58-67. Cambridge: Cambridge University Press.

Ortega Cebreros, A. M. 2002. A review of situational factors involved in students' discomfort when speaking foreign languages in class. *GRETA, Revista para Profesores de Inglés* 10, (1): 19-24.

—. 2003. Measuring Language Anxiety Perceived by Spanish University Students of English. *BELLS (Barcelona English Language and Literature Studies)* 12. Also in http://www.publicacions.ub.es/revistas/bells12/

Phillips, E. M. 1989. Anxiety and speaking in the foreign language classroom. *Texas Papers in Foreign Language Education* 1, (3): 191-206.

—. 1991. Anxiety and oral competence: Classroom dilemma. *The French Review* 65, (1): 1-14.

Price, M. L. 1991. The subjective experience of foreign language anxiety. In Language anxiety. From theory and research to classroom implications, eds. E. K. Horwitz and D. J. Young, 101-108. Englewood Cliffs: Prentice-Hall.

Revell, J., and S. Norman. 1997. *In your hands*. London: Saffire Press.

Rubio, F. D. 2004a. *Manual práctico de prevención y reducción de ansiedad en los exámenes y pruebas orales*. Archidona: Ediciones Aljibe.

—. 2004b. *La ansiedad en el aprendizaje de idiomas*. Huelva: Universidad de Huelva.

Scarcella, R.C., and R. L. Oxford. 1982. *The tapestry of language learning. The individual in the communicative classroom*. Boston: Heinle and Heinle.

Schumann, J. H. 1975. Affective factors and the problem of age in Second Language Acquisition. *Language Learning* 25, (2): 209-235.

—. 1978. The Acculturation Model for Second Language Acquisition. In *Second Language Acquisition and foreign language teaching*, ed. R. C. Gingras, 26-50. Arlington: Center for Applied Linguistics.

—. 1986. Research on the Acculturation Model for Second Language Acquisition. *Journal of Mulitilingual and Multicultural Development* 7: 379-392.

—. 1994. Where is cognition? Emotion and cognition in Second Language Acquisition. *Studies in Second Language Acquisition* 16: 231-242.

Scovel, T. 1978. The effect of affect on foreign language learning: A review of the anxiety research. *Language Learning* 28: 129-142.

Sharwood-Smith, M. 1981. Consciousness-raising and the second language learner. *Applied Linguistics* 2: 159-169.

Spitzberg, B.H., and W. R. Cupach. 1984. *Interpersonal communication competence.* Beverly Hills: Sage.

Tsui, A. B. M. 1996. Reticence and anxiety in second language learning. In *Voices from the language classroom. Qualitative research in second language education*, eds. K.M. Bailey and D. Nunan, 145-167. Cambridge: Cambridge University Press.

Williams, K. 1991. Anxiety and formal second/foreign language learning. *RELC Journal* 22: 19-28.

Williams, M., and R. L. Burden. 1997. *Psychology for language teachers. A social constructivist approach.* Cambridge: Cambridge University Press.

Young, D. J. 1990. An investigation of students' perspectives on anxiety and speaking. *Foreign Language Annals* 23, (6): 539-553.

—. 1991. Creating a low-anxiety classroom environment: What does language anxiety research suggest?. *The Modern Language Journal* 75: 426- 439.

—. 1992. Language anxiety from the foreign language specialist's perspective: Interviews with Krashen, Omaggio Hadley, Terrell, and Rardin. *Foreign Language Annals* 25, (2): 157-172.

—. ed. 1999. *Affect in foreign language and second language learning. A practical guide to creating a low-anxiety classroom atmosphere.* Boston: McGraw Hill.

# CHAPTER SEVEN

# FOSTERING TEENAGERS' WILLINGNESS TO LEARN A FOREIGN LANGUAGE

CARMEN FONSECA[1] AND CARMEN TOSCANO[2]
(UNIVERSITY OF HUELVA, SPAIN)

A People Place

If this is not a place where tears are understood,
Where do I go to cry?
If this is not a place where my spirits can take wing,
Where do I go to fly?
If this is not a place where my questions can be asked,
Where do I go to seek?
If this is not a place where my feelings can be heard,
Where do I go to speak?
If this is not a place where you'll accept me as I am,
Where can I go to be?
If this is not a place where I can try to learn and grow,
Where can I just be me?
—W.J. Crocker

---

[1] M. Carmen Fonseca Mora is Professor of Applied Linguistics at the University of Huelva. She has done research on learning styles, emotional intelligence, gender studies and the impact of melody on language learning. She has worked on cooperative curriculum development projects.

[2] Carmen Toscano Fuentes has taught Spanish language and literature at Harvard University and has been involved with teacher training with primary and secondary teachers of English. Her research interests centre on the role of music in the acquisition of a second language and on ways to incorporate music in the teaching of English.

*For most teachers teaching teenagers constitutes a very challenging experience that sometimes can be closer to a nightmare than to a rewarding situation. Teachers of teenagers complain about their students' behaviour, about their lack of interest in learning about other cultures, about many of them not being willing to participate in the classroom. While there are diverse variables that can contribute to this situation, the main aim of this chapter is to offer a description of ways to incorporate a concern for some of the affective factors in the language classroom that can help to transform a group of unwilling, uncooperative teenagers into a community of learners. This chapter will be partly based on research findings in the field of Psychology, Applied Linguistics and Neurobiology and partly on our own experiences and ideas as classroom teachers.*

## 1. Teaching teenagers

In the latter part of $20^{th}$ century, there was a growing concern in research done in the fields of Educational Psychology and Applied Linguistics with a learner-centred focus which stressed the importance for learning of the educational environment in addition to the individual's genetic endowment. Considering individual differences and matching them to appropriate learning conditions and instructional techniques has become an important research issue in Second Language Acquisition (SLA), as it affects classroom exposure and practice for second language learners (Robinson 2002, 114).

As has been said, teaching English to teenagers is not an easy task. According to MacIntyre et al. (2002, 560), second language communication is "heavily determined by fundamental characteristics of the learner" and this age group has peculiar characteristics that teachers constantly need to take into consideration because as Brown (1994, 138) explains,

> In adolescence, the physical, emotional, and cognitive changes of the pre-teenager and teenager bring on mounting defensive inhibitions to protect a fragile ego, to ward off ideas, experiences, and feelings that threaten to dismantle the organization of values and beliefs on which appraisals or self-esteem have been bound.

For instance, peer approval becomes more important than that of adults. There is a gradual increase in reasoning abilities and management of abstractions, but adolescent learners also need to talk and argue instead of only listening to the teacher when they are in the process of rebelling against adults and needing to express their own values. Cole also mentions teenagers' frequent swings in mood and adds that "these moods are usually the result of successes or failures in personal relationships or school work" (1964, 267).

Moskowitz (1978) remarks that teenagers are involved in the construction of their own identity, and, in fact, the image that teenagers have of themselves is vital for their whole growth. They are critical of others, but dislike others' criticism. Therefore, it is essential for them to learn to adopt others' perspectives as well, so they can assume their point of view and understand them. The use of language learning activities that include the development of empathetic behaviour can increase their sense of belonging to the group they are in and this will improve the quality of their relationships.

For learners' self-perception, the interaction in the classroom between them and their teachers is highly significant. For that reason, a supporting environment at school becomes crucial for them to develop self-acceptance and a sense of acceptance from others. In fact, Hadfield (1992, 10) observes that

> A positive group atmosphere can have a beneficial effect on the morale, motivation and self-image of its members, and thus significantly affect their learning, by developing in them a positive attitude to the language being learned, to the learning process, and to themselves as learners.

Not of less importance for teenagers' is their physical appearance. They are very concerned with their body image at a time when important changes are taking place. Another physical aspect is their high level of energy, something which justifies incorporating physical activities in the learning process. Drama, project work or interviewing are motivating activities for them.

All these characteristics certainly need to be considered to discover ways to foster teenagers' readiness to learn, but the discussion of some other psychologically-rooted constructs may throw light on how to initiate and how to maintain their willingness to cooperate in the language classroom.

## 2. Some affective factors revisited: motivation, language-aptitude skills and self-confidence

In the early seventies, humanistic psychologists such as Rogers or Maslow put forward theoretical bases for considering learning as it is understood in this chapter. They defined it as *an innate capacity for self-reflection and growth to achieve full potential*. Learning as *an innate capacity* means that everyone can learn provided the appropriate conditions are given, although there is variability in effort and in degree of achievement. Learning as *self-reflection* implies that learners' personal experience is considered as valuable knowledge that can be used as a resource for learning. Learners' different personal goals, needs and beliefs act as catalysts for their interest and involvement in any learning experience. For self-reflection to take place, learners need to be provided with adequate tools to explore and discover metacognitive knowledge about themselves, strategic knowledge of what learning techniques work best for them and task knowledge of how to accomplish a specific assignment (Flavell 1976; Wenden 1991). Finally, learning to *achieve full potential* entails the understanding that teaching a subject needs to connect to broader social roles. In fact, Arnold and Brown (1999, 2) postulate that, "As we teach the language, we can also educate learners to live more satisfying lives and to be responsible members of society".

## 2.1. Motivation and language aptitude

Motivation depends to a large extent on learners' beliefs about their coping potential. Feeling that they can succeed in a specific subject helps students to invest effort in learning. This does not mean merely that "ease in passing an exam" is a variable that promotes students' willingness to work; on the contrary, studies show that only challenging, but "manageable" learning experiences lead to higher performance (Locke and Kristof 1996).

Learners' beliefs about their language learning capacity may be attributed to personal internal causes, when, in fact, they could be a result of relational external factors. Sternberg (2002, 13) describes the different beliefs about his language-aptitude skills he had in his three language learning experiences. These beliefs were derived from his performance while learning Latin, French and Spanish and from his teachers' remarks on his language-aptitude skills. Being successful in two of those languages (Latin and Spanish) and unsuccessful in the third one indicated, as he said, that "my aptitude was not internal to me, but in the interaction between my abilities and the way I was being taught".

His analysis of the different teaching styles he was exposed to clearly suggests that successful language learning highly correlates with a teaching style that is based on "a balance of analytical, creative and practical abilities" (p.15) that fits learners' individual ability patterns. In the foreign language classroom the analytical ability is addressed, for instance, when students analyze texts to find out their meaning, or when formal instruction about prefixes and suffixes are given so that students can use this information to infer the meaning of certain words. The creative ability is connected to tasks where learners can create their own oral or written discourses, where, for instance, while observing any famous painting they are allowed to redefine any type of problem, to imagine, suppose or invent what the characters are saying and feeling.

The practical intelligence involves "individuals applying their abilities to the kinds of problems that confront them in daily life" (Sternberg 2002, 29). Gardner and Krechevsky (1993, 123) include among the foundations of their model of educating the practical intelligence at the middle school level the need to know oneself, which refers to the knowledge of "one's own intellectual profile, learning styles and strategies".

Learning a language is a process that requires a great investment in time[3]; therefore, initiating and sustaining the motivation to acquire this skill is of high importance. From an affective point of view, initiating motivation often relates to goal setting, while sustaining motivation may depend more on the quality of the language experience. Although many teenagers in FL context may consider that beginning to learn a foreign language is not a goal freely chosen by them, it is possible to initiate and even to maintain their language learning motivation if they feel emotionally connected to what they are learning as "emotional reactions influence the attention and effort devoted to learning" (Schumann 1997, 8).

For education to be an enriching experience, it needs to be a significant and meaningful part of the person's life (Williams and Burden 1997). It has been found that learners give importance to internal and external influences depending on the personal significance they have for them, on social aspects and on environmental factors. Personal meaning is mediated, according to Williams and Burden (1997), by internal factors such us curiosity, degree of challenge, learners' ability to set goals, learners' feeling of competence, learners' attitudes, gender and age, among others. Under the label of external factors, they consider significance of language learning for parents, teachers and peers, the type of positive interaction it entails, the comfort that the learning environment provides and the societal and cultural appreciation of the language learning activity.

Dörnyei's motivation model (2003) comprises three different levels that influence motivation: the language level, the learner level and the language situation level. Learners' goals, learners' self-confidence in achieving those goals and elements such as language use anxiety, perceived L2 competence, causal attributions, learners' expectancy of success and learners' sense of satisfaction from the outcomes achieved are relevant factors that determine students' level of motivation. Relational elements such as teaching style, teacher behaviour and the characteristics of the learner group are also relevant.

Both Dörnyei's and Williams and Burden's models refer to the need to provide resources to help teachers to increase motivation in their classrooms. Schumann (1999, 29-30) explains how to make language learning tasks more attractive. Following Scherer's stimulus appraisal model, he points out that tasks that relate to novelty, pleasantness, relevance to the individual's needs and goals, the individual's ability to cope with the event, and the compatibility of the

[3] Exceptional language learners are those that master a L2 in a period of two and a half or three years.

event with socio-cultural norms or with the individual's self concept have an influence on the maintenance of motivation. All these dimensions affect students' executive motivation in language learning, although there can be variation among learners depending on their goals, preferences and talents.

Dörnyei's explanations about how appraisal can be transferred from a general to a more concrete level is also very much to the point as he states that established attitudes about the whole school can profoundly affect one's specific L2 learning disposition ("I dislike everything that's going on in this building") and that "negative attitudes evoked by failure in doing a particular task can easily be generalised to the whole language course or to the whole of language learning ("I'm just not good at languages…"), which is also related to learners' self-confidence.

## 2.2. Self-confidence

Ehrman and Dörnyei (1998, 282) define self-confidence as "a general belief by an individual in his or her competence and acceptability, a general expectation of success". Several studies (MacIntyre et al. 1997, Cheng et al. 1999, Matsuda and Gobel 2004) show correlations between anxiety and self-confidence. Matsuda and Gobel (2004) investigated the relationships between general foreign language classroom anxiety, foreign language anxiety, gender, extended overseas experience, and classroom performance. Their results point to the fact that low self-confidence is a significant component in the general and reading anxiety scales they used. They also report a clear connection between self-confidence and overseas experience, which was also the case in Labrie and Clement's study (1986) that showed that while learning English, their Francophone students' contact with native Anglophone speakers was strongly related to self-confidence and motivation. Further on, Matsuda and Gobel's study (2004) support Clément et al.'s (1994, 441) statement that "Self-confidence influences L2 proficiency both directly and indirectly through the students' attitude toward an effort expanded [sic] on learning English".

Matsuda and Gobel explain that students need to become accustomed to a variety of activities that can help them to feel comfortable with each other in the classroom (2004, 33); self-confidence is a step by step by-product of an non-threatening and effective classroom atmosphere. Finally, they cite one student's comment on the teacher's positive behaviour, rating it as relaxed and friendly. Some teachers' behaviours that help to develop secondary learners' self-concept are avoiding empty praising, creating careful planning of minimal steps, selecting challenging activities, teaching metacognitive strategies, offering new material in a multi-sensory way, listening actively to what learners say, providing affective feedback on errors and accepting students' strengths and weaknesses as natural and different ways of absorbing information.

## 3. The teacher as a facilitator: Language and behaviour

Understanding teaching from the perspective described above implies a more highly developed role for teachers. Underhill (1999, 126) presents a view of the teacher as facilitator. By facilitator he means "a teacher …who understands the topic, is skilled in the use of current teaching methods and techniques, and who actively studies and pays attention to the psychological learning atmosphere and the inner processes of learning…with the aim of enabling learners to take as much responsibility for their learning as they can".

Secondary teachers often mention disruptive behaviour as one of the main characteristics of their students. Disciplinary problems may arise, and students "may push teachers to the limit, but they are much happier if that challenge is met, if the teacher actually manages to control them, and if this is done in a supportive and constructive way so that he or she helps rather than shouts" (Harmer 2001, 39).

Bad behaviour, however, is not the problem but teenagers' solution to their problems. It is necessary to consider that behind disruptive behaviour there is frequently conflict at the level of beliefs about their own capabilities. For instance, failure to succeed at school may be interpreted by adolescents as an attack against their self and social image.

Boredom can also lie behind disruptive behaviour. Puchta and Schratz (1993, 4) state that some problems in secondary schools may arise from "teacher's failure to build bridges between what they want and have to teach and their students' worlds of thought and experience". Engaging learners emotionally, that is to say, proposing them tasks that help them to express their own views and experience, instead of asking them to do mechanical exercises, may help learners to overcome boredom and to feel more capable of becoming successful.

Moreover, teachers' approach to errors has a significant effect on learners' willingness to participate in the classroom. For example, being critical of everything learners do, can increase inhibition. As teachers, we send verbal and non-verbal messages that can make students feel "real or unreal, accepted or rejected, valued or scorned, understood or misunderstood, humanized or objectified" (Sieburg 1985, 188). Learners need to feel that they can contribute, that what they can say and do is important for the group. This need to belong and to feel valued has an effect on behaviour, as when teenagers feel rejected, alone, not noticed, they call for attention through bullying others or defying the teacher's authority. Teachers can elicit responses in a way that produces negative affect; for example, their verbal expression ("Let's see if this time you can get it right") may be reinforced by their tone of voice, facial expression, etc. which imply that they do not expect a correct answer. On the contrary, they can smile and simply nominate a student to answer, facilitating the student's willingness to communicate.

When determining their policy on error correction, teachers need to consider not only what they want to correct but what type of feedback they are providing. Constant praise or empty praise should also be avoided as students know perfectly well when they have accomplished something in an appropriate way. Instead, it is preferable to praise that part of an action that is correct and to signal what needs to be improved, for example, "You were able to complete some of the exercises correctly, but you still need to work on verb tenses". Knoll and Patti (2003, 42) add "…teachers also know that true praise is specific rather than general. Instead of repeatedly saying, 'Good job', they specify precisely what was good about the job, for example, "You identified some excellent resources for your group to use".

## 4. Smith's model for fostering willingness to learn a foreign language

Smith's (1999) BASICS model may help to illustrate with different tasks how teachers may create a willing language learning community, how to generate an affective-effective class atmosphere to optimize language learning. The name BASICS is an acronym that encompasses six elements: belonging, aspirations, safety, identity, challenge and success. The following activities have been used with teenagers and the results point to an increase in motivation, and in language proficiency. However, when using them for the first time, it is advisable to ensure that learners understand the purpose and the usefulness of these tasks as learners need to "know why they are being asked to perform a task to appreciate its significance" (Wenden 1991, 42).

### 4.1. Belonging

The sense of belonging is very relevant for adolescents who need friendship and peer approval. To cooperate effectively, learners need to know each other and how to work in groups, to have the opportunity of making decisions together, of sharing ideas and of agreeing on how best to accomplish a task.

When learners feel they belong to a group, they normally act in a much more responsible way. According to Dörnyei and Murphy (2003), group cohesiveness increases productivity, and Diaz's study (2001) on how to raise Spanish secondary school learners' motivation towards English as a foreign language also showed the positive influence of humanistic activities as they promote class interaction, reinforce learners' self-esteem and help to encourage good relations in the group. "A magic guide to who we are" is a type of activity that could develop this sense of belonging. The teacher asks students to find their "group" identity related to certain topics such as physical ability, physical appearance, school performance, relation with people, hobbies or state of mind. Students in groups of five have to find out the statements that best describe them as a group. Then, they create a magazine with these sections where they write, draw and/or glue pictures that represent themselves as a group. The title of the magazine is A MAGIC GUIDE. They present their magazine to the whole class.

## 4.2. Aspirations

As already mentioned, initiating motivation relates to goal setting, which is in the case of teenagers of special difficulty, as they normally see a foreign language as a compulsory subject in which they have to pass an exam. However, it can be useful to offer them a questionnaire on reasons for learning the language. Items such as "I study this foreign language, because I have to pass an exam/I want to speak to people on holiday/ I need it for my job/I like understanding songs/I like to know more about its culture/I like speaking to many people through Messenger/I want to understand more web pages/…" may develop awareness of the different goals the members of a class can have. Later, they can have a group discussion about the best strategies to be used to achieve each goal and even to negotiate priorities the group may have.

## 4.3. Safety

The sense of security refers to physical and emotional security. Both are of essential importance in the secondary school classrooms. Experienced teachers know that many learners feel insecure when they have to take risks expressing themselves in front of others in a language they have not fully mastered. A relaxed classroom atmosphere is of crucial importance, as peer and teacher pressure can become a real handicap and can only be avoided when the teacher and the group create rules that build self-respect, when learners know what is expected of them, when the teacher projects a supporting image and avoids learner humiliation, and when disciplinary procedures are used to help students make better decisions (Andrés 1999).

The following activity could help to reinforce this sense of security as students can find out what a classmate, the teacher and their family like about them and at the same time, how they are in relationship to others. In groups of three, students each have sheet of paper and have to create their own coat óf arms. They divide their coat óf arms into four parts. In one of the four parts, they have to write two positive adjectives about themselves. When they have finished this, they exchange their coat of arms with someone else in the group who will write two different adjectives that describe the owner. The third area will be for the teacher who will have to write down other two qualities and in the fourth area, a member of their family has to do the same (students need to translate if family members do not know the foreign language). Once the students have the adjectives that suit them, they can decorate their coat of arms with drawings or stickers. The teacher will put them all up on the wall as if they were in a museum and students walk around and look at them to find a classmate who shares at least two of the adjectives that describe them.

## 4.4. Identity

The sense of identity or the image teenagers have of themselves will depend on their beliefs about their potential and on how they perceive their influence on others. These aspects can be considered from a physical and an emotional perspective. Teenagers' perception of their own bodies can affect self-esteem as contemporary culture focuses on an ideal body image that not everyone can have. Also, they may not be aware of or appreciate their abilities. Often when teenagers are asked what they are very good at, they do not know what to answer. Planning activities that give students the chance to explore different forms of art, music, crafts, drama and games[4] can increase learners' knowledge about their talents and abilities. Thinking-aloud procedures, where different learners explain how they accomplished a specific task, can help them to discover if the learning strategies they use are the most appropriate ones. Questions such as "who is the person who has had the most positive influence on your life and why?" can activate self-knowledge and initiate lively verbal exchanges. Visualizing and using music to relax and meditate on a personal experience, while the teacher's voice guides them with questions that help them to relive it mentally and to analyse what they did and how they did it is another technique that develops students' emotional intelligence and sense of self.

Another example of how to focus on teenagers' sense of identity in the language classroom is the following activity where teacher and students stand in a circle. After brainstorming positive words to describe people and putting these on the board, the teacher plays relaxing music and asks students to select a positive word or expression that describes themselves and an action related to that word. The teacher starts by giving a sentence using a word that describes

---

[4] See Fonseca (2002).

himself: "I am a cheerful person and I like being with people". The activity finishes when everyone in the circle has said his/her sentence.

### 4.5. Challenge

A significant change in the cognitive domain is teenagers' gradual increase in reasoning abilities and management of abstractions. Their intellectual growth demands challenge, problem-solving activities and thought-provoking tasks where not only linguistic information has to be used but also real-life knowledge and procedures need to be put into practice. Predicting what is going to happen in a story, inferring the steps to follow in order to solve a problem, analysing the cause and effects of incidents reported in newspapers are tasks that challenge teenagers' reasoning ability and connect them with their cultural environment. Referring to learning in general, Armstrong (1999, 99) recommends several tactics that can be used at different phases of problem solving:

> Find analogies; separate the various parts of a problem; propose a possible solution and then work backward; describe the characteristics that a solution should have; assume the opposite of what you are trying to prove, generalize (proceed from a given set of conditions to a larger set that contains the given one) or specialize (move from a given set of conditions to a smaller set).

### 4.6. Success

The sense of success is very much related to achieving goals. Competent learners have a positive self-image, a belief that they can face reasonable challenges and achieve success. Learners who are trained to set realistic and achievable goals feel internal motivation and are more likely to become successful. Tasks that include the presentation of an end-product can enhance the sense of competence. Teaching students how to create a project using the lyrics of a song they like, to design a power-point presentation that illustrates the best places to visit in their hometown or to write a self-portrait with pictures of special moments in their lives are possibilities with interesting end-products that can be exhibited to give them a sense of pride in their accomplishments.

## 5. Conclusion

The review of ways to transform a group of unwilling, uncooperative teenagers into a community of learners strongly suggests that affective concerns such as goal setting, developing a sense of belonging, creating a positive classroom atmosphere, offering challenging activities that are not only linguistically but also personally significant for learners, finding out their needs and accepting teenagers as they are, can help to ensure a successful language learning experience.

The way teachers present material to their students and the steps followed to involve learners in language learning influence learners' belief about their ability to participate successfully in any language task. For instance, a bad learning experience can influence learners' opinion about their coping potential, about their belief about their capacity to carry out a task. It can affect their willingness to take risks in other learning situations. Chastain (1988, 167) states that "experiences that have positive results tend to be repeated and those with negative outcomes avoided".

Different motivation models and the stimulus appraisal concept provide support for planning and using learning activities that address teenage learners' analytical, creative and practical abilities. Learning tasks need to be varied so that at least some of them relate to learners' strengths and needs, others connect with real-life situations, and others have a strategic focus that allows the students to overcome linguistic difficulties. Taking affective factors into consideration in the language classroom helps us as teachers to face the challenging task of initiating and sustaining teenagers' motivation, of enhancing their coping ability, and definitely, of fostering their willingness to learn a foreign language.

## Works Cited

Armstrong, T. 1999. *Seven kinds of smarts*. New York: Penguin Group.

Andrés, V. de. 1999. Self-esteem in the classroom or the metamorphosis of butterflies. In *Affect in language learning*, ed. J. Arnold. Cambridge: Cambridge University Press.

Arnold, J., and H.D. Brown. 1999. A map of the terrain. In *Affect in language learning*, ed. J. Arnold. Cambridge: Cambridge University Press.

Ausubel, S. A. 1968. *Educational psychology: A cognitive view.* New York: Holt, Rinehart &Winston.

Brown, H. D. 1994. *Principles of language learning and teaching*. New Jersey: Prentice Hall Regents.

Chastain, K. 1988. *Developing second-language skills. Theory and practice.* San Diego: Harcourt Brace Jovanovich Publishers.

Clark, A., H. Clemes, and R. Bean.1993. *Cómo desarrollar la autoestima en los adolescentes.* Madrid: Debate.

Cheng, Y., E.K. Horwitz, and D.L. Schallert. 1999. Language Anxiety: Differentiating writing and speaking components. *Language Learning* 49: 417-446.

Clément, R., Z. Dörnyei, and K.A. Noels. 1994. Motivation, self-confidence, and group cohesion in the foreign language classroom. *Language Learning* 44, (3): 417–448.

Cole, L. 1964. *Psychology of adolescence*. New York: Holt, Rinehart, and Winston, Inc.

Díaz Pinto, E. 2001. El ejercicio humanístico en la clase de inglés para alumnos de 1° de ESO: Una experiencia piloto. *Boletín de Lenguas* 9: 22-25.

—. 2002. La metodología humanística en la ESO y el desarrollo de las inteligencias múltiples. In *Inteligencias múltiples, múltiples formas de enseñar inglés,* ed. M. C. Fonseca Mora. Sevilla: Mergablum.

Dörnyei, Z. 2003. *Attitudes, orientations, and motivations in language learning: Advances in theory, research, and applications.* Oxford: Blackwell.

Dornyei, Z., and T. Murphey. 2003. *Group dynamics in the language classroom*. Cambridge: Cambridge University Press.

Ehrman, M., and Z. Dörnyei. 1998. *Interpersonal dynamics in second language education*. Thousand Oaks: Sage.

Ellis, R. 1985. *Understanding Second Language Acquisition*. Oxford: Oxford University Press.

Flavell, J. H. 1976. Metacognitive aspects of problem solving. In *The nature of intelligence*, ed. L.B. Resnick. Hillsdale: Erlbaum.

Fonseca Mora, M. C., ed. 2002. *Inteligencias múltiples, múltiples formas de enseñar inglés*. Sevilla: Mergablum.

—. 2004. Multiple Intelligences Theory as a framework for teaching English to teenagers in Spanish context. In *Broadening Horizons. A TEFL Methodology,* ed. P. Montijano. Málaga: Aljibe.

—. 2005. Individual characteristics of secondary school students. In *TEFL in Secondary Education,* ed. N. McLaren, D. Madrid and A. Bueno. Granada: Editorial Universidad de Granada.

Gardner, R. 1985. *Social psychology and second language learning: The role of attitudes and motivation*. London: Edward Arnold.

Gardner, H., and M. Krechevsky. 1993. Approaching School Intelligently: Practical Intelligence at the Middle School level. In *Frames of the mind: The theory of multiple intelligences 10th Anniversary Edition*, H. Gardner. New York: Basic Books.

Hadfield, J. 1992. *Classroom dynamics*. Oxford: Oxford University Press.

Hargreaves, A., L. Earl, and J. Ryan. 1998. *Una educación para el cambio. Reinventar la educación de los adolescentes*. Barcelona: Octaedro.

Harmer, J. 2001. *The practice of English language teaching*. Harlow, Essex: Pearson Education.

Knoll, M., and J. Patti. 2003. Social-Emotional learning and academic achievement. In *EQ +IQ= Best leadership practices for caring and successful schools*, M.J. Elias, H. Arnold and C. Steiger Hussey. Thousand Oaks: Corwin Press.

Labrie, N., and R. Clément. 1986. Ethnolinguistic vitality, self-confidence and second language proficiency: An investigation. *Journal of Multilingual and Multicultural Development* 7, (4): 269-282.

Locke, E. A., and A. L. Kristof. 1996. Volitional choices in the goal achievement process. In *The psychology of action: Linking cognition and motivation to behaviour*, ed. P.M. Gollwitzer and J. A. Bargh, 363-384. New York: Guilford Press.

MacIntyre, P.D., and R.C. Gardner. 1994. The effects of induced anxiety on three stages of cognitive processing in computerized vocabulary learning. *Studies in Second Language Learning* 16: 1-17.

MacIntyre, P.D., S.C. Baker, R. Clement, and L.A. Donovan. 2002. Sex and age effects on willingness to communicate, anxiety, perceived competence, and L2 motivation among junior high school French immersion students. *Language Learning* 52, (3): 537-564.

Matsuda, S., and P. Gobel. 2004. Anxiety and predictors of performance in the foreign language classroom. *System* 32, (1): 21-36.

Moskowitz, G. 1978. *Caring and sharing in the foreign language class: A sourcebook on humanistic techniques.* Rowley: Newbury House.

Puchta, H., and M. Schratz. 1993. *Teaching teenagers.* Pilgrims/Longman.

Robinson, P., ed. 2002. *Individual differences and instructed language learning.* Philadelphia: John Benjamins Publishing Company.

Schumann, J. H. 1997. *The neurobiology of affect in language.* Boston: Blackwell.

—. 1999. A neurobiological perspective on affect. In *Affect in language learning,* ed. J. Arnold. Cambridge: Cambridge University Press.

Sieburg, E. 1985. *Family communication: An integrated systems approach.* New York: Gardner Press.

Smith, A. 1999. *Accelerated learning in practice.* Stafford. Network Educational Press.

Sternberg, R. 2002. The Theory of Successful Intelligence. In *Individual differences and instructed language learning,* ed. P. Robinson. Philadelphia: John Benjamins Publishing Company.

Stevick, E. W. 1990. *Humanism in language teaching.* Oxford: Oxford University Press.

Underhill, A. 1999. Facilitation in language teaching. In *Affect in language learning,* ed. J. Arnold. Cambridge: Cambridge University Press.

Wenden, A. 1991. *Learners strategies for learner autonomy.* Englewood Cliffs: Prentice Hall.

White, M. 1992. *Self-esteem: Its meaning and value in schools.* Sets A and B. Dunetable: Folens.

Williams, M., and R. Burden. 1997. *Psychology for language teachers.* Cambridge: Cambridge University Press.

# Part III:

# Implementation and Classroom Applications

# CHAPTER EIGHT

# STORIES: WHO WE ARE AND ARE WE OK?


## ANDREW WRIGHT[1] (ILI INTERNATIONAL LANGUAGES INSTITUTE, GODOLLO, HUNGARY)



*In this chapter it is assumed that self-esteem is an aspect of a sense of personal identity, which we all need in order to live, sanely, with the infinite complexity of information assailing our senses at every moment of every day. The role of stories in establishing identity and self esteem in foreign language teaching is discussed. Acknowledgement is given to the idea that each culture and sub-culture has its own view on what a healthy sense of personal identity and self-esteem is.*


## 1. Introduction

### 1.1. A sense of personal identity

In this chapter, a sense of personal identity is taken to mean that we have a sense of who we are: I am... I can... I know... I come from... I belong to... I believe in... This is my community... This is my role... This is what I do... This is what I am like.

### 1.2. Self esteem

It is taken to mean a deep sense of confidence in the value of our personal identity, a sense of our independence, of our responsibility for what happens to

---

[1] Andrew Wright is an author, illustrator, storyteller, storymaker and teacher trainer. He has written a number of books for different publishers: *Five minute activities* for Cambridge University Press, *Storytelling with children* for Oxford University Press and *1000 pictures for teachers to copy* for Longman. He has worked as a storyteller and storymaker for approximately 50,000 students during the last 15 years in many different countries. He has worked as a teacher trainer in over 30 countries. E-mail: andrew@ili.hu; http://www.teachertraining.hu

us, and of our ability to deal with experience. Healthy self esteem is good for the individual but it is also good for society. Unhealthy self esteem may lead to selfishness, self aggrandisement, intolerance and xenophobia; we may prefer to categorise unhealthy self-esteem as a desperate manifestation of low self-esteem.

## 1.3. Stories

Stories are taken here to include: traditional stories and legends, selected and heightened anecdotes from history, commercial advertising and institutional propaganda, family stories of individuals and incidents, news stories. In the English speaking world the news is often introduced with the phrase, "The top stories today are..." And journalists say, "I am working on a story about..." All stories offer examples of concepts, values, perceptions, behaviour from which we can choose to build our sense of identity.

## 1.4. Foreign language teaching

The most common aim in foreign language teaching, worldwide, is: helping people to learn a foreign language so that they can use it rather than just knowing the grammar. Some teachers work towards this aim with a focus on the study of grammatical points and the application of those points in communicative situations. On the other hand, some teachers prefer to base their teaching on the creation of living communicative events and activities involving language in the classroom and to help the students to tease out the grammatical generalisations which are one of the key elements in successful communication. Finally, some other teachers combine these two approaches. The full potential of stories fits in very well with the second approach. Stories offer not only language in action but offer perceptions, values and ways of behaving, and in this sense stories both transcend and underlie the more apparent aims of foreign language teaching. Teachers of adults can reasonably concentrate on the teaching of the foreign language but teachers of children up to eighteen often consider that they have considerable responsibility to contribute to the child's overall development. With this responsibility in mind, stories, used in foreign language teaching, can play a major role.

It may be argued that the language proficiency of the students in the foreign language may limit their power to create and to respond to stories. I would say, perhaps limit but rarely prevent. Indeed one sometimes hears students say that they feel creatively liberated by working in a foreign language because they feel free from the responsibility for being a genius. One can be creative with a single word: try saying, "Hello", in five different ways. Tie limited language to the leg of art and watch it soar.

### 1.5. Culture and sub-culture

Each culture and sub-culture holds a different view, partly expressed through stories, of what a healthy sense of identity might be and these differences are reflected in the stories which are written or told in each society.

In some societies it is widely believed that the individual should feel positive about him or herself by belonging to a group and being happy to have a role in it. In other societies much more emphasis is given to the cultivation of the individual and his or her personal potential. This must be taken into account when we talk about a "healthy" self esteem. What is healthy in one country might be somewhat different from that of another.

My own view, derived from my own cultural background, is that it is important for the individual to flower and flourish, confident in his or her abilities and filled with self acceptance and self respect: important for the individual but also important for society. This view guides my work and my writing about my work.

In this chapter I will focus on the role of stories in the establishment of healthy and unhealthy self-esteem set against this view of identity. I will begin by describing my ideas about the link between stories, self-esteem and society (Section One) and then, later, describe, in very practical terms, my work on telling and making stories with young people (Section Two).

## 2. Section One

### 2.1. Stories and their role in our lives: Looking for patterns in infinite complexity

The Plough[2] is an arrangement of stars which many people can recognise. I remember my mother when I was a little boy, drawing the shape of the plough with her finger dark against the bright night sky. "There is its handle and there is the blade in the ground for cutting the furrow". The seven stars on which this shape is based are not all at an equal distance from us…they are many light years away from us and from each other. Amongst the plethora of stars in the

---

[2] The "Plough" is also called the "Big Dipper" and is a group of seven stars within the Ursula Major constellation of stars. The two stars which make up the leading edge of the plough are called Merek and Dubhe. The distance we see between them multiplied by five leads to the North Star, traditionally a key reference for navigational purposes.

heavens we try to find patterns and something we can recognise and name. Naming that configuration of stars as the Plough is part of story making and telling. We need to impose a pattern on aspects of infinite complexity not only in the night sky but in our daily lives and that is the role of stories. Incidentally, by taking the distance between the two stars on the right and multiplying it by five we find the North Star; and that star has offered a geographical point of direction and guidance from the beginnings of human time. Stories offer a lit path for us to follow.

## 2.2. Values, perceptions and behaviour in stories

We live in stories. Not only do the perceptions and values in stories give us guidance in dealing with our experiences, but they partially determine the experiences which occur, in the first place.

Stories guide us in determining whether something is right or wrong, important or of no consequence. They tell us what is expected of boys and girls and of grandparents and of marriage. Stories tell us what it is to be brave or to be wicked and how important it is to persevere. Partly because many traditional stories are about boys setting off to discover the world that is what many boys try to do. Partly because many traditional stories are about girls being beautiful and loving and loyal, that is what many girls try to be and do. Stories help to create experience not just show us how to deal with it.

In many cultures, particularly in the past, the range of stories told to children (and adults) was limited and values and perceptions were similar. The child was, thus, more likely to build an identity which was shared with others of his or her generation and social group. In our contemporary times children are subject to many stories from many different cultures in books, on television, through the internet and as part of their own local and national society. They are offered a great variety of values and ways of behaving. How confusing for them it must be! How easy it must be for children to adopt values and behaviour from this plethora of paths which are inappropriate, even harmful, both for them and for society!

## 2.3. An album of ourselves

Each one of us has an album of stories or bits of stories which are important to us. Here are a few images from my album:

When I was six my mother told me the story about the shepherd boy who cried, “Wolf!” in order to persuade the village people to join him in the mountain pastures even though there was no wolf. The people stopped coming when he shouted, “Wolf”, day after day and then a wolf really did come and ate him up (these days the wolf in the story doesn't eat up the boy, just frightens him a little. Society's story is softer now). This story became a part of my album of stories and led me to believe that I have no right to impose myself on other people.

When I was eight years old I read, *David Copperfield*, by Charles Dickens, from cover to cover. In later years my mother reported to me that I chuckled all the way through the book. Through Dickens I came to love the richness of different characters and I became more aware of the interweaving of events and people through time. I found the twistings and slimy wheedlings of Uriah Heap abhorrent and I valued the good nature of the simple and unassuming family living in the upturned boat.

Titus Oates went on the expedition with Scott to reach the South Pole. On the way back he became sick and had to walk more slowly than the others. He realised that he might endanger the team so he decided to leave the tent one night and went out into the storm, howling outside, at many minus degrees. As he went out he said, "I'm going outside. I might be some time". He sacrificed his life in order to save the others.

So many, many other stories in my story album, some from fiction and some from true happenings. I put some of the images there and others were put in by my family, my teachers and others in society around me. I am made of these story images.

The ubiquitous family photograph album is a deliberate piece of storymaking. We take the photos and choose which ones to put in the album. But wait a minute! We not only take the photos, we arrange the photograph to help to create the story we want ourselves and our family to live in! "Stand close together! Closer! Smile please! Say Cheese!". We must all look happy. "Look at great grandfather Jones with his foot on the lion he killed in Africa! Look at his splendid moustache. Look at those African chaps who had to carry his bags. Your great grandfather Jones was a real adventurer!".

To some considerable extent we create, select and mould the stories we live in. They sometimes coincide with our true identity but so often they hide a very different life and set of personal characteristics. "We" create? Very often the stories are chosen for us by our parents, teachers and the great institutions of the state. Thus, we are partly created by others.

## 2.4. Living in the right story

If we live in the "right" story and as the "right" character, life ticks over and there are no serious problems. If we are not able, truly, to be the character we have chosen and if the values, perceptions and behaviour of the character do not help us to cope with our actual experience of living then we have problems and society around has problems as well.

The wrong identity and falsely based self-concept may be fostered by well-meaning adults who say "You are a wonderful artist, etc.". Although the child may have done a few pictures which please the adults the child may have many more things which he or she can do and may want to do. How many little girls, labelled as "pretty", find it difficult to be sensitive to other aspects of themselves which they might explore and develop? How many little boys, labelled as naughty, find it difficult to give up this "charming" image and develop more fundamentally meaningful interests and abilities? Praise is not necessarily helpful! Sustained criticism or expressions of rejection and dismissal are even more undermining for the creation of self-esteem. My view is that stories written by the students should not be stamped with a grade by the teacher, but rather be bound as a book and made available to everyone to read or not to read.

We may hold an aspect of self-esteem from which others suffer as a consequence. The self-esteem of some teachers is based on being unchallenged for many years and being always "right". Such unhealthy self esteem leads to confidence for the teacher but may completely undermine the development of the children in her care when their flowering ideas are of the wrong species, in the opinion of the teacher. At the far end of the scale, xenophobia may provide a strong sensation of self-esteem for some people but the consequences for the people who do not belong to the same racial group may be grim. There must be many other examples of unhealthy self esteem bestowing on the holder a state of confidence but on others utter dismay.

Stories can be used to fashion other people and to control their behaviour, for example, to determine what loyalty is and even to place it at the top of our values and endeavours. It is a part of our daily news stories that people are willing to kill other people whose story does not fit with their own.

Stories offering clear values and rules of behaviour offer the relief of a well lit path guiding us through the dark onslaught of infinite, unpatterned experience. How tempting to follow such stories! But clear stories can contain the risk that many experiences are not catered for and the action taken does not lead to a satisfactory life for anybody. The map of the London underground is wonderfully useful if you are travelling on the underground but is of no use if you wish to drive by car from one side of London to the other. It's the wrong map. We can live in the wrong story.

Gersie (1997, 46) expresses another side to this idea very well:

> This tendency to render myths absolute continues to this day. It has all the manner of undesirable consequences: wars, lack of forgiveness and shunning are but some of these. How to develop a human relationship with the sacred, which is

built upon respect, compassion and tolerance, is an enduring challenge for all myth-makers.

Later in her book Gersie (1997, 226) quotes Ashley Ramsden, the British storyteller:

Rabbi Zoshia was a wise man. Once, while speaking about God, Rabbi Zoshia said: "Remember, when I die God will not say to me, Rabbi Zoshia, why weren't you more like Father Abraham? No, he will say, why weren't you more like Rabbi Zoshia?

We must help children (and adults as well) to find the right story to live in.

## 3. Section Two

### 3.1. My work as a story teller and storymaker with children

Over the last fifteen years I have worked, as a storyteller and storymaker, with approximately 50,000 young people aged mainly between 10 and 16, but also many very young children and many older teenagers in about twenty countries from Japan to Venezuela. I have always had the role of a visiting storyman rather than being a class teacher working with the same students throughout a whole year. This role has its advantages and its disadvantages. The disadvantages include not being able to spend time developing story awareness, knowledge and skill in individual students and my not being able to benefit from this huge, potential richness. The advantage of the peripatetic nature of my work is to have had the privilege of trying out ideas with a very wide spectrum of ages of students and from a very wide range of cultural background.

In this section I would like to describe practical aspects of this work which have focussed on the development of personal identity and healthy self-esteem.

### 3.2. Stories, education and healthy self-esteem: A summary

All the ideas given in the first section above have contributed to the development of the points below.

Stories are based on values, perceptions and behaviour which in turn derive from a sense of personal identity. Stories allow us to reflect on the validity and potential value to us of these values and to question and to work on our own sense of identity. Stories also offer many alternatives and this tells the student that there are alternatives to the view they hold of themselves.

Stories are the common thread of community and invite us to share ideas, feelings and experiences, not only with our contemporaries but with our antecedents. In the foreign language classroom creating stories encourage students to work together, asking each other for greater clarity of meaning, and offering opportunities for support and a sense of belonging. Furthermore, the stories are important and the students want to get them right…they want to "get the grammar right" because they want their creation to be as good as possible…this is strikingly the case if the stories are produced in book form.

An ambience in which stories are important and shared can offer an experience of love, trust and giving which is an ideal climate for the growth of confident and concerned individuals.

## 3.3. The importance of the story ambience

### Traditional examinations and traditional teaching focus on correctness of form

In order to use stories to foster healthy self esteem in second language teaching we should help the students to reflect on the content of the story given to them or on exploring and expressing ideas in the stories they make. Concern with formal accuracy can be related to the need for precision in thinking and communicating rather than concern for the application of rules for their own sake.

To develop student story awareness and related skills the teacher must respond to ideas first and form second…and only then related to the success or lack of success in expressing of ideas.

### Telling and retelling stories

Telling stories, both orally and in writing, is an essential experience for all of us in thinking and re-thinking the values and perceptions represented by them. Not telling and retelling stories bottles up experience and leaves it unexplained and increasingly unsorted and threatening or leaves it filed in a way which is no longer relevant as a guide to dealing with life around us. If the students are to *experience* the foreign language then they must use it for things which are important for them. For this reason the foreign language lesson provides an opportunity, through stories, for this experience to take place.

### Empathetic listening

If stories are to be told then there must be listeners and readers. It is important that all the students spend as much time on listening to, reading and reflecting on stories as on making and telling them. It is most important that the listener's empathetic feeling dominates his or her intellectual analysis. There should be a general delight in creativity both serious and light. Sensitive listening teases shy and lurking stories out of the shadowy corridors of the teller's memory.

Listening skills are based on:

a. A genuine interest in the teller.
b. Showing interest with eye contact and body language.
c. Not interrupting unless to make confirmatory noises or possibly to ask a question for further clarification or possibly occasional summaries to show that the gist of the story is being understood, for example, "so it was a very difficult time?".
d. Watching for non-verbal language as a contribution to the story's meaning.

All of these skills offer each individual student the opportunity to reflect, albeit unconsciously, on their own sense of identity and to work towards a stronger basis for a healthy self-esteem.

### Alternatives and misguided analysis

It is important for us all to experience alternatives: alternative roles, alternative orders of value, alternative ways of relating cause and effect. Thinking about the art and craft of storytelling relates very closely to the ability to reflect on experience and to learn how to live with it, by developing a healthy sense of personal identity.

Also, it is important to accept, positively, not always being able to understand the, "why's and wherefore's", of experience. Glib and misguided analysis does more harm than leaving some questions unanswered. In Goya's paintings there are many things to recognise but there are also forms which are ambiguous and un-nameable.

## 3.4. Choosing and adapting stories

In most classes there is a wide variety of needs represented by the different students. Some children may need to build their identity and gain more confidence…others should, perhaps, re order their values altogether if they want to live in harmony with themselves and with people around them. Some children may have to cope with bullying, poverty or death or some with lack of parental time and interest.

I have found a number of traditional stories which I like very much but which contain a value, originating in a past culture, which I do not accept. I change this aspect. The most obvious change is to make girls into the main protagonists whenever I can. I want to place in peoples' values and perceptions that girls as well as boys can go out and explore the world if they want to.

In the well known contemporary fairy tale, *The Paper Bag Princess*, it is the princess who saves the prince from the dragon, not the other way round.

Sometimes, I find a story which I like enormously but it seems to have a stumbling block for me of an unacceptable perception. There is a traditional story about six blind men who feel an elephant to find out what it is like. One of the men feels its leg and says that an elephant is like a tree. Another man feels its ear and says an elephant is like a blanket…and so on. A great story with a great message…that each person may experience a different aspect of something and thus perceive it quite differently. Unfortunately, for me, it also implies that blind people are incapable of knowing that they are each grasping a different part of the same animal! Such a story encourages a demeaning attitude to blind and other disabled people. How can we adapt the story in order not to risk damaging the self-esteem of people with disabilities?

*Little Red Riding Hood* is normally known through the late eighteenth century version which encourages us to think that little girls are incapable of looking after themselves and need a man (the woodcutter) to sort it all out. Jack Zipes in his book, *The Trials and Tribulations of Little Red Riding Hood*, recounts how an earlier version of the same story, deriving from country people, has Little Red Riding Hood as a girl with considerable "self esteem" and tough shrewdness. She beats the wolf.

These are a few examples of the way in which stories might be changed in order to support values which are likely to strengthen a healthy sense of personal identity for the listener without producing perceptions likely to damage society around them.

Stories should be chosen which help students to reflect on the nature of the individual, the relationship between the individual and society, the idea of cause and effect, the value of responsibility and the possibility of seeing experience in a new light and making changes. Some stories confirm unhelpful stereotyping and offer models of behaviour which are unhelpful for people who need to deal successfully with their experiences rather than to escape from them.

## 3.5. Techniques for responding to stories

There are many interesting, rich and useful ideas for helping children to respond to stories. I am noting here a selection of ways of responding to stories which have a good chance of promoting a healthy and strong sense of personal identity.

### Imagining

As you tell or read the story stop it and ask the children to look carefully at what they can see in their imaginations: What does Little Red Riding Hood look like? What does the forest look like? How does the wolf behave? Such an activity brings home how we all see things differently and there can be no right and wrong answers in such an activity. Furthermore, this activity offers the option to each participant to change his or her mind instead of taking the first impression. Experiencing and reflecting on and choosing from a range of alternatives is an essential part of establishing self esteem and of refreshing the student's existing self esteem.

### Personalising creation

The children can be asked to choose and to perform or draw the parts of the story which seem important for them. Once more the children experience alternatives. By responding creatively rather than objectively the children offer a variety of feelings and ideas which adds, still further, to the sense of choice, liberating the student who is unnecessarily trapped in an unhelpful perception of him or herself. Again there is no right or wrong answer.

### Retelling and adding

The children can be asked to retell or add to the story and in doing so must weigh up all the submerged values which he or she feels or even consciously thinks are implied by the story. Retelling can be made through a different medium which encourages recreation rather than regurgitation.

### Making it relevant

Particular focuses in stories which are relevant to developing a healthy sense of self identity include:

a. Awareness of alternative ways of being.
b. Awareness that change is possible.
c. Ability to assert oneself without damaging others.
d. Order of values…what do you really think and value?
e. Cause and effect and the possibility of intervention.
f. Criticism.
g. Managing stress.
h. Problem solving.

## 3.6. Techniques for promoting story making from experience

### Asking questions

Cezanne, the great French artist of the late nineteenth century, said "Back to nature". He meant that we should study experience directly rather than through accepted "ways of looking". That is still too broad an idea to be helpful. I have found that it is useful to help to focus the students' minds on details and to side-step reaching for tenth hand storylines, by asking questions:

What did you see?
What did you hear?
What did you feel, taste and smell?
What did you think and feel?
What did you say?
What did you do?

I also use questions to push the students from generalised information to highly particular information. "But tell me just how she sat. Exactly. Was her back straight or hollowed or bent? And her arms? Exactly? And her hands? And how did her appearance, her body position, face and clothes express how she felt? Etc.".

I once used questions with a large class of seventeen and eighteen year olds. They created a woman. They told me exactly how she looked and exactly how she was sitting. They had told me that she was sophisticated and that she was nervous. I asked, "Sophisticated suggests someone who is in control of things…but you said she was nervous. How was she smoking?". One student called out, "She was sophisticated so she was smoking, slowly". Another student added, "But she was nervous so her fingers were trembling".

Questions about appearance, behaviour, thinking and feeling can drive one forward into areas of the mind normally left vague. From here we can sometimes find new understandings of ourselves and of others. This, in turn, may lead to a re-thinking of one's own sense of identity.

When I use the question technique for helping students to create a story I, as matter of principle, always accept every suggestion. I do this in order to communicate that it is not my story and that they are responsible for it. I try not to respond to suggestions with favour or disfavour but with a general enthusiasm for the story as a whole. If I were to express my joy and admiration for one suggestion but offer impassive tolerance for another then that might be damaging for the student who had not affected me.

Sometimes when I am using the question technique the students cannot offer an idea…in these cases I often make suggestions which are so wide ranging that the students still feel that the suggestion they offer is their choice.

### Projects

I once carried out a project week with children in the Alps. A common story association related to the Alps is, "a mountain range covered with snow and a deep blue sky behind and the dancing figure of Julie Andrews coming over the meadow, singing as she skips". Rather than ask them to look at the great sweep of Alps rising above them and invite "pass me down" stories, I asked the students to find one metre of ground which they would like to be custodians of and to study for one week. Everyday, with the distant mountains rearing in the postcard panorama behind them, the students studied in detail what had not been "storied" for them. They studied their tiny plots as naturalists but they also peopled them with their imagination and created societies and alternative ways of life. On the last evening they wrote letters to themselves in twenty years time and the next day they buried the letters in solid plastic bags in their metre of ground.

I cannot assert that this helped to fortify their positive self-esteem. But I imagine it might have helped to do so both directly and indirectly. Directly because they would be able to write down matters of current concern and were able to bury them for the time being. They, hopefully, developed further the ability to look at themselves and to feel that nothing need be permanent…so much depends on how you look at it. Indirectly because, perhaps, they learned to create their own stories rather than to accept the often limiting stories offered to them.

### Story seeds

I help the students to recognise the many story seeds in our daily lives. A story seed is, for me, "a problem". You want something but it is difficult for you to have it. The story arising from this story seed is about how you deal with the problem. In working on ideas you learn how to search, find, weigh up and try out alternative ways of looking and being. This skill provides a basis for reflecting on and for reforming the nature of one's self-esteem.

## 3.7. Techniques for making fictional or fantasy stories

Sometimes it may help to let the students invent a protagonist and to write a story for them, instead of writing about themselves. The student can then decide how factually or how imaginatively the story should relate to his or her own life. In doing this, the student should be encouraged to concentrate on detail and to derive much of this from observation of real life. Also, ensure there is a "story seed" based on a "desire" and a "problem". In discussing how to create a character the student has the opportunity to reflect on his view of him or herself. Headings might include:

a. Personality.
b. Appearance.
c. Talents and skills.
d. Hopes, aims and difficulties.
e. Difficulties to overcome.
f. Likes and dislikes.
g. What is his or her opinion about him or herself?

For each of these guiding categories, you should give a summary of its meaning but also give detailed, actual examples.

To develop the feeling that it is possible to see things differently ask the students to write a story from the point of view of three different protagonists. You can limit this if you wish to one section of a story. You can also show the class three pictures one by one. Each student should write the start of a story based on the first picture and then read that beginning to their neighbour. It is enlightening and enriching to hear their neighbours very different story based on the same pictures. And nobody can be wrong. The students continue the same story related to the second picture and finally the third picture, each time reading their story to their neighbour (Maley and Duff 1978).

## 3.8. Edit, publish and perform

By editing I mean the work which students do to help each other by reading or listening to the stories of others and asking questions which drive the teller to be clearer and more precise about his or her telling. With this communal editing method, power and responsibility is put into the hands of the students. The feedback is not simply from the authority figure of the teacher. The teacher can eventually take on the role of the senior desk editor (as they are called in publishing).

By publishing I mean making their story available beyond the single reader or listener through books, magazines, posters, web sites, blogs, and email. As a principle every student has his or her story in the final collection, if it is to be a bound copy of a book. I do not select what I think are the best stories. The children experience their work in a public place for all to see. They can reflect on what they have done and what others have done and decide what to think about it. No story is highlighted by me or the teachers as being exceptional. In this way children with low self esteem have the satisfaction of seeing their work included. Children of high esteem are not misled into a state of hubris by having their work picked out and named as "excellent". All are rewarded by seeing their work become part of something which stands as a living object. As for many artists the object they have created matters to them, but it has taken on its own existence, like a growing child it must stand on its own feet.

By performing I mean dramatising their story and making it available to more people through live performance, through audio or video recording.

The advantage of publishing and performing is that the student feels directly responsible to him or herself for his or her product. This leads to a heightened sense of responsibility and wish to do a "good job". And this feeling is conducive to developing in the student responsibility for the identity of themselves manifested in their story which is offered to the society. Publishing and performing also offer huge opportunities for a sense of achievement and one which can be referred to for years to come. In one example of this I remember the grandparents of a child visiting the Sheffield City Library exhibition of student-made books which arose out of a story making and telling project I worked on. "Ee, look at that! It's our lad's book. You would never have believed it, would you?".

Some years ago I was working in a town in Austria when a woman stopped me in the street. She said, "Are you the man who is working in the local school on stories?" I told her that I was. She continued, "I want to tell you that I have always had difficulty getting my boy out of bed in the morning. He has never felt that he was any good at school. But this week he has been setting his alarm clock for an hour earlier every morning so that he can go into school and work with his group on writing and illustrating their storybook. He is so excited about it".

## Works Cited

Gersie[3], A. 1997. *Reflections on therapeutic storymaking*. London: Jessica Kingsley Publishers.

Maley, A. and A. Duff. 1978. *Drama techniques in language learning*[4]. Cambridge: Cambridge University Press.

[3] Alida Gersie has built up an extensive experience of therapeutic storytelling. All her books are wonderfully rich.

[4] This classic book launched many ideas for storymaking which are as valid and vibrant to day as they were in 1978.

## Further Reading

Cattanach, A., ed. 2002. *The story so far. Play therapy narratives*. New York: Routledge.

Gersie, A., and N. King. 1990. *Storymaking in education and therapy*[5]. London: Jessica Kingsley Publishers.

Rosen[6], B. 1980. *And none of it was nonsense*. London: Mary Glasgow Publications.

—. 1991. *Shapers and polishers*. London: Mary Glasgow Publications.

Wagner, B. J. 1976. *Dorothy Heathcote: Drama as a living medium*[7]. Washington, D.C.: National Education Association.

Wright, A. 1995. *Creating stories with children*[8]. Oxford: Oxford University Press.

—. 1997. *Storytelling with children*[9]. Oxford: Oxford University Press.

Zipes, J. 1993. *Little Red Riding Hood*[10]. New York: Routledge.

—. 1997. *Creative storytelling*[11].New York: Routledge.

---

[5] Such a wonderful collection of myths related to personal development.

[6] Betty Rosen's two books listed here pass on richly and practically stories and ideas for classroom use based on her work in inner city schools with tough teenagers.

[7] Dorothy Heathcote was a pioneer in helping children to make stories and of making them responsible for the direction of those stories and for the values and behaviour they raised.

[8] Ways of creating stories with students with suggestions on book making and shadow theatre production, etc.

[9] Ways of using stories in the classroom with 94 different activities and 63 stories and lesson plans.

[10] A fascinating comparison of the different ways in which this well known story has been told each representing very different values and perceptions.

[11] A rich book of ideas for helping young people to create stories.

# CHAPTER NINE

# TASKS AND ACTIVITIES TO PROMOTE SELF-ESTEEM IN THE ENGLISH PRIMARY CLASSROOM

MARINA ARCOS[1]
(POLYTECHNIC UNIVERSITY OF MADRID)

> Any system of education, any theory of pedagogy, any 'great national policy' that minimizes the role of schools to nourish self-esteem in its students fails in one of its primary functions.
> —Bruner (1997)

*Outcomes in education today are being increasingly criticised from different sectors of society and changes in education are constantly demanded. The reasons and solutions for this state of affairs vary according to the viewpoint of the person or group. Sometimes learners are blamed for their lack of interest. From the perspective of education as a process to cater for the whole person, that is to say, for their affective and cognitive domains, we look at other possibilities. One of these is lack of self-esteem in the learners. In this chapter we will explain the importance of self-esteem as a psychological factor in education and will suggest practical ways to incorporate self-esteem in the classroom, namely through classroom management and activities. Although children are the main focus here, other ages can also benefit from doing the activities.*

---

[1] Marina Arcos has taught at different levels from nursery school to university. She is currently teaching ESP at the Polytechnic University of Madrid. Her main field of research is materials development. She is also interested in learning styles and experiential learning. E-mail: marina.arcos@telefonica.net

# 1. Introduction

> The difference between a lady and a flower girl is not how she behaves, but how she's treated. I shall always be a flower girl to Professor Higgins, because he always treats me as a flower girl, and always will; but I know I can be a lady to you, because you always treat me as a lady, and always will.
> —*Pygmalion,* George Bernard Shaw

Our picture of what education is like nowadays is rather bleak. The poor results that different surveys show about children's performance at school together with complaints about their lack of interest and curiosity for knowledge and their inability to concentrate on their learning are becoming a topic of major concern. Some people might think that one of the causes of this state of affairs is that students are getting lazy. Although education is a very complex matter, perhaps one of the reasons for this possible disinterest could be that students do not feel confident enough about their capability to learn or perhaps they do not feel competent after having tried to learn.

In order to teach, we not only have to take into account the object of the learning (in our case the English language), but also the subject of the teaching: the learners. Traditionally, one of the major concerns of education has been to cater for students' cognitive needs but ignoring their affective ones. As Arnold and Brown (1999, 1) have stated, "The affective side of learning is not in opposition to the cognitive side. When both are used together, the learning process can be constructed on a firmer foundation". Students will have difficulties in learning the language unless they are psychologically ready to do so. And as teachers we can contribute to this if we plan, organize and manage our classes bearing in mind the psychological aspect of learning as well. One way to contribute to it is through attention to learners' self-esteem.

Self-esteem is an area which has attracted a great deal of interest among psychologists and educators over the last three decades. Our concern in this chapter is with the practical aspects of tasks and activities to promote self-esteem while learning English.

# 2. Working definition of self-esteem

Although a definition of self-esteem has already been provided in this book, to be able to better understand our practical proposals it is important to keep in mind first a working definition and state the underlying reasons that have made us select the tasks and activities. According to Coopersmith (1967 in Andrés 1999, 88) "Self-esteem is a personal judgement of worthiness that is expressed in the attitudes that the individual holds towards himself". The two main factors shared by different psychological theories that make up self-esteem are self-value and self-efficacy. The former refers to a sense of security, of feeling confident and worthy for what one is. The latter is related to a sense of feeling competent and capable for what one does. Both are considered psychological factors that can influence learning and as teachers, we are in an ideal position to promote or hinder self-esteem. Some of the key aspects of building up self-esteem in our students are to teach them how to be aware and have respect for their value, capacity, ability, knowledge and skills. This is what we are going to propose to do through different tasks and activities as we will see later on in this chapter. However, before embarking on the subject we should deal with some preliminary questions.

## 3. Reasons for not getting involved in self-esteem

The first of these questions is the fact that we might find it difficult to get involved in the challenge of enhancing self-esteem in the classroom for a number of reasons: we have many students; they are disruptive and lack motivation; we have a whole syllabus to cover and very few hours; the layout of the classroom does not help; we do not feel confident and/or competent to include this type of teaching in our repertoire. The school and/or our colleagues do not appreciate it. Nevertheless, if we are convinced that this is the right thing to do we should find a way to overcome these difficulties. In fact, according to Hoffman and Bartkowicz (1999, 4), "Research shows that stress and low self-esteem are responsible for most learning difficulties". So we should do something about it.

## 4. Classroom management and the role of the teacher

The second question deals with classroom management and the role of the teacher. The school is a microcosmos where children socialize and learn not only the contents of a subject, but also values, attitudes and ways of understanding the world and themselves. As Andrés (1999, 87) says, "The strong link between self-esteem and social relationships and academic performance can be witnessed in the everyday world of the classroom". Bearing this in mind, we should incorporate self-esteem in everything we do in the classroom, namely, classroom management and the tasks and activities that we implement.

Fig. 9-1. Classroom management and self-esteem.

With respect to classroom management, it is essential that we devise a system of classroom interaction based on confidence, competence and respect as a way of promoting self-esteem. It would include: classroom layout, grouping of students, and classroom routines. It is important for children to know what they are expected to do based on fair and reasonable principles. As part of the management of the class, students should be given the opportunity to discuss and agree to the directions for handling and organizing materials, the way they treat each other, how they will work in groups, how they will take turns and perform active listening. Moreover, from a linguistic point of view, classroom routines are also important because as Cameron (2001, 11) states, they "can provide opportunities for meaningful language development; they allow the child to actively make sense of new language from familiar experience and provide space for language growth".

## 4.1. The classroom as a cosy spot

Even if our students are not infants any more, they are still in need of feeling at ease in the classroom so that they find talking about themselves much easier and natural. Instead of the traditional distance imposed by rows of desks and chairs we should find a way to make the classroom a cosy spot where learning, being oneself and socializing go hand in hand. We can use it as a reading, activity or assembly corner. We can put a mat, some cushions, a bench, a table there or whatever we have to hand to make it inviting.

## 4.2. Circle time or assembly

Neither isolation nor teacher talking time should monopolise the action of the classroom. We have to give way to group activities that allow students to express themselves as individuals. To have children gathered together is a perfect opportunity for them to feel part of a community by listening and being listened to. It is a very motivating setting as students are able to put into practice, orally, what they know in English, and at the same time, they are learning new ways of expressing exactly what they want to convey. It is even a good opportunity for shy children to have their say. It is also a good source of information for the teachers to find out what their students feel, need and want. Through this format we can implement a number of different activities. The way to ensure that circle time is a success is for the children to know its rules. They should know that they have to accept other students' opinions, speak from their own point of view, and respect other people's turn to speak. They should also know that they cannot use pejorative language or physical force in order to solve a situation of conflict. It could be useful if the children decide the rules after reflecting on an experience where they did not comply with the rules and underwent its negative effects.

## 4.3. Teacher role

Teachers should show high and positive expectations of children because what we expect is a very powerful tool that turns into self-fulfilling prophecies in the classroom and produces the *Pygmalion effect*. Another important aspect of our teaching is the interest we show in the children. Students appreciate and benefit from teachers who are genuinely interested in them and care for them. We should avoid negative criticism, ridicule or favouritism and impede bullying, name calling, quarrelling, cheating, bragging and all sorts of unfair and discriminatory behaviour. We understand that to capacitate our students, value what they do or say, give them our best feedback and believe in them, will contribute immensely to them fulfilling their maximum potential. These four elements are as essential to self-esteem and teaching as water is to life. We cannot forget also that a great deal of their learning comes through observing and modelling us so it is necessary that we practice what we preach.

Getting to know our students is indispensable for affective effective teaching. We propose a motto to help ourselves to be on the watch out for discovering children's competence and confidence: "Every child has enough competence to be confident". We just have to look for it and let them be aware of what we know and from there to build up a whole world of self-esteem that will make learning easier, faster and more enjoyable.

# 5. Tasks and activities to promote self-esteem

We can incorporate self-esteem into tasks and activities in two different ways: overtly and covertly. When we deal overtly with self-esteem in a task, our main objective is to develop some of its components. However, when an activity is focused on, let us say, some more linguistic skills or specific topics, we may still be promoting self-esteem through management or by incorporating some self-esteem element to it.

The tasks and activities that we suggest in this chapter are aimed overtly at promoting children's sense of security and competence along with a sense of identity and belonging. We recommend adapting the suggested tasks and activities whenever it feels necessary to better cater for the needs of your students. In order to do so you may want to break down the tasks into more detailed steps or make more specific rules. These tasks are meant to provide you with ideas to spark the imagination so you and your students can create your own ones.

## 5.1. Tasks and activities which encourage students to focus on their own feelings, values and attainments

### Task 1: When do you feel…?

Purpose: To motivate students to talk about emotions and to make them aware that these can be of different nature: emotions might make them feel good or bad. However, they have to come to terms with the latter in a constructive way.

Procedure: 1) Warming up: ask students to mime the emotions included in the task to make sure they understand them. The teacher can mime them or explain them if necessary. 2) Ask students to express in what situations they would feel these emotions. If the students do not know how to express what they want to say in English the teacher can translate it into the target language at any time.

Fig. 9-2. Negative feelings.

Fig. 9-3. Positive feelings.

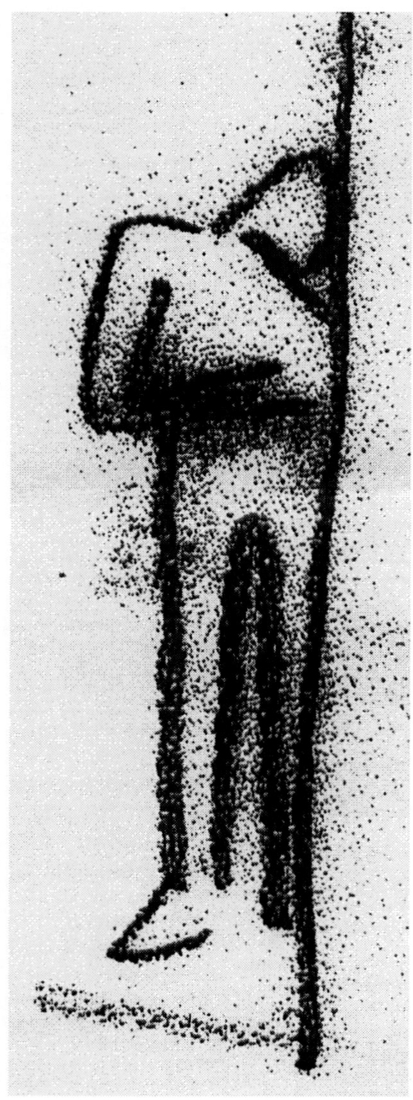

Fig. 9-4. How do you feel?

When do you feel…?
I feel/am happy when

..........................................................................................................

I feel/am proud when

..........................................................................................................

I feel/am loved when

..........................................................................................................

I feel/am appreciated when

..........................................................................................................

I feel/am excited when

..........................................................................................................

I feel/am useful when

..........................................................................................................

I feel/am kind when

..........................................................................................................

I feel/am secure when

..........................................................................................................

I feel/am worried when

..........................................................................................................

I feel/am scared when

..........................................................................................................

I feel/am nervous when

..........................................................................................................

I feel/am angry when

..........................................................................................................

I feel/am disappointed when

..........................................................................................................

I feel/am useless when

..........................................................................................................

I feel/am unkind when

..........................................................................................................

I feel/am insecure when

..........................................................................................................

**Task 2: The treasure in me**

Purpose: To help students value the big treasure they have in themselves which they can resort to whenever they need it.

Procedure: Ask students to think about all sorts of capacities, abilities and possessions they have in order to improve or overcome a difficult situation. Ask students to draw two columns on a sheet of paper. One with the heading "my capacities" and the other "my possessions". Ask the children to keep them handy whenever they are performing a task and they come up with a problem or get discouraged. Here are some ideas to fill them:

My capacities: to ask, read, write, explain, learn, think, concentrate, create, relax, try again, feel proud of myself, cheer myself up, etc.

My possessions: my intelligence, my effort, my persistence, my trust in myself, my family, my teachers, my friends, my books, my pet, etc.

### Task 3: My "I'm special" book. Art and craft activity

Purpose: To promote positive self-image through the opinion of people around children.

Procedure: After doing the "treasure in me" task, tell students that their capacities and characteristics are appreciated and valued by the people who care for them such as parents, relatives, friends, neighbours, teachers, schoolmates, etc.; (students can add other people). Ask students to make a mini-book in the shape of a star (the patterns are provided below in Figure 9-5) where the people who care for them are going to write what they like and appreciate about them or what things the child has done for them. In order to assemble the mini-book they will have to cut out the suns and punch a hole in each; put the pages in order; write their names on the back cover, and insert the pages with the comments between the cover pages. They can use a metal ring to hold the book together and add as many pages as they wish at any time.

Acknowledgement: The content of this activity was partly inspired by Hoffman and Bartkowicz (1999).

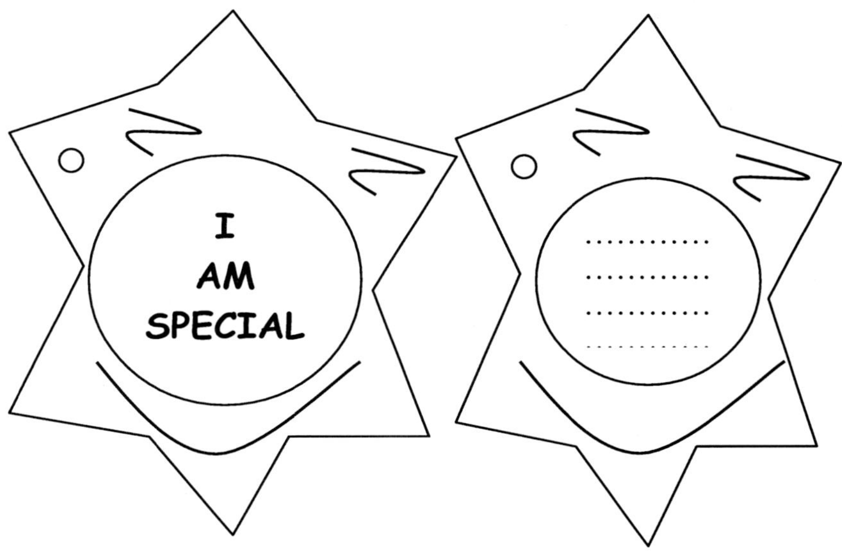


Fig. 9-5. My "I'm special" book.

### Task 4: My friendly diary

Purpose: To make students reflect on their actions and feelings to promote self-acceptance, self-understanding and find ways of changing their own behaviour.

Procedure: Ask students to keep a diary at the back of their notebook. On the right hand side page they could write some positive things they have felt or done during the lesson and on the opposite page some less positive things they have felt or done. Set a moment in your daily routine for the children to do it. Read their notes regularly otherwise they will think that the task is unimportant and they will stop doing it. You can expand this task by asking them to think and write about what they could do to minimise or overcome the less positive things they have experienced.

### Task 5: Slogans to promote self-esteem and to stamp out criticism, doubts and fears

Purpose: To surround them with permanent positive messages of self-esteem.

Procedure: Write the slogans on separate slips of paper and pin them up on the walls. Ask students to read them regularly by themselves and/or they can read them aloud and comment on them from time to time. Children can write the slogans and illustrate them with drawings. Throughout the school year ask children to add more slogans. They can also write the slogans down to take home and stick them on the wall in their bedrooms:

Mistakes are here to teach us, not to embarrass or upset us.
Mistakes are no excuse not to try again.
A mistake? Oops, no big deal. I'll correct it straight away.
A mistake? Never mind. I'll try not to make it again.
I always learn a lesson when I make a mistake.
Practice makes me improve and get what I want.
It's good to know we are the same and different at the same time.
It's good to notice and accept differences and similarities between people.
A joke which hurts other people is not a good joke at all!
I like to listen and to be listened to.
I'm proud of being different.
I like myself so I treat myself well.
I'm learning to know my strengths and weaknesses and make the most of them.
I express my thoughts and feelings without hurting my classmates and without falling out with them.
The only important competition is the competition with myself.
Hands are for helping not for hurting.
When I keep my promises, I respect myself.
I believe that what I think or do is right so I will not let any comment to put me off.
I help my friends, they help me, we are a great team!
When I'm angry I relax and I try to see things in a more positive light.

Acknowledgement: Some of these ideas come from Hoffman and Bartkowicz (1999).

### Task 6: The right frame of mind

Purpose: To make children aware of how their initial attitude towards things can influence a great deal the outcomes.

Procedure: 1) Warming-up: Ask students to choose a song they know in order to sing it to different moods, for example, a sad, happy, angry, scared mood. Encourage the use of body language for emphasis. 2) Ask students to choose a familiar story whose characters are easy to identify with different moods. Divide the class into small groups and assign each group a different character. Ask students to change the mood of their character and think about how they would react to the events of the story according to their new 'personality". Once the changes have been decided one member of each group can act out the new version of the story. The teacher may write on the blackboard the new reactions of the characters and the effects they produce on the events of the story. The children with the help of the teacher can reflect on the task to realise that a change of mood can bring about a change in events and outcomes. One reflection can be that if we face a situation in a positive light, if we get the right frame of mind, we will come up with ideas and ways of doing things that will help us to overcome the situation positively. Follow-up task: the class can write down the story in book format which will become part of the class library. Illustrations can be included. The book would be also a good example of team work and group self-esteem.

Tip: the teacher can illustrate the task before performing it with their students. S/he can act out the mood of a story character well-known by the children and write on the blackboard the name of the character and his/her habitual mood under the heading "old mood". Then, the teacher mimes and talks about the new mood that, let us say, a fairy godmother has conferred to the character, and writes it under the heading "new mood". The teacher proceeds by talking and enacting the positive consequences of the new mood and writing them on the board under the heading "positive consequences".

## 5.2. Tasks and activities which encourage students to appreciate other people's feelings, values and attainments

### Task 7: This is the biography of my friend

Purpose: to enhance appreciation for others and enjoy the benefits of being appreciated.

Procedure: After having talked about biographies, children will play the role of a biographer of an outstanding character whose merits, deeds and other personal details should be known by the general public. In this case, the outstanding character will be a friend.

"This is the biography of my friend"

Write the story of one of your friend's lives. Learn as much as you can about your friend. We will give you some ideas to guide you to fulfil your task.

My friend's name is .................................................................
She/he is............years old.
Her/his birthday is on...............................................................
She/he lives at ........................................................................

She/he has ........................................................ eyes.
She/he has .......................................................... hair.
In her/his house lives.....................................................................
Her/his favourite game is ...............................................................
Her/his favourite toy is....................................................................
Her/his favourite sport is.................................................................
Her/his favourite food is .................................................................
Her/his favourite drink is ...............................................................
Her/his favourite book is.................................................................
Her/his favourite school subject is ..............................................
Her/his favourite TV programme is ...........................................
Her/his favourite film is .................................................................
Her/his favourite place to go is .....................................................
When she/he grows up she/he wants to be a/an ..........................
I like her/him because She/he .......................................................
....................................................................................................
....................................................................................................
....................................................................................................
....................................................................................................

Acknowledgement: This task is an adaptation and expansion of one presented by Borba and Borba (1982, 84).

**Task 8: Problem solving report**

Purpose: To make children think of solutions to everyday problems.

Procedure: Have copies of the problem report to hand and give one to any child involved in a conflictive situation to fill it in on his/her own. Offer your help for any doubts that they might have about the task.

Tip: The problem report should be explained to the children by the teacher beforehand including an example so that they would be able to complete the form by themselves in the future.

"Problem solving report"

Name:...............................................................Date....................................
Who was involved?...........................................................................................
Where did it happen? .......................................................................................
Tell what happened ............................................................................................

What did you really want to happen?..............................................................
..........................................................................................................
..........................................................................................................
..........................................................................................................

How do you feel about what happened?
..........................................................................................................
..........................................................................................................
..........................................................................................................
..........................................................................................................
..........................................................................................................

How do you think the other person feels?
..........................................................................................................
..........................................................................................................
..........................................................................................................
..........................................................................................................
..........................................................................................................

Name some ways you could have prevented the problem from happening.
..........................................................................................................
..........................................................................................................

Name two ways you can still solve the problem.
..........................................................................................................
..........................................................................................................

What will you do the next time something similar happens?
..........................................................................................................
..........................................................................................................
..........................................................................................................

Acknowledgement: This task has been drawn from the book by Borba (2001, 117). Question number 9 has been added, and some wording and the name of the activity have been partially changed.

### Task 9: Today's achievement

Purpose: To make children aware of their confidence and competence and to integrate both of them in their everyday experiences.

Procedure: Ask the children, after an activity or at the end of the class, how they feel about what they have done. If they are not familiar with language of feelings, you can work on that first. It is a good idea to have a poster or flashcards at sight illustrating different feelings.

Today's achievement

Today ............................................ of us (number of students or names) have felt
..........................................................................................................................
because we have been able to.................................................................................
..........................................................................................................................
..........................................................................................................................
..........................................................................................................................

**Task 10: A classroom with a view**

Purpose: Allow children imagine what they will be in the future as a way of building hope and setting objectives for the future.

Procedures: Ask each student using different techniques (drawing, colouring, writing, pasting…) to express on a A3 cardboard sheet what they want to be, do, have, feel, and think when they are twenty years old, or other age. You could bind the sheets together and write on the front cover the title *A Classroom with a View* and also messages to encourage students to strive for their aims such as: This is what we want, this is what we'll get, we'll work hard for it and we'll ask people for help. During the process the teacher can go around the class and discuss with the children what they what to include on the sheet, why and how.

Note: The book can be used many times as raw material to talk and work on related topics. For instance children can work out how a long term objective can be split down into smaller easier and more manageable objectives.

## 5.3. Reading books as key material on which to build up self-value and self-efficacy

The value of children's literature to promote language learning is widely accepted among other reasons because reading books are good examples of language in context and in use, and in the case of stories children can easily interact with the themes, events and characters in them. Beside the common use of reading books to develop children's linguistic skills they can also be employed to work on any aspect of children's self-esteem which Borba and Borba (1982) call *bibliotherapy*. Two examples of how to exploit books is this sense are going to be given: one refers to a story book and the other is a book of poems.

### Task 11: Story book: A cultivated Wolf[2]

Purpose: To make students reflect on making positive choices, goal setting efforts, believing in themselves and being able to accept criticism.

Procedure: Read the story to the children as a group. Differentiate this part with a special name such as "story time", and depending on children's age, a chant and some actions can be included. Practice some deduction skills about what the story is going to be about based on the front page and carry on reading it making sure that children understand it and by letting children give their own interpretation of the story. Deal with it, not only at a factual level, but at an interpretative one in which children can identify and talk about their feelings, opinions or misunderstandings.

Note: This activity is also ideal to practice classroom management. For more details about how to incorporate stories into teaching, see Morgan and Rinvolucri (1988), Wright (1996), Arcos (2002) and Wright's chapter in this book.

### Task 12: Using poems[3]

Purpose: To enhance self-esteem through appreciating things and people, raising self-competence, learning from mistakes, making efforts to improve, keeping your word, quarrelling and sharing. As an example we reproduce the following two poems:

**"I didn't believe I could do it"**

I didn't believe I could do it.
I was afraid to try.
My teacher believed I could do it,
And next time, so will I.

---

[2] Bloom and Biet (1998). London: Siphano.

[3] Fom the book *I like being me*. Lalli and Mason-Fry. (1997) Minneapolis: Free Spirit Publishing.

**"Someone Else's Chairs"**

What to learn about each other?
What to show how much you care?
Just imagine what it's like
To sit in someone else's chair.

Note: We highly recommend these poems not only because of their self-esteem building content but also because their stress and intonation patterns facilitate the retention of useful large chunks of language. It is not uncommon to be able to recite poems or sayings years after learning them.

Procedure: We propose four ways of exploiting the poems:

To read and discuss the poems one at a time during assembly.
To act them out (if the topic permits).
To ask children to copy them and memorize their favourites.
To graph the children's favourite poems.

Other suggested story books and some of the aspects connected with self-esteem that are dealt with:

*Where the wild things are*. Sendak (1963). Harper Collins. (Isolation, misbehaviour and love).

*Princess smartypants.* Cole (1986). London: Puffin. (Self-determination and daring decisions).

*This is the bear and the picnic lunch*. Hayes and Craing (1986). London: walker books. (Overcoming disappointment).

*Kirsty knows best.* McAfee and Browne (1987). London: Julia MacRae Books. (Exposing and fighting bulling).

*Elmer*. McKee (1989). London: Red Fox. (Accepting differences).

*Nobody cares about me!* Ritchie and Kronheimen (1997). London: Bloomsbury Publishing. (disappointment, reluctance to share).

*I wish I were a dog*. Monks (1998). London: Mammoth. (Accepting differences and coping with dissatisfaction).

*A great attitude*. Hill (1998). Cypres: Creative Teaching Press. (Independence, responsibility and coping with problems).

*Mr wolf's pancakes*. Fearnley (1999). London: Mammoth. (Lack of cooperation, selfishness and drastic solutions).

*Eat your peas*. Gray and Sharratt (2000). London: Red Fox. (Self-determination and accepting faults).

## 6. Conclusions

Self-esteem will help children discover their true potential, to like themselves for who they are and to believe that they are capable of changing and setting goals to improve themselves. We should not confuse self-esteem with arrogance or selfishness because a sense of responsibility, sharing and respect is part and parcel of the approach to learning that we have been discussing here.

Through the type of tasks and activities suggested in this chapter to promote self-esteem children can learn a great deal of English in a very experiential and meaningful way. Teachers can rediscover and experience that "*all children are born learners*" as Hoffman and Bartkowicz (1999, 4) say. Their interest for learning will flourish in a caring atmosphere influenced by the "you can do it" and "I can do it" principle.

At first activities for enhancing self-esteem may be new for some of us, but with time, practice and reflective thinking we can all come to see how the advantages and benefits for teachers and children alike make the whole process of promoting self-esteem more than worth the effort.

## Works Cited

Andrés, V. de. 1999. Self-esteem in the classroom or the metamorphosis of butterflies. In *Affect in language learning*, ed. J. Arnold. Cambridge: Cambridge University Press.

Arcos, M. 2002. El reto de despertar las inteligencias múltiples: El taller de lectura. *Inteligencias múltiples, múltiples formas de enseñar Inglés*, ed. M.C. Fonseca Mora. Seville: Mergablum.

Arnold, J., and H. D. Brown. 1999. A map of the terrain. *Affect in language learning*, ed. J. Arnold. Cambridge: Cambridge University Press.

Borba, M. 2001. *Building moral intelligence*. San Francisco: Jossey-Bass.

Borba, M., and C. Borba. 1982. *Self-esteem: A classroom affair. Volume 2. More ways to help children like themselves*. San Francisco: Harper Collins.

Bruner, J. 1997. *The culture of education*. Cambridge: Harvard University Press.

Cameron, L. 2001. *Teaching languages to young learners*. Cambridge: Cambridge University Press.

Hoffman, E., and Z. Bartkowicz. 1999. *The Learning adventure*. Middlewich: Learn to Learn.

Morgan, J., and Rinvolucri, M. 1988. *Once upon a time*. Cambridge: Cambridge University Press.

Wright, A. 1996. *A Storytelling with children*. Oxford: Oxford University Press.

# CHAPTER TEN

# PRACTICAL ACTIVITIES TO PROMOTE TEENAGERS' SELF-ESTEEM IN THE EFL CLASSROOM

CONCHA JULIÁN[1],
(UNIVERSITY OF SEVILLE, SPAIN)
AND EVA R. DÍAZ[2]
(UNIVERSITY OF HUELVA, SPAIN)

*There are not many examples of activities designed to foster self-esteem among teenagers in the EFL classroom. The implementation of such self-esteem building activities should be developed far more. This chapter contains ten activities teachers can use in class. Each class means different individual capabilities, potentials and social relationships. Teachers need to create new activities or adapt old ones that are tailored to the individuals in their class. The activities suggested below follow the steps Reasoner (1982) advises in any self-esteem program: building a sense of security, identity, belonging, purpose and competence.*

---

[1] Concha Julián has taught English as a foreign language in secondary education in Spain. She has been an advisor in a state in-service teaching training centre in Andalucía and is an advisor in the bilingual program in Andalucía. She has been involved in action research on sensory learning styles, Brain Gym© and the role of hemispheres in learning a foreign language. E-mail: concha.julian.ext@juntadeandalucia.es

[2] Eva R. Díaz has been working as a language teacher in Secondary Education since 1997. She is also a researcher at the University of Huelva, where her doctoral dissertation dealt with emotional intelligence and willingness to communicate in the EFL classroom. E-mail: ediazpinto@mtoscano.com

## 1. Introduction

To understand the full meaning and the sense of the activities in this chapter, it will be helpful to consider the characteristics of adolescents according to Cole (1964, 267):

1. They are critical of others yet sensitive to criticism about themselves. They feel this criticism is unjust because others do not really understand them.
2. They value their solitude for it allows them to think without distraction. At home they might seek refuge in their room. In school they might find a quiet corner.
3. They are preoccupied with their body and self. The changes which take place at the onset of pubescence in size, body proportions, and secondary sexual characteristics generally occur rapidly. Understandably, the body attains a new value. When physical changes are not concurrent with sexual development, the adolescent is likely to perceive this imbalance as evidence of sexual inadequacy.
4. They experience swings in mood from elation to depression. These moods are usually the result of successes or failures in personal relationships or school work.
5. They rebel against adults and their values. This derives from their fear of losing their individuality. Conflicts may arise because of dress styles, dating privileges, or eating habits.
6. They gravitate toward their peer group. The group provides them with a sense of belonging. But in seeking admission into the group, they must comply with the dictates of the group.
7. They revaluate their stand on issues such as religion, drugs, sex, and world affairs. They want to feel certain their moral standards reflect their values and not those of their parents.

These circumstances have an important influence on classroom behaviour. For that reason, special methodology should be adopted for language instruction. That is why interaction with peers, teachers and parents is fundamental for secondary school students who are physically, emotionally and cognitively in a state of change. Teenagers have to feel engaged in the activities and tasks they perform in the classroom. This way, their creativity and their capability to learn a foreign language is developed. Following Chastain (1988), some of the ingredients to consider when designing or adapting activities for secondary education are:

1. Avoiding empty praising
2. Careful planning of minimal steps
3. Selecting challenging activities
4. Teaching metacognitive strategies
5. Offering "new material" in a multi-sensory way
6. Listening actively
7. Accepting students' strengths and weaknesses

The last point is especially helpful in understanding and managing discipline problems. As it has been said above, teenagers have constant mood swings which, most of the time, are influenced by their relationships with parents, teachers, peers and their own self-image. If teachers manage to control discipline problems in a supportive and constructive way through talks and activities-for instance, role-plays about dealing with difficult situations-which are meaningful to teenage students, a great deal of improvement will be achieved in the teaching-learning process of a foreign language.

As Moskowitz (1978) points out, there is an important emotional feature in the teenagers′ involvement in the construction of their own identity. The image they have of themselves and their self-acceptance is vital for their whole growth and has to be taken into account in the language classroom. Teenagers are active participants who have to construct their personal understanding of the world and grow as learners and as individuals.

In this chapter, we propose ten activities that may help students to construct a strong sense of self-esteem. The activities can be used along with course book or at the beginning of the course year. The experience of the authors has been that the following activities have proven to make for a better atmosphere and reduce disruptive behaviour, as teachers and students are emotionally involved in a more constructive way.

## Activity 1: Medals

### Focus on competence

Level: Lower intermediate and above.
Skills: Writing.
Time: 60 minutes.
Special materials: Prepare some medals on coloured paper before the session. There must be enough medals for each student to have several of them.
Procedure:

Make a medal with some positive qualities such as “Patient teacher” or “Good friend” and wear them in class. Then, explain to the students your own feelings when nobody notices how much you care or work, so you have decided to make a medal for yourself. After that, tell the students that they are going to work on recognising how others are and that they are going to have a ceremony giving each other medals.

Ask the students to make a circle around the class. Each student is given a number of medals and works independently making medals for their classmates and also for themselves.

When they have finished, the ceremony will start, using music if possible. Every student will receive their medals and at the end, they will explain the qualities they have chosen for their own medal.

## Activity 2: We make posters

### Focus on belonging

Level: Lower intermediate and above.
Skills: Writing and speaking.
Time: 120 minutes.
Procedure:

Make groups of four. Each group should make a collage-poster representing their own lives. Each group should have a nickname based on something that all of them have in common.

In the collage, each student can add photos of their own family: parents wedding, birthdays, childhood, etc., anything they want to share and show to the rest of the classmates.

At the end, each group shows their poster to the rest of the students explaining their good qualities.

## Activity 3: Poems

### Focus on identity

Level: Lower intermediate and above.
Skills: Writing.
Time: 60 minutes.

Procedure:

Ask students about their likes and dislikes. Tell students to write a poem following the structure below. After that, they should make two more poems, one for a relative and the another one for a friend.

Line 1: Your name.
Line 2: Two adjectives describing yourself.
Line 3: Three verbs to indicate what you like to do.
Line 4: Another adjective.
Line 5: A Three-word description of yourself.

For example:

Mary
Organized, motivated
Cycles- runs- writes
Inspiring
Cares for others

Suggestions:

Line 1: Names.
Line 2: Responsible, punctual, sensitive, inspiring, clever, sporty, optimistic, open-minded, tolerant, thoughtful, writer, poet, generous, etc.
Line 3: writes e-mails, plays basket or football, goes shopping, goes jogging, reads, plays computer games, etc.
Line 4: Happy, romantic, passionate, sensible, humorous, hard-working, responsible, nice, powerful, energetic, attractive, confident, brilliant, radiant, intelligent, friendly, cheerful, etc.
Line 5: Listens to others, writes good stories, always tells the truth, loves their family, is a good thinker, hasn't got any patience, likes having pets, etc.

## Activity 4: Descriptive words

### Focus on identity and purpose

Level: Lower intermediate and above.
Skills: Reading and writing.
Time: 60 minutes.
Procedure:

First, tell the students to write the positive qualities that define their personality best. Then, tell them to add to the list five qualities or features that they would like to have in the future. Finally, make them describe five things that will help them to get those future qualities.

For example:
Now I am sporty, optimistic and generous.
In the future, I'd like to be more responsible, tolerant, intelligent, punctual and strong.
To be more responsible, I need to have my things tidier.
To be more tolerant, I need to respect others people's opinions without criticising them.
To be more intelligent, I need to study more.
To be more punctual, I need to get up earlier.
To be stronger, I need to do some more exercise.

## Activity 5: General performance

### Focus on purpose and competence

Level: Lower intermediate and above.
Skills: Reading and writing.
Time: 30 minutes.
Special materials: Prepare a photocopy with a circle divided in different parts. In each part, there is the name of a subject or skill.
Procedure:
Using colours, as it is detailed below, every student will draw each area:
Green (1): I've made excellent growth in this area and I feel good about it.
Blue (2): I've made fairly good progress but I feel I could do better.
Yellow (3): I haven't made much change.
Red (4): This is an area I should work on next term.

For example:

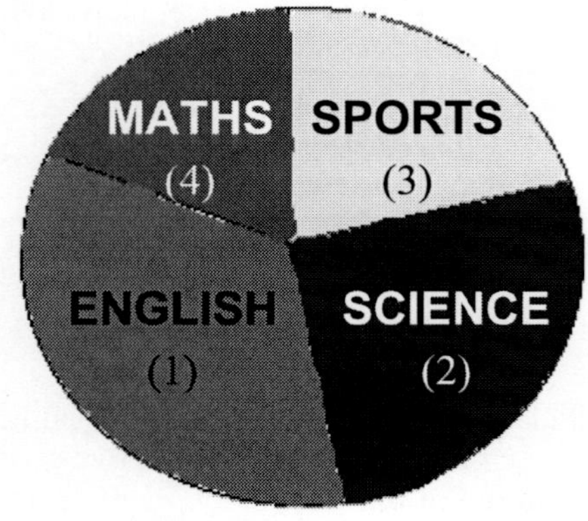

## Activity 6: Cooperative tale

### Focus on belonging

Level: Intermediate, upper intermediate.
Skills: Listening, speaking, writing and reading.
Time: 45 minutes.
Special materials: A soft ball.
Procedure:
Tell the class they are going to create a tale…

Part 1:

It would be helpful to revise and make a chart with the usual parts of a traditional folk tale and some typical expressions students can use depending of their level:

Organization of stories:
Opening: Once upon a time, there was/were …
Introduction of characters
Description of setting
Introduction of a problem
Events that lead to problem
The resolution of the problem
Closing the tale: They all lived happily ever after or a moral which may be or not be explicitly stated
Language usually used:
Parallelisms and Repetitions:
Grandmother, what big eyes you´ve got!
All the better to see you with, my dear
(ears-hear; hands-grab; teeth-eat)
Alliterations: (little) red riding, the deep dark (forest), big bad (wolf)
Contrasts: the good and the devil, youth-age
Metaphors: the forest as life outside the safety of the family, the wolf as the stranger that represents threat to innocence and safety.
Tenses: narrative with past tenses, dialogues with present tense.

Part 2:

The class should be arranged in a circle. One student starts: Once upon a time … and throws the soft ball to another student who adds something to the story. The students take it in turns to make up the story. The group decides when to finish the story.

One or two students take notes about what is said. When the tale is finished, a student writes it on the board helped by the whole class and the notes. The class decides on a title for the story.

Part 3:

A group of volunteers copy the final version of the tale on a piece of cardboard with a paper frame to be hung on the classroom wall.
This tale represents the effort of the whole group.
Leave 3 or 5 minutes every week in your class so the students can decide if they would like to change or add anything to the tale.

Part 4:

At the end of the term, give a copy of the tale to each student, so they can keep it in their diaries or note-books as a symbol of the group they belong to.

## Activity 7: Our school cultural week

### Focus on identity

Level: Intermediate and above.
Skills: Listening, speaking and writing.
Time: 120 minutes.
Special materials: A1 or A2 paper and party decorations.
Procedure:

Prepare some big posters with your students and make some decorations to hang around the classroom, so the cultural week should mean something special for students beyond their weekly routine.

Students individually or in pairs think about a hobby or a special holiday they enjoy and prepare a presentation using one or more of the following if possible: posters, role-plays, photos, computer presentations, videos, readings, short demonstrations. They will use these to show the rest of the class how they do that hobby or how they celebrate their special holiday. In the case of their hobby, they might need to say why it is important for them and what are the advantages and disadvantages of having that hobby. The students can encourage other people to try that hobby or to celebrate that special holiday.

## Activity 8: Music and moods

### Focus on identity

Level: Elementary and above.
Skills: Listening, writing and reading.
Time: 60 minutes
Special materials: tape or CD recorder or MP3.
Procedure:

Every week, students take it in turns to bring music which is special for them. The teacher should know previously the type of music students are going to bring, so s/he can bring a piece of music which is very different.

In class, play the student's piece of music for five or ten minutes. While listening, students should write some sentences or draw something about how the music makes them feel. Afterwards, they repeat the procedure but, this time, with the teacher's music.

In the end, the students who wish to read their pieces of writing or explain their drawings to the rest of the class and check whether their moods and feelings have changed with the different pieces of music played. This chart about moods could be used as a guide the first time. This way you provide those students with limited language with a means of doing the activity. In following lessons they continue to use the chart until they no longer need it.

| | | | | |
|---|---|---|---|---|
| HAPPY | FRIENDLY | BORED | NOISY | INTERESTED |
| PATIENT | SAD | EXCITED | TALKATIVE | SELFISH |
| LUCKY | AGGRESSIVE | TIRED | QUIET | SILLY |

Table 10-1. Activity inspired from Cranmer, D., and Cl. Laroy.1992. *Musical openings*. Harlow, Essex: Longman.

## Activity 9: Weaknesses and strengths

### Focus on security

Level: Intermediate and above.
Skills: Listening and speaking.
Time: 45 minutes.
Special materials: Soft ball.
Procedure:

Part 1

Brainstorm on board about abilities/positive qualities and fears (strengths and weaknesses) students have. For example: "I´m afraid of: spiders, exams, riding a bike, etc."; "I´m good at: catching insects, telling jokes, etc.".

Part 2

Put your students in a circle. The student who has the soft ball starts and says his/her name and a good quality s/he has. S/he then throws the ball to another student, who repeats the procedure. Once all students have had a turn, move on to the next part.

Part 3

This part is called *fears and solutions*. Every student in the circle in turn tells the class his/her fear or weakness. A student raises his/her hand if s/he has a solution. The student with the fear/weakness throws the soft ball to this person who gives a solution to overcome his/her problem. Students can use expressions such as: you can…, you could..., you should…, try to…, if I were you I… (Give help if necessary).

Source:
Idea modified and adapted from Torrego, J.C. 2003. *La alternativa al juego, y mediación de conflictos en instituciones educativas*. Madrid: Narcea S.A. Ediciones.

## Activity 10: Tutorial time

### Focus on security

Level: Upper intermediate.

Skills: Listening, speaking and writing.
Time: 45 minutes.
Special materials: note pads.
Procedure:

Part 1

Divide the class into groups of 5 or 6 students. Each group chooses a panel of "experts" (2 or 3) who are going to listen and give advice to the rest of the students in the group. The topic to be discussed is "Difficulties and concerns at school during the last week". Teachers can suggest some possibilities, for instance: feeling excluded from the group, changing the date of exams, punctuality, respecting others′ feelings, or any other problem they have had during the week. The role of the "experts" is:

Listening to the other students in their group.

Taking notes about the difficulties and concerns. Asking for clarification, if necessary.

Discussing the topic among themselves as 'experts'.

Giving possible solutions to the students in their group.

Part 2

The students reflect on the activity individually. A possible outline could be:

Have you enjoyed the activity?

Do you think it can be useful to you? In which way?

Have you discovered anything new about your classmates?

Do you agree with the given solutions?

Can you apply them at school or to your everyday learning?

Do you think this way of participation is important and needs to be taken into account by teachers and tutors? Why?

Part 3

Finally, discuss in L1 or L2 whether they have found the activity interesting and useful.

# CHAPTER ELEVEN

# TEACHER'S SELF-ESTEEM: THE ROLE OF CONFIRMATION


INMACULADA LEÓN[1]
(UNIVERSITY OF SEVILLE, SPAIN)



*When one speaks about self-esteem in the classroom the tendency is to associate it almost immediately with students. This chapter intends to change the focus, showing current teachers' needs at school-specially language teachers'-to have a higher self-esteem that allows them to do their best at work.* Confirmation*, the process by means of which we make others feel valued, recognized and acknowledged, is presented as an excellent ally for teachers to implement and care their self-esteem. The present work is structured into two parts, the first one being a description and reflection on teachers' daily reality and their needs, and the second part contains some comments and appreciations made by secondary language teachers about their self-esteem and about what they can do to foster it from their position.*


## 1. Introduction

> A tennis shoe in a laundry dryer. Probably no image captures so fully for me the life of an adult working in an elementary, middle, or senior high school. For educators schoolwork much of the time is turbulent, heated, confused, disoriented, congested, and full of recurring bumps.
> —Barth (1991, 1)

---


[1] Inmaculada León Moruno is a secondary English teacher in Badajoz, Spain. Especially interested in the affective dimension of language learning, she has done research on teacher confirmation in the English classroom and has developed scales for measuring teacher and learner confirmation. E-mail: inmile@hotmail.com

Throughout this book the topic of fostering self-esteem is addressed. In the literature on Second Language Acquisition the focus is mostly on the learners and their well-being, while teachers and their needs are very frequently consigned to oblivion. Indeed, we often speak about the obstacles students must overcome on their way to language acquisition, but what about teacher's vulnerability? The purpose of this chapter is to draw attention to teachers' perceptions in order to give insight into the daily obstacles they have to overcome within the classroom, as well as what they need in order to face them and foster their own self-esteem.

Teachers are sometimes erroneously supposed to be invulnerable individuals programmed to carry out their tasks every day and ready to overcome any obstacle on their own. However, teachers are not merely outside observers of the educational process. They are intellectually and emotionally involved in it, affected by everything that takes place in and around the classroom, as well as by the opinion of students, parents, colleagues and much of the whole social structure.

Our educational systems are in need of changes. Both scholars and educators themselves argue that our current form of schooling is often frustrating to teachers and does not really prepare students to face real life. Some pose changes in the legislation, the Curriculum, teachers' training, financing and management of money, staff salaries and a long so on so forth of possibilities. But, as Claxton (1989, 2) claimed, the place where these necessary changes should start to be achieved is "the state of mind of teachers themselves":

> The success of any reform, whether to curriculum, teaching method, school organization or administration depends upon teachers being "in-play", willing to participate in the search for a more powerful and enabling form of schooling, and to give proposed reforms (to quote the Americans)"their best shot".

For teachers to become willing agents of change, it is crucial to build up their self-esteem, which is recurrently endangered by many tense and difficult situations. Teaching has an important emotional component and to make it successful, programs should be carried out in schools to create a more solid base of emotional understanding among the members of the educational community, especially between teachers and students (Greta Morine-Oershimer 2000, 824). Education is a human process between human beings, both teachers and students need mutual respect and understanding to carry out their daily activity in the class, to give their best in what they do. Sometimes educators find themselves alone among troublesome students, insensitive parents and non-supportive Superiors. At those moments teachers need to have a positive *self-image*. It is here that the concept of *confirmation* can be an excellent allied for teachers, and provide support for their self-esteem.

Confirmation is the process by means of which we convey others that they are *recognized, endowed and acknowledged* as special and unique individual (Sieburg 1961; Ellis 1998). For more than forty years the term *confirmation* has been used in an interpersonal sense in literature belonging to different areas of knowledge such as Philosophy, Religion, Psychiatry, Sociology or Communication. Used first by the theologian Martin Buber in 1957, the implications and valuation of the construct of confirmation have evolved throughout the years by means of the several studies carried out about it (Laing 1961, 1969; Sieburg 1969, 1975, 1985; Cissna and Sieburg, 1981; Ellis 1998, 2000a, 2000b).

According to Buber, confirmation is a phenomenon which is deeply integrated within the interaction among human beings. Furthermore, he claims that it is by means of this process that humans are capable of discovering and establishing their own identity, and enables us to experience the *partnership of experience*. Confirmation is a phenomenon whose reason of being lies in the fact that its existence and validity are relevant as far as it is perceived by the receiver in the reception of messages that transmit it. These messages are codified by means of communicative behaviours that awaken in the receptor feelings of being "real or irreal (sic.), accepted or rejected, valued or despised, understood or misunderstood, humanized or cosified" by his interlocutor (Sieburg 1985, 188). That is to say, the communicative messages conveyed by means of those particular behaviours make the other feel confirmed or disconfirmed.

For teachers, being confirmed by others in school context is crucial, for they need to feel valued, recognized and acknowledged both as persons and professionals. Claxton (1989, 25-26) makes an interesting description of what teachers would need to feel positive. According to him, educators want to be effective in helping their students to develop and learn, and need to feel pleasure in the meanwhile and satisfaction after it. They also need their work and effort to be acknowledged, and to be optimistic about their skills and a better future for education. They would like to feel relaxed and businesslike within the classroom, keeping their students interested and involved; they want to be caring without limits or fear, to feel that they are making a reasonable living, and that they can ask for support or advice without being judged. Moreover, they want to be consulted and their opinions and views to be taken into account; they need a harmonious work environment where they feel part of a team.

Looking at all these requirements from the outside, it could seem out of teachers' power to make most of these things happen, but nothing is further from reality. All these things Claxton lists could be summarized in this sentence: teachers need to be confirmed and they can create the proper conditions for this to happen. Educators have power to decide; they can determine what they have to do, because nothing comes out of the blue. We must give to get back, plant to collect, support to be supported, care to be cared, and definitively, we must confirm to be confirmed. Sometimes confirming is hard when you have poor self-esteem, but it is necessary to make an effort to fight against hopelessness and conformism, to believe in our power to change our reality at school by initiating a confirming spiral beginning with our own behaviour in our educational centres.

Due to its reciprocal nature, confirmation can help teachers to prepare the way for that harmonious, efficient, cooperative atmosphere of work they need. Sundel (1972) carried out a study in which he underlined the reciprocity of communication. In his research on teacher-student interaction within the classroom, taking as his focus teachers' and students' confirming and disconfirming verbal behaviours, he concluded that when teachers confirmed students, students tended to do the same with their teachers, and when teachers were disconfirming so were students.

Ellis' research results also show evidence that the behaviours that seem to provoke in the receiver feelings of being recognized, acknowledged and valued-that is to say, confirmed-have a reciprocal effect, and the same happens with disconfirmation (Ellis 2002, 331). In the same way, as can be seen in the following quotation, Cissna and Sieburg (1981, 279) highlight the dialogic structure of confirmation, explaining how this is a reciprocal and complex activity in which participants who take part in a communicative act exchange the roles of subject and object, cause and effect:

> Confirming response is dialogic in structure; it is a reciprocal activity involving shared talk and sometimes shared silence. It is interactional in the broadest sense of the word. It is not a one-way flow of talk; it is not a trade-off in which each speaker pauses and appears to listen only in order to get a chance to speak again. It is a complex affair in which each participates as both subject and object, cause and effect, of the other's talk. In short, confirming response, like all communication, is not something one does, it is a process in which one shares.

In view of this, it would hardly be an exaggeration to claim that teachers' conscious acknowledgement of students and manifestation of confirming behaviour could help them to create a "boomerang effect", receiving back the recognition and acknowledgment which they need to do their best and which fosters their self-esteem and growth as persons and professionals.

After these reflections on how confirmation can have a positive effect upon teachers' self-esteem, we would like to turn now to language teachers' testimonies which convey how they feel at schools and what they need to create and maintain a stronger self-esteem. Four secondary school language teachers were interviewed in their High School during their morning break about what they would need to increase their self-esteem as teachers, and what they think they could do to get it. These teachers were: M. José and Víctor, both French teachers, and M. Ángeles and Nuria, both English teachers. All of them agree that language teachers' needs are basically the same as those of teachers of other subjects, though they feel there are some peculiarities about the foreign language classroom. This is what they say they need in order to increase their self-esteem:

1. More social recognition of the importance of the teaching profession:

> Mass media could become a useful instrument to promote a change in the way society understands and looks at teachers and their work. I'm fed up with hearing comments like "being a teacher means living it up. You only work in the mornings and very few hours, have plenty of holidays and get a lot of money just for playing or reading books with children". It really hurts, people don't really know how hard we have to work and struggle with our pupils, their disrespectful behaviour, our low salaries... (Víctor).

2. More support within the school (Directive Team, administration and parents' associations):

> Teachers have a first-rate social role-just as a doctor or a judge-and consequently they should be respected. Why is it that the decisions made by a judge or a doctor are never questioned, only discussed, and those made by us are daily called into question? My self-esteem gets lowered every time a pupil, a parent or the Headmaster tells me what to do or doubts about my way of correcting an exercise, keeping discipline in my class or doing an exam. (M. Ángeles).

3. A change in the educational system, with renewed disciplinary measures which give more authority and legal protection for teachers to act and prevent cases of *bullying*:

> Very often, due to current laws, the rights of those conflictive students who don't want to learn precede the right of students who really want to work. Some hard-working pupils come to my desk crying because they can't hear me when I explain because of the noise. For me it is really embarrassing and frustrating being forced to keep students in class who are always interrupting, insulting and threatening teachers and classmates. You cannot even send them to the Headmaster, the psychologist or the school social worker because these professionals are completely swamped with work. Schools need more professionals trained to cope with troublesome students and help them to solve their problems. (Nuria).

4. Open and more frequent channels of communication with parents:

> Parents should make themselves more available for us so that teachers and family can coordinate our efforts to give a better holistic education to children. Sometimes they argue they are too busy to come to school to speak with us, and they only come to our office when they are notified that their children have done something bad or have failed a subject. Very often when they come it is too late to solve the problem. (Víctor).

5. A higher salary.

6. An equal treatment for all teachers:

> Often your own colleagues distinguish between categories. When temporary teachers arrive at the School in September frequently they find a horrible situation: the members of the department have already chosen the groups and the timetables, giving them what they don't like. It's unfair and it really affects your self-esteem, it makes you feel rejected and inferior to others. (Nuria).

7. An increase in the offer of courses or other activities to complete teachers' training, especially on the application of new technologies in the classroom. As Víctor says "if you are better prepared you are more confident about yourself and what you do in class, therefore your self-esteem increases".

8. Classrooms just for foreign language teaching (when possible):

> We, language teachers, need many different materials for our classes. I have to go up and down stairs about ten times a day to give my lessons carrying my bag, dictionaries, books, posters, cards, cassettes and cds. I need all that to create a proper atmosphere for language learning. If I had my own class I could prepare all the material beforehand and welcome my students as they deserve, saving time and improving learning. (M. José).

9. Avoid the comparisons, established in our current society, between native and non-native speakers of the foreign language as far as their skills and capacity to teach the L2 is concerned:

> The question is not if you are a native or non-native speaker of the language, what really counts is if you are a good teacher and use an appealing and effective methodology. (Nuria).

10. More awareness of the importance of learning languages on the part of society and families:

> Frequently both pupils and parents, especially in rural areas, give importance to students' marks in what they call "basic subjects", as Mathematics or Science,

> with especially Foreign Languages being considered second-rate subjects which are not necessary for children's future. In fact, in these cases parents' reaction is not the same when their children fail Maths and when they fail a Foreign Language class. When you notify parents about their children's lack of interest in the L2 class, they usually ignore you or say that speaking a foreign language is not necessary to work. This attitude really affects your self-esteem. (M. Ángeles).

As can be inferred from all these comments, teachers are very aware of the things they need to foster their self-esteem. Making all these changes happen is not an easy task. Changes of this nature need time, a commitment spirit and a lot of effort to be materialized. Undoubtedly, many of the things language teachers require to strengthen their self-esteem are beyond their control. Nevertheless, there are many things educators can change on their own to foster their self-esteem and, consequently, to create a more comfortable and effective work atmosphere that leads to an improvement in the classroom. The following are suggestions which have been found to improve teachers' self-esteem and, by extension, the classroom climate:

Make an effort to face everyday work with positive thinking and a renewed mind. Create a habit of reflection, for example on your way home. During that time you can analyze what has happened that day at school and look for the good things you have achieved, everything counts: a pupil's smile a shy student's participation... Repeat encouraging words in your mind. Learn how to focus positively on the little wrongs of everyday, and use them to guide you in making changes in your next lesson.

If you teach a conflictive group try to take it as a challenge not as a punishment. Whatever happens in class, always go in and out of the class with a smile on your face and an "I can do it" spirit. Plan strategies to deal with the students in those groups together with their other teachers; coordinate efforts.

Bring new elements to your classroom, avoid monotony: use new technologies, photos, meaningful quotes or even decorate the classroom. In that way your students will be more willing to pay attention and participate.

Ask any member of the Guidance Department of your school if they have any books or material that can help you to understand better the stage of psychological and intellectual development of your students, and prepare activities designed to solve problems and establish affective links with them. This can help you to be more patient and understand their thoughts and behaviours better, and deal with them not as sources of a personal conflict with you, but as something which is part of their development or particular situation. Show interest in the personal or family situation of the more conflictive or shy students; it can explain their attitude and help you to find solutions.

Exchange teacher-pupil roles so that each can put himself in the other's shoes, developing empathy. One activity that really works, especially for disciplinary problems in the classroom, is to ask the conflictive student to prepare something to teach in the next class. The topic does not have to be necessarily related to your subject; the pupil can choose anything he/she likes: fishing, computer games, fashion... Motivate the students to prepare that class in depth offering them a reward, something they really appreciate, for example extra-credit points, a letter of acknowledgment for their parents or getting to be in charge of something they like in the class for a week. Making a written agreement with the student is crucial. In the next class you will change roles, you will sit at a student's desk and a student will occupy the teacher's place. When the student initiates the explanation behave as the student usually does in your class (interrupting, singing, making comments about how bored you are). It is amazing how the rest of the class will start playing along with you! The student will start to understand what you feel when he/she behaves like that in class. When you realize the student has learnt the "lesson", change your behaviour; act as you would like him/her to behave in class: pay attention, participate, smile... After the activity, you can ask the pupil how he/she felt and which one of your behaviours and those of the classmates s/he preferred. You can also organize a class debate in which students can express their opinion or ideas on the issue of discipline in their classroom, exchange views, and agree on rules of behaviour to apply in the language class. In groups, ask your pupils to make posters with those rules and pass them around so that everybody can read and sign them to promise fulfil them. Hang the posters on the classroom walls.

Accept the fact that you cannot control students' reaction to the materials and activities you propose in class, they have the ultimate word. However, you can control the way you feel about your effort. If you always prepare your lessons thoroughly, you will be satisfied with yourself and that is positive for your self-esteem. Sooner or later your pupils will appreciate your effort and your interest in them.

Take the initiative to carry out new projects, do not be afraid of taking risks, and make proposals to the members of your school community. Conformity leads to frustration.

Be ready to accept feedback, even criticism from students, parents and colleagues.

Convey enthusiasm in what you say and do; enthusiasm is almost always contagious.

Don't be afraid of asking for help or support.

Propose putting a notice board in a visible place in the school where everybody can ask for what they need, convey feelings or make suggestions. Communicative channels must be always open. For example, ask the cleaning staff to manifest their complaints about how dirty the corridors and classrooms are on the notice board, they can even put photos of the rubbish so that everybody can see what they mean. On the same board there will be also space for people to put notes back to them to apologize, give an explanation, or say thank you. Teachers can also communicate their requirements to the Headmaster, colleagues, parents or pupils and viceversa. People can remain anonymous if they want.

Create support groups of teachers. They can meet regularly to discuss or share their problems, worries or achievements in class or at school. Name a Chairperson to organize them. Sometimes sharing ideas and feelings helps to discover solutions and to foster a relaxed atmosphere.

Keep informed of your rights and obligations and those of the people around you. Everyone must assume his/her responsibilities.

Try to build up affective links with students and other teachers: activities to get to know each other, posters showing students information about their teacher's life that he/she would like them to know and the other way around. Include in your lessons time for sharing experiences or opinions. If teachers and students get to know each other, their relationship will be more productive.

Finally, and possibly the most effective instrument teachers have to create an excellent learning and teaching atmosphere in the foreign language class, confirm your pupils. Make them feel valued, recognized, and unique; and because of the reciprocal nature of confirmation you will also feel valued. Both your self-esteem and that of your students will increase. But the question any language teacher might ask is: how can I confirm my students? The result of a study (León, 2005) done to find an answer to that question is the ETCS (English Teacher Confirmation Scale). This scale contains the English teacher behaviours that are perceived by students as confirming and disconfirming. Confirming behaviours have proved to foster students' positive attitude towards the subject (Ellis 1998, 2000; León 2005). Students themselves claim that when they are confirmed, they feel more relaxed and comfortable, willing to participate in class and to use English to communicate, and affectively closer to their teachers.

A sample of 114 secondary school students participated in the study, representing all the stages of secondary education. A questionnaire was given to students and Flanagan's (1954) CIT (Critical Incident Technique) was used. The confirming behaviours included in the ETCS are the following:

BEHAVIOUR
MENTIONS
The confirming English teacher:

| | |
|---|---|
| Congratulates students verbal and non-verbally when they do something good (e.g.: "congratulations", "well done", "you're the best"; gestures like shaking hands or applauding). | 15 |
| Conveys to the pupils his confidence in their possibilities, encouraging them to keep on working to improve (e.g.: "come on, you can do it!", "don't give up!", "you can get what you want, you are hard-working"). | 13 |
| Pays attention to what students do or say, listening to them carefully. | 9 |
| Smiles at students frequently. | 9 |
| Conveys verbally and explicitly his/her happiness about students' achievements (e.g.: "I'm very happy for you", "I'm proud of you and your results", "you have improved a lot"). | 8 |
| Shows interest in answering students' questions. | 7 |
| Shows interest in the personal dimension of students-not only the academic one-asking them about their worries, goals and problems. | 7 |
| Asks questions frequently to make sure that students have understood everything perfectly (e.g.: "Have you got any questions or doubts?, "Is there anything that is not clear for you?", "Are you following me?"). | 7 |
| Keeps visual contact with students throughout the lesson. | 6 |
| Helps students when they need it, making him/herself available for them outside class. | 6 |
| Shows interest in correcting pupils' pronunciation (e.g.: "pronounce that sound again", "put your mouth like this to pronounce it accurately", "listen how I pronounce this word | 6 |

| | |
|---|---|
| and repeat after me", "this word can be pronounced in two different ways, either with British or American pronunciation"). | |
| Encourages students to ask all their doubts (e.g.: "ask me everything you don't know or understand, don't be shy", "I'm here to answer all your questions", "stop me if you don't understand what I'm explaining and I will repeat as many times as you need"). | 5 |
| Proposes practical lessons, based more on the oral than written language. | 5 |
| Treats all the students with equanimity. | 5 |
| Values and rewards pupils (giving them good marks, extra-credit points...). | 5 |
| Gives students enough time to think before they answer. | 5 |
| Makes students laugh (e.g.: makes jokes, explains contents as if they were interesting stories, share funny personal anecdotes with pupils). | 4 |
| Is patient, understanding and reasonable (e.g.: when a student forgets doing the homework, makes a mistake, pronounces a word wrong, does not understand anything or takes a long time to answer). | 4 |
| Explains things thoroughly as many times as necessary. | 3 |
| Shows concern about students who aren't doing well in the subject, trying to help them (e.g.: stays in class during the break to explain the contents to them or prepares remedial activities so that they can learn). | 3 |
| Challenges students intellectually, preparing varied activities and avoiding monotony (e.g. competitions, games, translations of current events, music, penfriends, …). | 3 |
| Gives useful vocabulary so that students can convey their ideas | 2 |

| | |
|---|---|
| and complete the classroom activities (lists, dictionaries, slang words, idioms...). | |
| Has a good English pronunciation. | 2 |
| Brings to class materials about the culture of the English-speaking countries, not only about the language. | 2 |
| Carries out individualized teaching, paying attention to each student's particular needs (e.g. prepares extra activities, advises every student about how they should organize their studies…). | 2 |
| Is positive, energetic and dynamic, conveying his enthusiasm about what he says or does (e.g.: he has got an energetic tone of voice, stands up while is explaining, moves around the classroom…). | 2 |
| Designs activities in which everybody can get involved and participate (e.g.: role plays or group work). | 2 |
| Rectifies when he makes a mistake and can say "sorry". | 2 |
| Presents in a clear way the purpose of each lesson. | 2 |
| Speaks English slowly. | 1 |
| Uses Spanish if it is necessary. | 1 |
| Never laughs at students' mistakes. | 1 |
| Creates and keeps discipline in the classroom. | 1 |
| Teaches techniques to memorize vocabulary. | 1 |
| Is concerned about his/her appearance (hygiene, clothing, etc.) | 1 |

Table 11-1. English teachers' behaviours perceived by pupils as confirming (ECPI).

To conclude, it is undeniably true that teachers' self-esteem is affected by the daily events they have to face in the classroom, and it seems that a number of changes should be made in the educational system to improve the quality of teaching and learning. It is also true that most of these changes are not under educators' control, but must be carried out by governments and other entities endowed with a greater legal power of decision. Parents, students and headmasters have also much to do to make teachers feel recognized, endorsed and acknowledged. However, there are things which are under teachers' control, which we teachers can do from our position to improve our daily practice and foster our self-esteem, and confirmation is a very important one of them. We cannot simply be led by others' decisions and designs; it is our duty and responsibility to promote changes for a better, more effective work atmosphere, creating affective relationships with those who surround us. This may seem a small step forward, but as Burke (quoted in Claxton 1989, 1) claimed once: "Nobody made a greater mistake than he who did nothing because he could only do a little".

## Works Cited

Barth, R.S. 1991. *Improving schools from within: Teachers, parents, and principals can make the difference.* San Francisco: Jossey-Bass Publishers.

Buber, M. 1957. Distance and relation. *Psychiatry* 20: 97-104.

Cissna, K.N., and E. Sieburg. 1981. Patterns of interactional confirmation and disconfirmation. In *Rigor and imagination: Essays from the legacy of Gregory Bateson*, ed. C. Wilder-Mott and J.H. Weasland, 253-282. New York: Praeger.

Claxton, G. 1989. *Being a teacher: A positive approach to change and stress.* London: Cassell.

Ellis, K. 1998. Perceived teacher confirmation. PhD. diss. (unpublished), Colorado Spring University.

—. 2000. Perceived teacher confirmation: The development and validation of an instrument of two studies of the relationship to cognitive and affective learning. *Human Communication Research* 26, (2): 264-291.

—. 2002. Perceived parental confirmation: Development and validation of an instrument. *Southern Communication Journal* 67, (4): 319-334.

Flanagan, J.C. 1954. The critical incident. *Psychological Bulletin* 52: 327-357.

Hargreaves, A. 2000. Mixed emotions: teachers' perceptions of their interactions with students. *Teaching and Teacher Education: An International Journal of Research and Studies* 6, (8): 811-826.

Laing, R.D. 1961. *The self and others.* New York: Pantheon.

—. 1969. Mystification, confusion, and conflict. In *Intensive family therapy,* eds. I. Boszormenyi-Nagy and J.D. Framo, 343-363. New York: Harper and Row.

León, I. 2005. La Confirmación del profesor de inglés percibida por el alumno en el aula de secundaria: Elaboración de la ECPI. PhD diss. (unpublished), University of Seville.

Sieburg, E. 1969. Dysfunctional communication and interpersonal responsiveness in small groups. PhD. diss. (unpublished), University of Denver.

—. 1975. Interpersonal confirmation: A paradigm for conceptualization and measurement. United States International University, (ERIC Document No. ED 983 634/ CS 500-881).

—. 1985. *Family communication: An integrated systems approach.* New York: Gardner Press, Inc.

Sundell, W. 1972. The Operation of confirming and disconfirming verbal behavior in selected teacher-student interaction. PhD diss. (unpublished), Denver University.

# CONTRIBUTORS

Verónica Andrés, Universidad del Salvador, Argentina
Marina Arcos, Polytechnic University of Madrid
Jane Arnold, University of Seville
Javier Avila, University of Cordoba
Sonia Casal, Pablo de Olavide University
Eva Diaz, University of Huelva
Carmen Fonseca, University of Huelva
Elaine Horwitz, University of Texas
Concha Julián, University of Seville
Inmaculada León, University of Seville
Ana Ortega, University of Jaén
Fernando Rubio, University of Huelva
Carmen Toscano, University of Huelva
Andrew Wright, ILI International Languages Institute, Hungary